THIS IS
VOCA
VOCABULARY

For Beginners

THIS IS VOCABULARY 초급

지은이 권기하
펴낸이 임상진
펴낸곳 (주)넥서스

출판신고 1992년 4월 3일 제311-2002-2호 2-16
10880 경기도 파주시 지목로 5
Tel (02)330-5500 Fax (02)330-5555

ISBN 979-11-6165-204-7 54740
      979-11-6165-203-0 (SET)

www.nexusbook.com

어휘의
기초를 다지는

THIS IS
VOCA
VOCABULARY

권기하 지음

초급
For Beginners

NEXUS Edu

Preface

영어에서 어휘는 듣기·말하기·읽기·쓰기의 기초를 이루는 핵심적인 요소입니다. 그리고 학습자들의 영어 실력이 높아질수록 어휘가 차지하는 비중이 높아집니다. 즉, 독해지문 읽기와 대화에서 발음이나 문법을 몰라서라기보다는 어휘의 정확한 의미나 쓰임을 알지 못해 문맥을 이해하는 데 어려움을 느끼거나 제대로 활용할 수 없는 경우가 많습니다. 더군다나 초등학교의 영어 노출 시기가 앞당겨지면서 중학교와 고등학교 과정에서 요구하는 어휘의 수준은 점점 높아지고 있습니다. 실제 각종 시험이나 수능에서 느끼는 체감 난이도도 평상시보다 높다는 것을 알 수 있습니다. 이것은 교과서나 한 권의 어휘 교재만으로는 해결할 수 없음을 의미합니다.

그렇다면 어떻게 어휘를 효과적으로 학습할 수 있을까요? 무조건 많은 양의 어휘를 기계적으로 외우기만 하면 될까요? 단순히 많은 양의 영단어를 암기하는 것도 어휘 학습의 한 방법이긴 합니다. 하지만 이러한 방법으로는 무수히 많은 어휘를 학습하기는 불가능하며, 암기하더라도 금방 잊어버리거나 외운 단어를 실제 생활이나 시험에서는 활용할 수 없게 됩니다. 따라서 단순히 어휘의 정의만이 아니라, 연어 또는 회화나 독해를 통해 문맥 속에서 어휘의 의미를 유추하고, 중심 개념, 어원의 이해 등을 통해 체계적으로 학습하는 것이 중요합니다.

〈This Is Vocabulary 최신개정판〉 시리즈는 어휘를 주제별로 정리해 의미의 연계성을 통해 학습자들이 각각의 어휘를 자연스럽게 학습하고 기억할 수 있도록 했습니다. 그리고 어휘 수준에 따라 초급, 중급, 고급, 어원편 등으로 구성, 다양한 어휘 활동을 추가하였으며, 학습 효과를 극대화하기 위해 빈도가 높은 연어, 파생어, 예문 등을 제시했습니다.

〈This Is Vocabulary 최신개정판〉 시리즈를 통해 언어의 기본 단위인 어휘를 효과적으로 학습하고 더 나아가 이 책의 다양한 어휘 학습 장치를 통해 영어의 4가지 skill을 모두 향상시킬 수 있었으면 합니다.

권기하

이것이 더 강력해진
"THIS IS VOCA"시리즈다!

✎ 효과적인 주제별 어휘 학습

〈This Is Vocabulary 최신개정판〉 시리즈는 어휘를 주제별로 분류하여, 학습자들이 각각의 어휘를 연상 작용을 통해 효과적으로 암기하고 쉽게 기억할 수 있도록 구성하였습니다.

✎ 문맥을 통한 어휘 학습

어휘는 단독으로 사용되지 않으므로 예문이나 어구의 형태에서 확인하는 과정이 필요합니다. 따라서 단순히 주제와 관련된 어휘만을 나열한 것이 아니라, 연어, 파생어, 주제와 관련된 예문을 함께 제시하여 가능한 한 다양한 표현을 반영, 문맥을 통해 학습할 수 있도록 구성하였습니다.

✎ 입문(주니어)부터 수능 완성, 고급 단계까지의 연계성

어휘 학습이 체계적이고 단계적으로 이루어질 수 있도록 입문(주니어)부터 초급, 중급, 수능 완성, 어원편, 고급, 그리고 뉴텝스까지 시리즈로 구성했습니다. 각 단계에 맞는 표제어를 선정하고 적절한 예문, 수능 기출 예문, 그리고 추가 어휘를 제시하여 보다 효과적으로 학습할 수 있도록 구성하였습니다.

✎ 다양한 학습 방법

레벨에 따라 Word Search, Word Bubbles, Crossword Puzzles, Word Mapping 등 다양한 활동을 추가함으로써 앞서 배운 어휘를 복습하는 과정을 자연스럽게 즐길 수 있도록 구성하였습니다. 또한 언제 어디서나 학습이 가능하도록 모바일로 영/미 발음을 확인하고, 모바일 VOCA TEST를 통해 자기주도학습을 할 수 있는 최적화된 학습 시스템을 제공합니다.

Features

Thematic Grouping

교육부 권장 초급 어휘를 주제별로 정리 총 11개의 챕터, 39개의 유닛으로 정리하였습니다.
제공되는 다양한 이미지를 통한 연상학습이 가능합니다.

Unit 07 Clothes

Basic Words

☐ skirt 치마
☐ dress 드레스
☐ wear 입고 있다
☐ socks 양말

☐ shoe 신발
☐ pants 바지
☐ wallet 지갑
☐ boot 부츠

☐ hat 모자
☐ cap 모자
☐ belt 허리띠
☐ bag 가방

Healthful Life

☐ ill 아픈
☐ nurse 간호사
☐ weak 약한
☐ flu 독감

☐ sick 아픈, 병든
☐ well 건강한
☐ hospital 병원
☐ health 건강

Basic Words

유닛마다 이미지와 함께 영어 교육과정에서 제시한 기본 단어를 다시 한 번 정리할 수 있도록
구성하였습니다.

품사 표시

ⓝ 명사 **ⓥ** 동사 **ⓐ** 형용사 **ad** 부사 **conj** 접속사 **prep** 전치사 **ant** 반의어 **syn** 동의어 **c.f.** 비교

Word Meaning

표제어 옆에 어휘의 의미를 제공하여 손쉽게 뜻을 가리고 암기한 어휘를 확인할 수 있습니다.

Daily Conversations

예문을 대화체로 제시하여 자연스럽게 표제어의 의미를 파악하고 실생활에서의 활용도를 높일 수 있습니다.

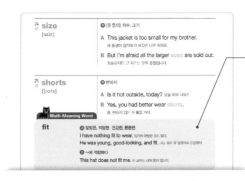

Multi-Meaning Word

다양한 뜻을 가진 단어를 소개하고 collocation(연어)을 통해서 간단명료하게 단어의 뜻을 확인할 수 있습니다.

Review Test

챕터마다 다양한 문제 형태로 구성된 Review Test를 제공해 학습한 단어를 확인하고 점검할 수 있습니다.

Voca Inn

단어의 유래나 추가 어휘 등을 정리해 다양한 어휘를 심화 학습할 수 있습니다.

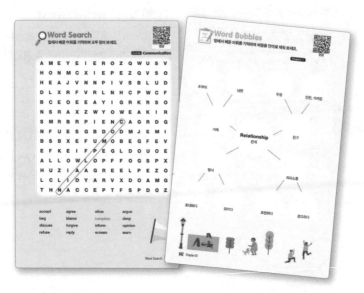

Word Search

유닛마다 앞에서 배운 단어를
워드 게임을 통해 자연스럽게
암기할 수 있습니다.

Word Bubbles

챕터마다 테마별 단어를
함께 묶어 봄으로써 단어들을
효과적으로 더 오래 암기할 수 있습니다.

추가 제공 자료

www.nexusbook.com

① 어휘리스트/테스트
② 테스트 도우미
③ 주제별 VOCA PLUS
④ Fun Fun한 보카 배경지식
⑤ MP3 듣기
⑥ 모바일 VOCA TEST
⑦ Word Search 정답
⑧ Word Bubbles 정답

어휘/뜻/예문 듣기
영/미 발음 MP3

모바일
VOCA TEST

Word Search
정답

Word Bubbles
정답

Contents

"THIS IS VOCA 초급"을
얼마나 알고 있는지 VOCA?

☑ 자신이 아는 단어를 체크하고 그 의미를 제대로 알고 있는지 확인해 보세요!

☐ belong	☐ expensive	☐ fair	☐ result	☐ prepare
☐ homework	☐ museum	☐ borrow	☐ recipe	☐ foreign
☐ bridge	☐ collect	☐ deliver	☐ history	☐ duty
☐ modern	☐ clap	☐ escape	☐ favorite	☐ tradition
☐ follow	☐ press	☐ hire	☐ advertise	☐ rule
☐ direction	☐ social	☐ profit	☐ cousin	☐ income

맞은 개수	권장 학습 방법
0~15	음원을 여러 번 듣고 따라 말하며, 직접 어휘도 써 보면서 반복 학습을 통해 공부해 보세요! 모바일 VOCA TEST로 학습한 내용을 수시로 점검해 보는 것이 어휘 암기에 큰 도움이 됩니다!
16~25	단어의 의미를 좀 더 깊게 파고들기 위해서는 표제어의 파생어도 함께 암기하는 것이 좋습니다. 또한 Review Test 문제도 빠짐없이 풀어 본다면 더욱 더 향상된 어휘력을 갖출 수 있습니다.
26~30	상당한 어휘 실력을 갖고 있네요! 단어와 뜻 그 자체도 중요하지만, 문장에서 해당 단어가 어떻게 쓰이는지 주어진 예문을 통해서 공부한다면 상당한 양의 어휘를 단숨에 마스터할 수 있습니다.

어휘 뜻 확인하기

☑ ____ / 30

☐ ~에 속하다, 소유이다	☐ 값비싼	☐ 공평한, 공정한	☐ 결과, 결말	☐ 준비하다
☐ 숙제	☐ 박물관	☐ 빌리다	☐ 요리법, 조리법	☐ 외국의
☐ 다리	☐ 수집하다, 모으다	☐ 배달하다, 전하다	☐ 역사, 역사학	☐ 의무
☐ 현대의, 근대의	☐ 손뼉을 치다	☐ 벗어나다, 달아나다	☐ 아주 좋아하는	☐ 전통
☐ 따라가다, 따르다	☐ 누르다, 밀다	☐ 고용하다	☐ 광고하다	☐ 규칙, 관례
☐ 방향, 방위	☐ 사회의, 사회적인	☐ 이익	☐ 사촌	☐ 소득

Chapter
01

Relationships

Unit 01 Family & Relatives

Basic Words

- parents 부모
- sister 여동생
- grandfather 할아버지
- home 집
- father 아버지
- brother 남동생
- son 아들
- family 가족
- mother 어머니
- aunt 고모, 이모
- daughter 딸
- love 사랑

01 birth
[bəːrθ]

ⓝ 탄생, 출생　　　　　**give birth to ~** ~을 낳다

A Congratulations on the birth of your baby.
아기가 태어난 걸 축하해.

B Thank you! 고마워!

02 couple
[kʌ́pəl]

ⓝ 부부, 한 쌍, 두 개　　**a couple of** 두 사람의, 두서너 개의

A Is the ring for your wife, sir?
손님, 반지는 아내에게 드리는 겁니까?

B No. We're not a couple.
아니오. 저희는 부부가 아니에요.

03 child
[tʃaild]

pl children 아이들
ant parent 부모

ⓝ 아이, 자식

A Do you think that an only child becomes spoiled? 외동아이는 버릇이 나빠진다고 생각하니?

B I don't think so.
난 그렇게 생각하지 않아.　　　　* spoil : 버릇없게 만들다

04 marry
[mǽri]

ⓝ marriage 결혼

ⓥ 결혼하다　　　　**be married to ~** ~와 결혼한 상태이다

A Are you really going to marry him?
너 정말로 그 남자랑 결혼할 거니?

B I don't know. I can't make up my mind.
모르겠어. 마음을 못 정하겠어.

05 single
[síŋɡəl]

ant married 기혼의, 결혼한

ⓐ 미혼의, 독신의

A Are you single or married?
당신은 미혼이십니까, 기혼이십니까?

B I am single. 미혼입니다.

06 niece
[niːs]

ⓝ 조카딸, 질녀

A Is she your daughter? She is so cute!
이 아이가 당신 딸이에요? 너무 귀엽네요!

B No, she's my niece. She is my sister's child.
아뇨, 제 조카딸이에요. 제 언니의 딸이죠.

07 relative
[rélətiv]

ⓝ 친척, 일가　　　　　　**a close relative** 가까운 친척

A Someone is in your room. Who is she?
네 방에 누군가가 있는데. 누구야?

B My relative came to stay with me.
내 친척이 나와 같이 지내려고 와 있어.

08 twin
[twin]

ⓝ 쌍둥이(중의 하나)　　　　**identical twins** 일란성 쌍둥이

A Isn't he James? How could he just pass by without saying hello?
저 사람 제임스 아니니? 어떻게 인사도 없이 그냥 지나갈 수가 있지?

B He is probably James' twin brother, Mike.
아마 제임스의 쌍둥이 형, 마이크일 거야.

09 respect
[rispékt]

ⓐ respectful 공손한

ⓥ 존경하다 **ⓝ** 존경　　　　**show respect** 존경을 표하다

A Who do you respect most?
넌 누구를 가장 존경하니?

B I respect my parents most.
난 내 부모님을 가장 존경해.

10 cousin
[kʌ́zn]

ⓝ 사촌

A Who is the handsome man in the picture?
사진 속에 잘 생긴 남자는 누구니?

B Oh, Jacob is my cousin. Do you want me to introduce him to you?
아, 제이콥은 내 사촌이야. 소개해 줄까?

11 husband
[hʌ́zbənd]

ⓝ 남편　　　　　　**husband and wife** 남편과 아내

A Have you made up your mind, Ms. Turner?
터너 부인, 결정은 하셨습니까?

B I'm sorry. Let me talk to my husband first.
죄송해요. 먼저 남편이랑 상의할게요.

12 relationship
[riléiʃənʃip]

v relate 관련시키다

n 관계, 관련

A How is your relationship with your sister?

언니하고의 관계는 어때요?

B We are very close. We get along very well.

우리는 매우 친해요. 매우 잘 지내죠.

13 engage
[ingéidʒ]

n engagement 약혼

v 약혼하다

A I heard James and Angela are engaged.

내가 듣기로 제임스와 앤젤라가 약혼했대.

B I can't believe he finally succeeded!

그가 마침내 성공했다는 것이 믿기지 않아!

14 grandparent
[grǽnpɛ̀ərənt]

ant grandchild 손자, 손녀

n 조부모

A Do you have any plans for this summer?

이번 여름에 계획 있니?

B Yes. I'm going to visit my grandparents.

응. 나는 조부모님 뵈러 갈 거야.

15 uncle
[ʌ́ŋkl]

n 삼촌

A The jacket looks good on you.

그 자켓 너에게 잘 어울린다.

B Thanks. My uncle bought me this jacket for my birthday present.

고마워. 나의 삼촌께서 내 생일선물로 사주셨어.

16 member
[mémbər]

n 일원, 회원

A How many family members does Jessica have? 제시카의 가족은 몇 명이니?

B She has five. 다섯 명이야.

17 grow
[grou]
(grow-grew-grown)

n growth 성장

v 성장하다, 자라다

A Lincoln grew up to be a great person with his mother's help.
링컨은 어머니의 도움으로 훌륭한 사람으로 성장할 수 있었어.

B A mother's love is great. 어머니의 힘은 위대해.

18 depend
[dipénd]

n dependence 의지

v 의존하다, 의지하다

A Children depend on their parents for everything. 아이들은 부모님에게 모든 것을 의존해.

B That's because they are young and small.
그건 그들이 어리고 작기 때문이야.

19 divorce
[divɔ́:rs]

v 이혼하다 **n** 이혼　　　　　**get a divorce** 이혼하다

A Will and Grace are going to divorce.
윌과 그레이스가 이혼할 거래.

B They were a lovely couple. What happened to them? 사랑스러운 부부였잖아. 그들에게 무슨 일이 있었니?

20 share
[ʃɛə:r]

v 공유하다, 분담하다

A I can't talk about my problem with my family.
내 문제를 가족들에게 얘기할 수가 없어.

B I think family should share everything.
가족이란 모든 것을 공유해야 한다고 생각해.

21 nephew
[néfju:]

n 조카

A What do you call your brother's son in English? 형제의 아들을 영어로 뭐라고 부르니?

B He's called my nephew. 조카라고 불러.

22 partner
[pá:rtnər]

ⓝ 배우자, 동료

A I heard you will marry a basketball player.
네가 농구 선수와 결혼할 거라고 들었어.

B Yes, I wonder what your marriage partner will be like. 응. 네 배우자는 어떤 사람일지 궁금해.

23 son-in-law
[sʌ́ninlɔ̀ː]

c.f. daughter-in-law
며느리

ⓝ 사위

A What are you so excited about?
뭐에 그렇게 흥분해 있니?

B My daughter and son-in-law will visit us from Japan. 딸과 사위가 일본에서 오거든.

24 support
[səpɔ́ːrt]

ⓥ 부양하다, 원조하다 **ⓝ** 지지, 부양

A What is Jim doing lately?
짐은 요즘 무엇을 하면서 지내니?

B He is working hard to support his family.
그는 가족을 부양하느라 열심히 일하고 있어.

25 unless
[ənlés]

conj 만일 ~이 아니면

A Life doesn't mean anything unless I have my family to share it with.
함께 공유할 가족이 없다면 삶은 아무런 의미도 없어.

B Oh honey, that's so sweet. 오 여보. 참 감동적이네요.

🐱 Multi-Meaning Word

single

ⓐ 단 하나의
They won the game by a **single** point.
그들은 단 일 점 차이로 게임을 이겼다.

ⓐ 독신의, 미혼의
Jeff is 38 years old and still **single**.
제프는 서른여덟 살이며 아직 미혼이다.

ⓐ 일인용의
We are looking for a **single** bed for our son.
우리는 아들이 쓸 일인용 침대를 찾고 있다.

Word Search

앞에서 배운 어휘를 기억하며 모두 찾아 보세요.

정답

O	G	I	X	G	K	M	F	U	E	T	H	N	A	Z
T	C	C	V	R	C	A	A	N	L	N	D	X	Z	B
P	P	E	U	O	R	R	Y	C	P	Z	G	P	T	S
K	W	F	I	W	E	R	Q	L	U	S	H	I	R	K
E	E	W	V	N	N	Y	H	E	O	H	N	V	O	G
N	V	L	C	L	T	B	T	U	C	E	H	U	P	D
M	I	O	A	H	R	I	R	T	S	D	L	A	P	N
Q	E	S	T	A	A	R	K	C	H	B	N	N	U	I
S	I	M	U	A	P	T	Y	E	T	S	A	L	S	W
I	Q	N	B	O	L	H	A	P	W	K	C	N	Q	T
D	P	X	O	E	B	E	O	S	W	O	N	L	B	O
C	H	I	L	D	R	W	R	E	E	G	A	G	N	E
E	L	G	N	I	S	M	X	R	D	N	E	P	E	D
E	F	D	W	E	H	P	E	N	M	S	H	A	R	E

birth	child	couple	depend
engage	grow	marry	member
nephew	partner	respect	share
single	support	twin	uncle

Unit 02 Friends & Neighbors

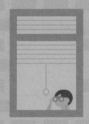  

Basic Words

- □ live 살다
- □ like 좋아하다
- □ dear 소중한
- □ and ~와
- □ friend 친구
- □ boy 소년
- □ dislike 싫어하다
- □ dog 개
- □ next to ~옆에
- □ girl 소녀
- □ window 창문
- □ park 공원

01 friendship
[fréndʃìp]

n 교우, 우정　　　　　　**real friendship** 진실된 우정

A We will still be friends after graduation, won't we? 우리 졸업 후에도 계속 친구 할거지, 그렇지 않니?

B Of course. Let's keep our friendship forever. 물론이지. 우리의 우정을 영원히 간직하자.

02 neighborhood
[néibərhùd]

n 근처, 이웃, 인근

A Is there a park in your neighborhood? 너의 집 근처에 공원이 있니?

B Yes, it is on the corner of Main Street and Arch Street. 응, 메인가와 아치가의 모퉁이에 있어.

03 community
[kəmjú:nəti]

n 지역 사회, 공동체

A The library will be made for the community. 도서관이 지역 사회를 위해서 만들어진다고 해.

B When does it open? 언제 개관하니?

04 area
[ɛ́əriə]

n 지역, 구역

A What area do you live in, Nancy? 낸시, 너는 어느 지방에 사니?

B I live in Arkansas. 아칸소주에 살아.

05 care
[kɛər]

a careful 주의 깊은

n 걱정, 조심　**v** 걱정하다

care for sick people 아픈 사람들을 돌보다

A Good-bye. I'll see you next year. 안녕. 내년에 보자.

B Take care! 몸조심하고 잘 있어!

06 neighbor
[néibər]

n 이웃 사람

A How do you know Jane? 제인을 어떻게 알게 되었니?

B She lives nearby. She is my neighbor. 우리 집 근처에 살아. 이웃 사람이야.

07 maintain
[meintéin]

ⓥ 유지하다

A How do you maintain a good relationship with everyone?
어떻게 모든 사람과 좋은 관계를 유지하니?

B The best way is to be honest with the other person. 최고의 방법은 상대방에게 정직하는 거야.

08 close
[klous]

ⓐ 친한, 친밀한, 가까운

A Sam and I were very close friends when we were young.
어릴 때 샘과 나는 정말 친한 친구였어.

B Why don't you call him and say hello?
그에게 전화해서 안부를 전하는 게 어때?

09 secret
[sí:krit]

ad secretly 비밀로, 은밀히

ⓝ 비밀 **ⓐ** 비밀의   **a secret plan** 비밀 작전

A Do you have a friend you can tell your secrets to? 네 비밀을 터놓고 이야기할 수 있는 친구가 있니?

B Yes, I can trust Helen with everything.
응, 나는 헬렌을 전적으로 믿어.

10 across
[əkrɔ́:s]

prep ~을 가로질러, ~의 맞은편으로

A Do you know who lives across your house?
너희 집 건너에 누가 사는지 아니?

B The Jacksons have just moved into. Why?
잭슨 가족이 막 이사 왔어. 왜?

11 trust
[trʌst]

ⓥ 믿다, 신뢰하다 **ⓝ** 신임, 신뢰

    put one's trust in ~ ~을 신뢰하다

A I know you are lying to me.
네가 나에게 거짓말하는 거 알고 있어.

B No, it is true. Please trust me.
아니야, 사실이란 말이야. 제발 날 좀 믿어.

12 □ introduce
[ìntrədʒúːs]

ⓝ introduction 소개

ⓥ 소개하다, 도입하다

introduce oneself 자기 자신을 소개하다

A Let me introduce my friend. This is Jenny.
너에게 내 친구를 소개할게. 이쪽이 제니야.

B Hi, Jenny. I'm Fred. 안녕, 제니. 난 프레드야.

13 □ village
[vílidʒ]

ⓝ 마을

a fishing village 어촌

A There are about 200 people in my village.
우리 마을에는 약 200명의 사람이 있어.

B People are pretty close to each other, aren't
they? 사람들이 서로 꽤 친하겠구나, 그렇지 않니?

14 □ fence
[fens]

ⓝ 울타리

put a fence 울타리를 치다

A What did you do last Sunday? Anything fun?
지난 일요일에 뭐했니? 재미있는 일 없었어?

B My neighbor and I painted the fence.
내 이웃과 울타리를 칠했어.

15 □ forever
[fərévər]

ad 영원히, 영구히

A Our friendship will last forever.
우리의 우정은 영원히 지속될 거야.

B It would be very nice to have such a close
friend. 그렇게 친한 친구가 있어서 참 좋겠다.

16 □ warmth
[wɔ́ːrmθ]

ⓐ warm 따뜻한

ⓝ 따뜻함, 온정

A Villagers here seem to be kind to us.
이곳 마을 사람들은 우리에게 친절한 것 같아.

B They welcome anybody with warmth.
그들은 어떤 사람이든 따뜻하게 환영해.

17 lifetime
[láiftàim]

ⓐ 일생의 ⓝ 일생, 평생

during one's lifetime ~의 일생 동안

A I wish I had a lifetime friend.
평생 함께할 친구가 있으면 좋겠어.

B Don't worry. You will meet someone soon.
걱정하지 마. 곧 누군가를 만날 거야.

18 friendly
[fréndli]

(friendly-friendlier-
friendliest)

ⓝ friend 친구

ⓐ 친한, 정다운

A Can't you be friendlier to Susan?
수잔에게 더 친절할 수 없니?

B I'm sorry. I didn't mean to be rude.
미안해. 무례하게 굴 생각은 없었어.

19 near
[niər]

ant far 멀리, 먼

ⓐ 가까운 ad 가까이, 접근하여

A Is your house near Sally's house?
너희 집은 샐리의 집과 가깝니?

B Yes, she lives just across the street.
응, 그녀는 바로 길 건너에 살아.

20 split
[splít]

(split-split-split)

ⓥ 쪼개다, 분열하다　　**split up with ~** ~와 헤어지다

A Are there any more cookies in the jar?
통에 쿠키 더 남았니?

B No, this is the last one. I'll split mine and give
you half. 아니, 이게 마지막이야. 내 것을 반 나눠줄게.

21 rumor
[rúmər]

ⓝ 소문

A There is a rumor that John is moving to
another city.
존이 다른 도시로 이사 갈 거라는 소문이 있어.

B I think we should ask John about it.
내 생각에는 존에게 물어보는 것이 좋을 것 같아.

22 next door
[nékstdɔ̀ːr]

ⓐ next-door 이웃의

ad 이웃에

A Josh and I have lived next door since we were little. 조쉬와 나는 어려서부터 옆집에 살았어.

B You two must be very close friends.
둘이 굉장히 친한 친구겠구나.

23 between
[bitwíːn]

prep ~ 사이에

A You have to keep this a secret between us.
이거 우리 사이에 비밀로 유지해야 해.

B You can trust me. 나를 믿어도 돼.

24 together
[təgéðər]

ad 함께, 같이   **get together** 모이다

A Let's all go to the concert together.
우리 모두 공연에 같이 가자.

B That sounds great! 좋아!

25 as
[æz]

conj ~한 것과 같이 **prep** ~로서

as a birthday present 생일 선물로

A Why are you doing this to me, Sally?
샐리, 나한테 왜 이러는 거야?

B Don't act as if you don't know!
모르는 것 같이 굴지 마!

Multi-Meaning Word

close

ⓥ 닫다(= shut) [klouz]
It's getting dark. **Close** the window. 날이 어두워져. 창문을 닫아.

ⓐ 종결하다, 끝내다 [klouz]
I will now **close** the meeting. 이제 회의를 끝냅니다.

ⓐ 가까운(= near)[klous]
Alaska is **close** to Russia. 알래스카는 러시아와 가깝다.

ⓐ (관계가)밀접한[klous]
Dad and I have always been very **close**.
아빠와 나는 항상 매우 친하게 지낸다.

Word Search

앞에서 배운 어휘를 기억하며 모두 찾아 보세요.

정답

```
R G R R F T H V G H W C Y Q J
U K O I E R E W I T E A E W E
M D M D X V I R F V S R N A H
O X I R P P E A C T Q E E R O
R R S V D W I R N E T B I M R
S P L I T U L H O D S R G T X
L I F E T I M E S F L M H H X
T O G E T H E R V D A Y B P T
I N T R O D U C E I N S O Z S
V I L L A G E J N E S E R Q U
W R A R E A K T N O S I I X R
F E N C E R A W R B R O Z R T
P H V E I I H C N E A R L L F
N T B M N Y A H J G W Y E C R
```

across	area	care	close
fence	friendship	introduce	lifetime
near	neighbor	rumor	split
together	trust	village	warmth

Unit 03 Celebration & Events

□ gift 선물
□ happy 행복한
□ party 파티

□ candle 양초
□ card 카드
□ Christmas 크리스마스

□ want 원하다
□ give 주다
□ get 얻다

□ smile 미소 짓다
□ fun 즐거운
□ buy 사다

01 birthday
[bə́:rθdèi]

ⓝ 생일   **a birthday gift** 생일 선물

A Can I bring my friends to my birthday party, Dad? 아빠, 제 생일 파티에 친구들 데려와도 돼요?

B Sure. Bring all your pals. 물론이지. 네 친구 다 데려오렴.

02 celebration
[sèləbréiʃən]

ⓥ celebrate 축하하다, 기념하다

ⓝ 축하, 축전   **a celebration party** 축하 파티

A What is the party for? 무슨 파티니?

B It's the celebration for our anniversary.
우리의 기념일을 축하하는 거야.

03 invite
[inváit]

ⓝ invitation 초대

ⓥ 초대하다

A Do you want to watch a movie on Sunday?
일요일에 영화 보러 가지 않을래?

B I'm sorry, but I'll be out of town. My uncle invited me to his house.
미안하지만, 나 동네에 없을 거야. 삼촌께서 집으로 초대하셨거든.

04 dine
[dain]

ⓝ dinner 저녁 식사, 정찬

ⓥ 식사를 하다

A Happy birthday, Tom! Do you have any plans today? 생일 축하해, 톰! 오늘 계획 있니?

B Thank you. I am going to dine out with my parents. 고마워. 부모님하고 외식하기로 했어.

05 holiday
[hálədèi]

ⓝ 휴일, 공휴일, 휴가   **go on holiday** 휴가를 가다

A What are you doing for the holiday?
너 휴일에 무엇을 할 거니?

B I'm thinking about taking a trip somewhere.
어디론가 여행을 떠날까 해.

06 ☑ graduate

[grǽdʒuèit]

ⓝ graduation 졸업

ⓥ 졸업하다

　graduate from middle school 중학교를 졸업하다

A I graduated from ABC Elementary School last year. 난 작년에 ABC 초등학교를 졸업했어.

B Really? Me, too. 정말? 나도 그래.

07 ☑ gather

[gǽðər]

ⓝ gathering 모임, 집회

ⓥ 모이다

A Lots of people gathered downtown to see the fireworks. 많은 사람이 불꽃놀이를 보려고 시내에 모였어.

B I wanted to see them, too. 나도 보고 싶었는데.

　　　　　　　　　　　　　* firework : 불꽃놀이

08 ☑ congratulation

[kəngrætʃəléiʃən]

ⓥ congratulate 축하하다

ⓝ 축하

A I won first place in the contest!
나 대회에서 일등 했어!

B Congratulations! 축하해!

09 ☑ guest

[gest]

ant host 주인, 사회자

ⓝ 손님

A Honey, can you help me set the table? The guests are arriving soon.
여보, 식탁 차리는 것 좀 도와줄래요? 손님들이 곧 도착하실 거예요.

B Okay, I will. 알았어. 도와줄게.

10 ☑ thank

[θæŋk]

ⓐ thankful 감사하는

ⓥ 감사하다 **ⓝ** 감사　　　**return thanks** 답례하다, 감사하다

A I don't know how to thank you!
어떻게 감사를 드려야 할지 모르겠어요!

B It's okay. I'm sure you would have done the same. 괜찮아요. 틀림없이 당신도 똑같이 하셨을 거예요.

11 event
[ivént]

ⓝ 행사, 사건

A Thank you for inviting me to this great event.
이 멋진 행사에 절 초대해주셔서 감사합니다.

B The pleasure is all mine to have you here.
당신이 오셔서 오히려 제가 기쁩니다.

12 anniversary
[ӕnəvə́:rsəri]

ⓝ 기념일

A Are you looking for a gift, sir?
선물을 찾으시는 건가요, 손님?

B Yes, it's my parents' wedding anniversary.
네, 저희 부모님 결혼기념일이에요.

13 festival
[féstəvəl]

ⓝ 축제, 축제일   **hold a festival** 축제를 열다

A I'm planning to go to Kyoto. 나 교토에 갈 계획이야.

B I heard it's the festival season there.
거기 축제 기간이라고 들었어.

14 present
[prézənt]

ⓝ 선물

A Where did you get that lovely hat?
그 멋진 모자 어디서 났니?

B I got it as a birthday present from my friend.
내 친구한테서 생일 선물로 받은 거야.

15 occasion
[əkéiʒən]

ⓝ 특별한 일, 행사, 경우

A I went to a fancy restaurant yesterday.
나 어제 고급 레스토랑에 갔었어.

B That's nice. What was the occasion?
좋았겠네. 무슨 날이었니?

16 special
[spéʃəl]

ⓐ 특별한, 전문의

A The chef made a special cake for her birthday. 요리사가 그녀의 생일을 위해 특별 케이크를 만들었어.

B She is such a lucky girl! 그녀는 참 복이 많은 여자야!

---

17 during
[djúəriŋ]

prep ~동안, ~사이에

A Ashley, when did you meet your husband?
애슐리, 남편을 언제 만났어요?

B I met him during my senior year of college.
대학 졸업반 때 만났어요.

---

18 hold
[hould]
(hold-held-held)

ⓥ 개최하다, 열다　　　　**hold a meeting** 회의를 열다

A I heard Jane is holding a party for her birthday. 제인이 생일에 파티를 연다고 들었어.

B Yes, I got the invitation, too. 응, 나도 초대장 받았어.

---

19 prize
[praiz]

ⓝ 상품, 상

A What is the prize for the contest?
대회 상품이 무엇인가요?

B It's a laptop computer. 노트북 컴퓨터입니다.

---

20 wedding
[wédiŋ]

ⓝ 혼례, 결혼식　　　　**a wedding ceremony** 결혼식

A I want to have a big wedding.
나는 성대한 결혼식을 하고 싶어.

B So do I. 나도 그래.

---

21 memory
[méməri]
ⓥ memorize 기억하다

ⓝ 추억, 기억

A Mom, how was your college life?
엄마, 엄마의 대학 생활을 어땠어요?

B The memories of my college life are still fresh. 대학 생활의 추억이 아직도 생생해.

22 cancel
[kǽnsəl]

ⓥ 취소하다, 중지하다

A I am afraid to tell you that the party was cancelled. 유감스럽게도 파티가 취소되었어.

B Oh, I was looking forward to it so much! 이런, 정말 기대하고 있었는데!

23 happiness
[hǽpinis]

ⓐ happy 행복한

ⓝ 행복, 기쁨

A Everybody wants to make much money. 모든 사람이 많은 돈을 벌길 원해.

B I think happiness is more important than money. 난 행복이 돈보다 더 중요한 것 같아.

24 welcome
[wélkəm]

ⓥ 환영하다 **ⓝ** 환영, 환대   a warm welcome 따뜻한 환영

A The host welcomed the guests at the door. 주인이 손님을 문 앞에서 기쁘게 맞이했어.

B Yes, he looked very happy that night. 응, 그날 밤 그는 굉장히 행복해 보였어.

25 without
[wiðáut]

ant with ~와 함께, 더불어

prep ~없이, ~하지 않고

A Congratulations! You finally passed the exam! 축하해! 드디어 시험에 합격했구나!

B I couldn't have done it without you. 당신 없이는 해내지 못했을 거야.

Multi-Meaning Word

present

ⓐ 현재의[prézənt] /출석하고 있는[prézənt]

He moved to his **present** home last year. 그는 작년에 현재의 집으로 이사 왔다.
I was **present** at the meeting. 나는 그 집회에 참석했다.

ⓥ 수여하다, 주다[prizént]

A girl **presented** a basket of flowers to me.
한 소녀가 내게 꽃바구니를 주었다.

ⓝ 선물[prézənt]

I am making a special Christmas **present** for my parents.
나는 부모님께 드릴 특별한 크리스마스 선물을 만들고 있다.

Word Search

앞에서 배운 어휘를 기억하며 모두 찾아 보세요.

정답

M	O	G	E	G	E	A	H	U	B	O	O	T	Q	W
E	G	U	N	R	A	O	R	I	S	C	T	U	M	F
M	J	R	E	A	L	T	R	L	E	C	S	C	T	J
O	E	J	A	I	D	H	H	M	N	A	E	M	J	T
R	H	Z	D	D	H	D	O	E	T	S	U	L	W	N
Y	J	A	E	D	U	C	E	H	R	I	G	E	C	S
H	Y	R	A	R	L	A	A	W	K	O	Y	K	P	P
O	F	Y	U	E	P	N	T	W	D	N	N	R	P	E
L	Y	F	W	Q	K	A	M	E	D	U	E	J	M	C
D	H	W	I	T	H	O	U	T	N	S	R	E	E	I
I	N	V	I	T	E	N	E	C	E	U	V	I	Q	A
F	E	S	T	I	V	A	L	N	G	E	Z	E	N	L
C	A	N	C	E	L	S	T	H	N	A	P	Y	N	G
A	W	P	L	R	Y	O	E	T	Z	W	P	U	X	S

cancel   during   event   festival

gather   graduate   guest   hold

holiday   invite   memory   occasion

present   special   thank   without

Unit 04 Communication

Basic Words

- □ speak 말하다
- □ ask 물어보다
- □ say 말하다
- □ letter 편지
- □ talk 대화하다
- □ call (큰소리로) 부르다
- □ listen 듣다
- □ meeting 회의
- □ tell 말하다
- □ fight 싸우다
- □ phone 전화하다, 전화
- □ speech 연설

01 express
[iksprés]

n expression 표현

v 표현하다, 나타내다

A I heard you won first prize in the speech contest. 네가 웅변대회에서 일등을 했다고 들었어.

B I cannot express how happy I was then.
그때 얼마나 행복했던지 말로 표현할 수 없어.

---

02 complain
[kəmpléin]

n complaint 불평, 불만

v 불평하다

complain about the noise 소음에 대해 불평하다

A Our food is coming too late.
우리 음식이 너무 늦게 나온다.

B I agree. Let's complain to the manager.
맞아. 지배인에게 불평해야겠어.

---

03 conversation
[kànvərséiʃən]

n 회화, 대화　　　**make conversations** 대화를 나누다

A Dad, why can't I go to the party?
아빠, 저 왜 파티에 가면 안돼요?

B We already had this conversation, Jenny.
이것에 대해서 이미 대화했잖니, 제니야.

---

04 discuss
[diskʌs]

v 토론하다, 논의하다

A Fred, I have something to talk to you.
프레드, 너에게 할 말이 있어.

B I'm sorry, Sue. Let's discuss it later.
미안해, 수. 나중에 논의하자.

---

05 apologize
[əpálədʒàiz]

n apology 사죄, 사과

v 사과하다, 사죄하다

A Did you apologize to Clara, yet?
클라라에게 사과했니?

B I did, but she is still angry.
사과했는데 아직도 화가 나 있어.

06 communicate
[kəmjúːnəkèit]

ⓝ communication
의사소통

Ⓥ 의사소통하다

A Do you get along well with your father?
너는 아버지와 친하게 지내니?

B No, it's hard for us to communicate.
아니, 의사소통하기가 너무 어려워.

07 refuse
[rifjúːz]

Ⓥ 거절하다

A Did Susan tell you why she was mad?
수잔이 자기가 왜 화났는지 얘기했니?

B No, she still refuses to talk to me.
아니, 아직도 나와 대화하기를 거부해.

08 blame
[bleim]

Ⓥ 나무라다, 비난하다

A I'm so sorry, Bella. 벨라, 정말 미안해.

B It's all right. I don't blame you.
괜찮아. 너를 탓하진 않아.

09 warn
[wɔːrn]

Ⓥ 경고하다, 주의하다

A Don't break the rules again! I warn you!
다시는 규칙을 어기지 마라! 경고하는 거야!

B Yes, Ms. Marge. 네, 마지 선생님.

10 argue
[áːrgjuː]

ⓝ argument 논쟁

Ⓥ 논쟁하다, 논하다

A How could you do this to me?
어떻게 나한테 이럴 수 있어?

B I don't want to argue, but it's really not my
fault. 논쟁하고 싶지는 않지만, 정말 내 탓이 아냐.

11 allow
[əláu]

Ⓥ 허락하다

A Dad, can I go to the party tonight?
아빠, 오늘 밤 파티에 가도 돼요?

B No, Sally. I won't allow it. 안 된다, 샐리. 허락할 수 없어.

12 excuse
[ikskjúːz]

ⓝ 변명 **ⓥ** 용서하다, 변명하다

excuse a fault 잘못을 용서하다

A Tina, why were you late for school?
티나, 오늘 학교에 왜 늦었어?

B I'm sorry, Mr. Charlie. I have no excuses.
죄송합니다. 찰리 선생님. 변명의 여지가 없습니다.

13 opinion
[əpínjən]

ⓝ 의견, 견해   **express one's opinion** 의견을 표하다

A What do you think about this office?
이 사무실 어떻게 생각하세요?

B In my opinion, it's too large for us.
제 생각에는 우리에겐 너무 넓은 것 같아요.

14 offer
[ɔ́(ː)fər]

ⓝ 권유, 제의 **ⓥ** 권하다, 제공하다

offer a free gift 무료 선물을 제공하다

A Would you like some tea, John? 존. 차 마실래요?

B No, I'm fine. Thanks for the offer.
아뇨, 괜찮아요. 그래도 권해주셔서 고마워요.

15 suggest
[sədʒést]
ⓝ suggestion 제안

ⓥ 제안하다, 제의하다

A We lost ourselves. What should we do now?
길을 잃었어. 우리 이제 어떻게 하지?

B I suggest we stay here and wait for help.
내가 제안하는 것은 여기서 도움을 기다리는 거야.

16 accept
[æksépt]
ant refuse 거절하다

ⓥ 받아들이다, 동의하다

A It takes much courage to accept that you are wrong.
네가 틀렸다는 사실을 받아들이는 데는 많은 용기가 필요해.

B Yes, it is harder than it sounds.
맞아, 생각보다 어려운 일이지.

17 forgive
[fəːrgív]
(forgive-forgave-forgiven)

ⓥ 용서하다　　　　**forgive and forget** 용서하고 잊다

A I made a big mistake. Please forgive me.
내가 큰 실수를 했어. 용서해 줘.

B It's okay. Don't worry about it. 괜찮아. 마음 쓰지 마.

18 language
[lǽŋgwidʒ]

ⓝ 언어　　　　**a body language** 몸짓 언어

A Many people watch American sitcoms to learn the English language.
많은 사람이 영어를 배우기 위해 미국 시트콤을 봐.

B I guess studying won't be boring.
공부하는 게 지루하지 않겠구나.

19 beg
[beg]
ⓝ beggar 거지, 걸인

ⓥ 간청하다, 구걸하다

A Why did you lend him so much money?
왜 그에게 그렇게 많은 돈을 빌려줬니?

B He was begging. His mother is in hospital.
그 사람이 간청했어. 그의 어머니께서 입원해 계셔.

20 scream
[skriːm]

ⓥ 비명을 지르다　**ⓝ** 비명　　**hear a scream** 비명 소리를 듣다

A Was the movie scary? 영화 무서웠니?

B Yes, my wife was screaming the whole time.
응, 내 아내는 영화 내내 비명을 질렀어.

21 deny
[dináí]

ⓥ 부정하다, 인정하지 않다

deny the truth 진실을 인정하지 않다

A Did Henry really do such a thing?
헨리가 정말 그런 짓을 했니?

B I'm not sure, but I heard him deny it.
나도 잘 모르겠는데, 그가 인정하지 않는 걸 들었어.

22 inform

[infɔ́ːrm]

n information 정보

v 알리다

A I didn't know that the party was cancelled.
나는 파티가 취소된 걸 몰랐어.

B I am sorry that they didn't inform you.
그들이 너에게 알려주지 않아서 유감스럽군.

23 agree

[əgríː]

n agreement 동의

v 동의하다, 의견이 일치하다

A I think people need to love each other more.
나는 사람들이 서로를 더 사랑해야 한다고 생각해.

B I agree with you. 네 말에 동의해.

24 reply

[riplái]

n 대답, 답변 **v** 대답하다, 답장하다

A Have you written a reply to John, yet?
존에게 답장 썼니?

B No, I haven't had the time to even read his letter. 아니, 그의 편지를 읽을 시간도 없었어.

25 mention

[menʃən]

v 말하다, 언급하다

A Did the teacher mention the test?
선생님께서 시험에 대해 언급하셨니?

B No, not yet. 아니, 아직 안 하셨어.

Multi-Meaning Word

express

v 표현하다
Words cannot **express** it. 말로는 그것을 표현할 수 없다.

a 급행의
I'm planning to take an **express** bus to Seoul.
나는 서울까지 고속버스를 타고 갈 예정이야.

a 속달의
I sent the package by **express** post, so you can receive it by tomorrow.
내가 그 소포를 속달 우편으로 보냈으니까 내일까지는 받을 수 있을 거야.

Word Search

앞에서 배운 어휘를 기억하며 모두 찾아 보세요.

정답

A	M	E	Y	E	I	E	R	O	Z	Q	W	U	S	V
H	O	N	M	C	X	I	E	P	E	Z	Q	V	S	O
H	E	A	J	V	N	N	P	I	V	S	B	L	U	D
D	L	X	R	F	V	R	L	N	H	C	P	W	C	F
B	C	E	O	E	E	A	Y	I	G	R	K	R	S	O
N	S	R	A	X	Z	W	Y	O	W	E	A	K	I	R
S	M	R	B	R	P	I	E	N	C	A	G	R	D	G
N	F	U	E	S	G	B	D	O	D	M	J	E	M	I
B	S	B	X	E	F	U	M	O	B	E	G	F	E	V
E	F	K	E	I	F	P	E	G	L	D	O	U	O	E
A	L	L	O	W	L	O	P	F	F	O	G	S	P	X
H	U	Z	I	A	A	G	R	E	E	L	P	E	Z	O
L	C	L	I	D	Y	A	R	V	X	D	O	A	M	G
T	H	N	A	C	C	E	P	T	F	S	P	D	O	Z

accept	agree	allow	argue
beg	blame	complain	deny
discuss	forgive	inform	opinion
refuse	reply	scream	warn

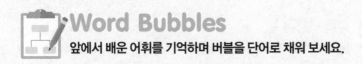

조부모　　　　남편　　　　우정　　　　친한, 가까운

가족　　　　**Relationship**
관계　　　　친구

행사　　　　의사소통

초대하다　　　모이다　　　표현하다　　　경고하다

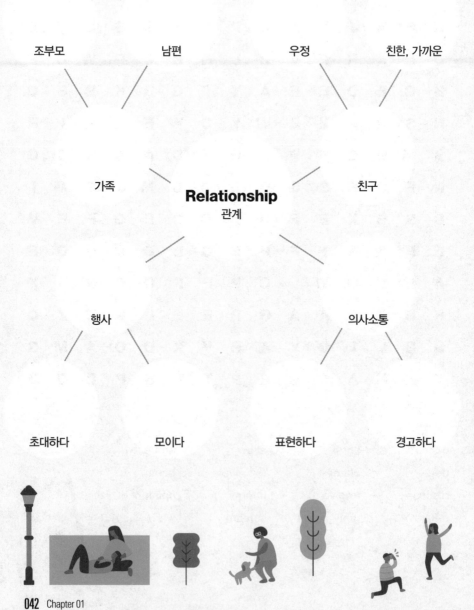

A 우리말을 영어로, 영어를 우리말로 쓰시오.

01 비밀	_____	08 marry	_____
02 사촌	_____	09 guest	_____
03 추억, 기억	_____	10 respect	_____
04 거절하다	_____	11 dine	_____
05 이웃사람	_____	12 conversation	_____
06 비명	_____	13 friendship	_____
07 의존하다	_____	14 welcome	_____

B 빈칸에 알맞은 단어를 쓰시오.

01 일란성 쌍둥이	identical _____	
02 모이다	get _____	
03 축제를 열다	hold a _____	
04 cancel a match	시합을 _____	
05 complain about the noises	소음에 대해 _____	
06 during one's lifetime	~의 _____ 동안	

C 단어의 관계에 맞게 빈칸을 채우시오.

01 남편	: 아내	= husband	: _____
02 초대	: 초대하다	= invitation	: _____
03 따뜻한	: 온정	= warm	: _____
04 congratulate	: congratulation	= 축하하다	: _____
05 single	: married	= 독신의	: _____
06 graduation	: graduate	= 졸업	: _____

D 배운 단어를 사용하여 문장을 완성하시오. (필요하면 형태를 바꾸시오.)

01 South Korea _____ the Olympics in 1988 and 2018.

한국은 1988년과 2018년에 올림픽을 개최했다.

02 Nick always _____ others for his faults.

닉은 항상 자신의 잘못을 다른 사람 탓으로 돌린다.

03 Sam and Linda have three _____.

샘과 린다에게는 세 명의 아이가 있다.

04 Cindy is a(n) _____ of the book club.

신디는 그 북 클럽의 회원이다.

05 It took me three hours to put up the _____.

나는 울타리를 세우는 데 세 시간이 걸렸다.

E 빈칸에 알맞은 말을 보기에서 찾아 쓰시오.

accept	grandparents	birthday	between	holidays

01 **A** Did you apologize to her for lying?

  B I did, but she didn't _____ my apology.

02 **A** Are there any problems _____ you and your son?

  B Actually, we had a big argument the other day.

03 **A** Do you have any plans for the winter _____?

  B I will visit my _____ in China.

04 **A** Oh, you have such a nice bike.

  B My uncle bought me as a _____ gift.

F 밑줄 친 부분을 우리말로 옮기시오.

01 Would you like to send it by <u>express mail</u> or regular mail?

02 Debby is one of my <u>close friends</u>.

Chapter
02

Describing People

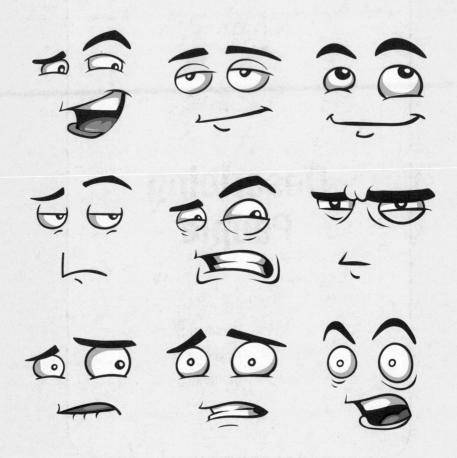

Basic Words

□ good 착한, 선량한	□ bad 나쁜	□ quiet 조용한
□ loud (소리가) 큰, 시끄러운	□ funny 재미있는	□ kind 다정한, 친절한
□ smart 똑똑한, 영리한	□ foolish 어리석은	□ shy 수줍음을 많이 타는
□ nice 친절한, 좋은	□ easy 쉬운, 수월한	□ honest 정직한

01 active
[ǽktiv]
v act 행동하다, 활동하다

ⓐ 활동적인, 활기 있는

A My grandmother is over 80, but is still very active. 내 할머니는 팔십 세가 넘으셨지만, 여전히 활동적이셔.

B I wonder what the secret is.
그 비결이 무엇인지 궁금해.

02 curious
[kjúəriəs]
ⓝ curiosity 호기심

ⓐ 호기심 있는, 기이한

be curious about ~ ~에 대해 궁금해하다

A William asks questions about everything.
윌리엄은 모든 것에 대해 질문을 해.

B He seems curious about many things.
그는 많은 것에 호기심이 있는 것 같아.

03 alone
[əlóun]

ⓐ 혼자의 **ad** 홀로, 외로이 　　**live alone** 혼자 살다

A Leave me alone, Sam. I don't want to talk to you. 날 좀 내버려 둬, 샘. 너하고 얘기하고 싶지 않아.

B I said I was sorry. 미안하다고 했잖아.

04 calm
[kɑːm]

v 가라앉히다, 달래다 **ⓐ** 침착한, 고요한

become calm 침착해지다

A Calm down, James. There is no point in fighting. 침착해, 제임스. 싸워서 이로울 게 없어.

B But he's the one who started it first.
하지만, 먼저 시작한 건 저쪽이야.

05 cheerful
[tʃíərfəl]
ⓝ cheer 기쁨, 환호

ⓐ 기분 좋은, 명랑한　　**a cheerful person** 쾌활한 사람

A There hasn't been any cheerful news for a long time. 오랫동안 기분 좋은 뉴스가 없었구나.

B We can always hope for some tomorrow.
언제나 내일이 있을 거라고 기대할 수는 있잖아.

06 strict
[strikt]

ⓐ 엄격한, 엄한   **strict school rules** 엄격한 교칙

A Hurry up! We are going to be late. 서둘러! 늦겠어.

B Oh, no. My teacher is very strict about being late. 오, 안 돼. 선생님은 지각하는 거에 정말 엄격하신데.

07 gentle
[dʒéntl]

ⓐ 온화한, 부드러운

A What do you like so much about her?
그녀의 어디가 그렇게 좋아?

B She is so gentle and wise.
그녀는 정말 온화하고 현명해.

08 clever
[klévər]

ant stupid 어리석은

ⓐ 영리한, 똑똑한

A Nick is such a clever boy! 닉은 정말 영리한 소년이야!

B What makes you think so? 왜 그렇게 생각하니?

09 hasty
[héisti]

ⓝ haste 급함. 서두름

ⓐ 급한, 조급한

A I was so hasty that I made a terrible mistake.
너무 조급해서 엄청난 실수를 저질렀어.

B I think haste always makes things worst!
조급함은 항상 일을 최악으로 만드는 것 같아!

10 lazy
[léizi]

ant diligent 부지런한

ⓐ 게으른, 나태한

A Honey, stop being lazy and wake up!
여보, 그만 게으름 피우고 일어나!

B Just give me five more minutes. 5분만 더 줘.

11 serious
[síəriəs]

ⓐ 진지한, 심각한

A Are you feeling all right? 너 괜찮니?

B It's just a cold. Nothing serious.
그냥 감기야. 심각한 거 아니야.

12 rude
[ruːd]

ⓐ 무례한, 버릇없는　　　**a rude manner** 무례한 태도

A It's rude to talk with your mouth full.
입에 음식물이 있을 때 말하는 건 무례하단다.

B I'm sorry, Mom. 죄송해요, 엄마.

13 wonder
[wʌ́ndər]

ⓐ **wonderful** 불가사의한, 훌륭한

ⓥ 이상하게 여기다, 궁금해하다 ⓝ 경이, 놀라움

A I always wonder about life after death.
나는 사후의 인생이 항상 궁금했어.

B Only a dead man knows that.
죽은 사람만이 그것을 알겠지.

14 cruel
[krúːəl]

ⓝ **cruelty** 잔인함

ⓐ 잔인한, 무자비한　　　**a cruel fate** 잔혹한 운명

A Why did you get in a fight with Sally?
샐리와 왜 싸우게 되었니?

B She did something cruel to my dog.
내 개에게 잔인한 짓을 하잖아.

15 brave
[breiv]

ⓝ **bravery** 용감

ⓐ 용감한　　　**a brave warrior** 용감한 용사

A What kind of person is your uncle?
너희 삼촌은 어떤 분이시니?

B He is a very brave person.
그는 매우 용감한 분이셔.

16 patience
[péiʃəns]

ⓐ **patient** 인내력 있는

ⓝ 인내, 끈기

A I'm running out of patience, Lenny.
레니, 내 인내력이 바닥나고 있어.

B I'm sorry. It won't take any longer.
미안해. 더 이상 오래 안 걸릴 거야.

17 honesty

[ánisti]

a honest 정직한

n 정직, 성실

A There is a saying "Honesty is the best policy." '정직이 가장 좋은 정책이다'라는 격언이 있어.

B Yes, it is best to always tell the truth.
맞아, 항상 진실을 이야기하는 것이 가장 좋지.

18 doubt

[daut]

a doubtful 의심스러운

v 의심하다 **n** 의심　　**have no doubt** 의심치 않다, 확신하다

A Do you think what she said is true?
그녀가 얘기한 것이 사실이라고 생각해?

B I doubt it. 좀 미심쩍어.

19 polite

[pəláit]

ant impolite
버릇 없는, 무례한

a 공손한, 예의 바른

A I've never met someone as polite as Jack.
나는 잭만큼 예의 바른 사람을 만난 적이 없어.

B Yes, it feels good to be around him.
맞아, 그 사람 주변에 있으면 기분이 좋아.

20 certain

[sə́ːrtn]

a 확신하는, 확실한　　**be certain of ~** ~을 확신하다

A I am not certain whether it will succeed.
그것의 성공 여부에 대해서는 자신이 없어.

B Try being more positive about everything.
모든 것에 대해 더 긍정적으로 생각해 봐.

21 careful

[kɛ́ərfəl]

ant careless 부주의한

a 주의 깊은, 신중한

A Be careful in deciding what to study.
무엇을 공부할지 결정할 때는 신중해야 해.

B I know, but there aren't many choices.
저도 알지만, 선택의 여지가 많지 않아요.

22 unkind
[ʌ̀nkáind]

ant kind 친절한

ⓐ 불친절한, 매정한

A She was so unkind to say such harsh words to him. 그에게 그런 심한 말을 하다니 그녀는 정말 매정해.

B He deserves it. 그는 그렇게 당해도 싸.

* deserve : ~할 만하다

23 proud
[praud]

ⓝ pride 자부심

ⓐ 자랑으로 여기는, 거만한

A Jenny is too proud of herself sometimes.
제니는 가끔 너무 거만해.

B She may seem so, but I think she's a good person. 그렇게 보일 수도 있지만, 그녀가 좋은 사람이라고 생각해.

24 annoy
[ənɔ́i]

ⓥ 괴롭히다, 귀찮게 굴다

A There is so much work to do. Cleaning is so annoying! 할 일이 너무 많아. 청소하는 건 정말 성가셔!

B But someone has to do it.
하지만, 누군가는 해야 하는 법이야.

25 brilliant
[bríljənt]

ⓐ 똑똑한

A How did John do at school? 존은 학교에서 어땠어?

B He was a brilliant student. 똑똑한 학생이었지.

🐱 Multi-Meaning Word

wonder

ⓥ 궁금해하다
I **wondered** where he was.
나는 그가 어디에 있는지 궁금했다.

ⓝ 감탄, 놀라움
It's a **wonder** no one got hurt.
아무도 다치지 않은 것은 놀라워.

ⓝ 놀랄만한 것, 불가사의
What are the seven **wonders** of the world?
세계 7대 불가사의는 무엇입니까?

Word Search

앞에서 배운 어휘를 기억하며 모두 찾아 보세요.

정답

J	I	L	R	T	F	T	C	E	W	R	P	O	A	G
F	H	P	B	R	H	U	C	J	Q	U	R	C	C	E
J	F	U	H	L	R	O	L	I	G	D	O	A	T	N
R	O	V	J	A	G	N	N	E	R	E	U	R	I	T
D	W	Q	O	L	E	N	Q	E	A	T	D	E	V	L
T	F	U	A	E	E	Y	F	R	S	R	S	F	E	E
F	S	Y	V	R	U	P	B	Y	O	T	C	U	H	P
C	N	A	I	C	E	R	T	A	I	N	Y	L	T	O
Z	R	O	M	J	Y	B	M	R	E	V	E	L	C	L
B	U	L	E	T	E	O	W	O	N	D	E	R	U	I
S	A	A	L	O	N	E	A	Q	Q	U	Y	E	D	T
C	G	E	C	Y	O	I	O	N	Z	F	B	M	E	E
A	B	N	D	E	T	G	Q	S	A	L	A	Z	Y	B
U	Z	E	L	M	P	M	I	Z	E	Z	N	L	R	Z

active	alone	brave	calm
careful	certain	clever	doubt
gentle	honesty	lazy	polite
proud	rude	strict	wonder

Unit 06 Appearance

□ old 늙은
□ young 어린
□ fat 살찐
□ thin 얇은, 가는
□ short 키가 작은
□ tall 키가 큰
□ pretty 예쁜
□ handsome 잘생긴
□ beautiful 아름다운
□ lovely 사랑스러운
□ fantastic 환상적인
□ giant 거대한

01 alike
[əláik]

ⓐ 서로 닮은, 비슷한 **ad** 똑같이   **treat alike** 차별 없이 대우하다

A This is a picture of my family. 이건 우리 가족사진이야.

B Your sisters look so alike!
너희 자매들은 서로 정말 닮았구나!

02 appearance
[əpíərəns]

ⓥ appear 나타나다

ⓝ 외모, 겉모습

A You should not judge people by their
appearance. 사람을 외모로 판단하면 안 돼.

B Yes, I think it is unfair to do so.
맞아, 그렇게 하는 건 불공평한 것 같아.

03 blond
[blɑnd]

ⓐ 금발의 ⓝ 금발   **a lady with blond hair** 금발의 숙녀

A What does your brother look like, Jason?
제이슨, 네 남동생은 어떻게 생겼니?

B He is tall and blond, and wears glasses.
키가 크고, 금발이며 안경을 써.

04 charming
[tʃáːrmiŋ]

ⓥ charm 매혹시키다

ⓐ 매력적인, 호감이 가는   **a charming smile** 매력적인 미소

A Who is that charming man you came in with?
너랑 같이 온 저 매력적인 남자는 누구니?

B He's just a friend from work. 그냥 직장 동료야.

05 attractive
[ətrǽktiv]

ⓥ attract 매혹하다

ⓐ 마음을 끄는, 매력적인   **an attractive job** 매력적인 직업

A That actress is very attractive.
저 여배우 정말 매력 있어.

B Yes, people even watch the movie just to see
her. 응, 사람들은 심지어 단지 그녀를 보려고 영화를 보기도 해.

06 bald
[bɔːld]

ⓐ 대머리의, 머리카락이 없는

A Does my forehead look wider? I think I'm going bald.
내 이마가 더 넓어 보이니? 나 대머리가 돼가는 것 같아.

B Don't worry. It looks fine. 걱정하지 마. 괜찮아 보여.

07 pale
[peil]

ⓐ (얼굴이) 창백한, (빛깔 등이) 엷은　　**pale blue** 엷은 파랑

A I don't feel well. 몸이 안 좋아.

B You look so pale! Did you go see a doctor?
얼굴이 너무 창백하구나! 진찰은 받았니?

08 gracefully
[gréisfəli]
ⓐ graceful 우아한

ad 우아하게

A Look, isn't she Amy? 저기 봐. 에이미 아니니?

B I didn't know that she walked so gracefully.
그녀가 저렇게 우아하게 걷는지 몰랐어.

09 neat
[niːt]

ⓐ 단정한, 깔끔한　　**neat and clean** 단정하고 깨끗한

A Your sweater is very neat. 네 스웨터 참 단정하다.

B Thank you. I bought it last spring.
고마워. 지난봄에 산 거야.

10 heavy
[hévi]
ant light 가벼운

ⓐ 무거운

A I feel heavier than before. 예전보다 몸이 무거워.

B You'd better work out. 운동을 해 봐.

11 cute
[kjuːt]

ⓐ 귀여운, 예쁜

A Sue, your baby is so cute! 수. 네 아기 너무 귀엽다!

B Thank you. Doesn't she take after me?
고마워. 아기가 나 닮지 않았니?

12 good-looking
[gúdlúkiŋ]

ⓐ 잘 생긴, 아름다운

A Who is that good-looking man in the picture? 사진에 있는 잘 생긴 남자는 누구야?

B He's my father when he was young.
우리 아버지 젊었을 때야.

13 weight
[weit]

ⓥ weigh 무게를 달다

ⓝ 체중, 무게　　　　　　　**weight control** 체중 조절

A I have put on a lot of weight.
나 체중이 많이 늘었어.

B You don't seem to gain weight at all.
전혀 체중이 는 것 같지 않은데.

14 beard
[biərd]

c.f. mustache 콧수염

ⓝ 턱수염

A I have wanted to grow a beard since I was 17. 난 열일곱 살 때부터 턱수염을 기르고 싶었어.

B Why don't you grow it? It may look good on you. 한 번 길러보지 그래? 어울릴지도 몰라.

15 curly
[kə́ːrli]

ⓐ 곱슬머리의, 고수머리의　　　**curly hair** 곱슬머리

A I liked your hair better when it was curly.
나는 네 머리가 곱슬머리였을 때가 더 좋았어.

B You think I should get a perm again?
다시 파마해야 할 것 같니?

16 stranger
[stréindʒər]

ⓝ 낯선 사람　　　　　**a total stranger** 전혀 모르는 사람

A Can you tell me where the art museum is?
미술관이 어디 있는지 알려주시겠어요?

B Sorry, I am a stranger here, too.
죄송한데요, 저도 여기가 처음입니다.

17 skinny
[skíni]

n skin 피부

a 바싹 여윈, 깡마른

A Women on television are so skinny these days. 요즘 텔레비전에 나오는 여자들은 너무 말랐어.

B Yeah, I don't know why it doesn't show any overweight girls.   * overweight : 과체중의
맞아. 왜 과체중의 여자들이 안 나오는지 모르겠어.

18 ugly
[ʌ́gli]

a 추한, 추악한   **an ugly monster** 추한 괴물

A Being ugly depends on your heart rather than your appearance. 추해 보이는 것은 외모보다는 마음에 달렸어.

B I agree with that completely.
나는 그 말에 전적으로 동의해.

19 similar
[símələːr]

a 유사한, 닮은

A My sister and I look quite similar.
우리 언니하고 나는 제법 닮았어.

B Really? Do you have a picture of her with you? 정말이야? 언니 사진 가지고 있니?

20 beauty
[bjúːti]

a beautiful 아름다운

n 아름다움, 미인   **the beauty of nature** 자연의 아름다움

A This is a picture of my mother.
이게 우리 엄마 사진이야.

B I can see where you got your beauty!
네가 엄마를 닮아서 미인인가보다!

21 different
[dífərənt]

ant same 같은

a 다른, 상이한   **be different from ~** ~와 다르다

A Does your brother look like you?
너희 형은 너와 닮았니?

B No, we look totally different.
아니, 우린 서로 완전히 달라.

22 straight
[streit]

ⓐ 곧은, 직선의

A I heard you had a blind date. How does she look? 너 소개팅 했다고 들었어. 그녀는 어떻게 생겼니?

B She has black straight hair with brown eyes.
갈색 눈에 검은 생머리였어.

23 height
[hait]

ⓐ high 높은

ⓝ 키, 높이

A How tall are you? 네 키가 얼마니?

B I was six feet the last time I measured my height. 마지막으로 키를 쟀을 때 6피트였어.

* foot [feet]: 30.48cm

24 perfect
[pə́:rfikt]

ⓐ 완벽한   **perfect in all things** 모든 점에서 완벽한

A Jenny has a perfect body like a fashion model. 제니는 모델처럼 완벽한 몸매를 가지고 있어.

B I wish I had that body. 나도 그런 몸매를 가졌으면.

25 unlike
[ʌnláik]

prep ~와 다른, 닮지 않은

A Unlike his brother, Jasper is very tall.
그의 형과는 달리 제스퍼는 정말 키가 커.

B How tall is his brother? 그의 형은 키가 몇인데?

Multi-Meaning Word

heavy

ⓐ 무거운

How **heavy** is the bed?
그 침대는 얼마나 무겁니?

ⓐ 격렬한, 강한

The baseball game was cancelled because of the **heavy** rain.
폭우 때문에 야구 경기가 취소되었다.

ⓐ 다량의, 대량 소비의

My grandfather was a **heavy** smoker.
나의 할아버지는 담배를 많이 피는 분이셨다.

Word Search

앞에서 배운 어휘를 기억하며 모두 찾아 보세요.

정답

F	C	P	J	E	G	L	W	D	D	E	K	O	C	C
Y	E	H	T	Y	W	X	I	L	D	R	Q	X	T	K
T	N	U	E	F	F	F	C	C	O	N	A	O	S	S
H	C	M	B	R	F	T	S	H	X	Y	F	E	R	F
G	X	D	I	E	M	B	B	P	K	H	L	O	B	S
I	F	I	R	K	U	I	T	H	G	I	A	R	T	S
E	A	E	E	G	S	G	N	W	E	I	G	H	T	Y
H	N	F	L	V	O	X	V	G	C	N	E	C	T	A
T	L	Y	D	T	C	E	F	R	E	P	L	U	D	L
H	Y	L	R	U	C	M	W	E	K	B	E	F	L	I
E	V	I	T	C	A	R	F	T	A	E	L	E	A	K
H	E	A	V	Y	O	T	C	D	B	T	L	O	B	E
R	A	L	I	M	I	S	H	M	K	A	G	B	N	G
N	E	A	T	Z	D	Z	I	N	P	M	H	L	D	D

alike	bald	beard	blond
curly	cute	different	heavy
height	neat	pale	perfect
similar	straight	ugly	weight

Basic Words

☐ skirt 치마	☐ shoes 신발	☐ hat 모자
☐ dress 드레스	☐ pants 바지	☐ cap (야구) 모자
☐ button 단추	☐ wallet 지갑	☐ belt 허리띠
☐ socks 양말	☐ boots 부츠	☐ bag 가방

01 clothes
[klouðz]

C.f. cloth 천, 옷감

N 옷, 의복   Fine clothes make the man. 옷이 날개다.

A It's eight o'clock. It's time to go to school.
여덟 시야. 학교 갈 시간이야.

B Hurry up and put your clothes on.
서둘러 옷을 입어라.

02 jewelry
[dʒúːəlri]

C.f. jewel 보석

N 보석(류)

A Did you see the new jewelry store near the station? 역 근처에 새로 생긴 보석 가게 봤니?

B Yes, I found a very pretty ring there.
응. 거기서 정말 예쁜 반지 하나를 봤어.

03 sew
[sou]

(sew-sow-sewn)

V 바느질하다
      sew a button onto the shirt 셔츠에 단추를 달다

A Mom, is my skirt ready? 엄마. 제 치마 준비되었나요?

B No, I still have to sew the edges.
아니. 끄트머리를 바느질해야 돼.

04 wear
[wɛər]

(wear-wore-worn)

V 입다

A Why don't you wear this coat? It's really cold outside. 이 코트를 입는 게 어때? 밖이 정말 추워.

B Okay, thanks. 응. 고마워.

05 sweater
[swétər]

N 스웨터   knit a sweater 스웨터를 뜨다

A What did you get for Christmas last year?
작년 크리스마스에 무엇을 받았니?

B My parents got me a nice sweater.
부모님이 멋진 스웨터를 사주셨어.

06 change
[tʃeindʒ]

ⓥ 갈아입다, 바꾸다 **ⓝ** 변화

a change in appearance 외모의 변화

A Mom, I'm home. It's raining heavily.
엄마, 저 집에 왔어요. 비가 억수같이 와요.

B You are all wet. Change your wet clothes before you catch a cold.
너 흠뻑 젖었구나. 감기 들기 전에 젖은 옷을 갈아입으렴.

07 blouse
[blaus]

ⓝ 블라우스

A You spilled milk on my blouse!
내 블라우스에 우유를 쏟았잖아!

B I'm so sorry. Here are some napkins.
정말 미안해. 여기 냅킨 줄게.

08 fashion
[fǽʃən]

ⓐ fashionable
최신 유행의, 유행하는

ⓝ 유행, 패션　　**a fashion magazine** 패션 잡지

A You're tall enough to be a fashion model.
너 패션모델 할 만큼 키가 크구나.

B Do you think so? I want to be one, too.
그렇게 생각하니? 나도 패션모델이 되고 싶어.

09 patch
[pætʃ]

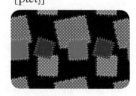

ⓥ 헝겊을 대고 깁다

A Mom, my pants got torn.
엄마, 바지가 찢어졌어요.　　* tear-tore-torn : 찢다

B Don't worry. I'll patch it up for you.
걱정하지 마. 엄마가 기워줄게.

10 trousers
[tráuzəːrz]

ⓢⓨⓝ pants 바지

ⓝ 바지

A Can I try these trousers on?
이 바지 입어 봐도 되나요?

B Yes, sir. The fitting room is this way.
네, 손님. 탈의실은 이쪽입니다.

11 sneaker
[sníːkər]

ⓝ (고무로 창을 댄) 운동화

A I need a new pair of sneakers.
나 새 운동화 한 켤레가 필요해.

B Why don't we go shopping? 쇼핑 가는 게 어때?

12 swimsuit
[swímsùːt]

ⓝ 수영복

A It's so nice out at the beach! Let's swim!
해변에 오니 정말 좋다! 우리 수영하자!

B Alright. But we need to change into our swimsuits first. 좋아. 그런데 먼저 수영복으로 갈아입어야 해.

13 purse
[pəːrs]

ⓝ 지갑

A Nancy, do you have any money? I lost my wallet. 낸시, 혹시 돈 있니? 나 지갑을 잃어버렸어.

B Wait a minute. I'll go get my purse.
잠깐만 기다려. 내 지갑을 가져올게.

14 cotton
[kátn]

ⓝ 면직물, 솜

A This shirt is made of pure cotton.
이 셔츠는 순면으로 만든 것이야.

B Yes, I like its soft feeling. 응. 부드러운 감촉이 좋아.

15 pocket
[pákit]

ⓝ 호주머니, 포켓

A The pockets on my pants are worn out.
바지 주머니가 다 닳았어.

B Make sure you don't keep any money in there. 거기에 돈을 넣어두지 않도록 해.

16 suit
[suːt]

n (의복)한 벌 **v** 어울리다, 적합하다　　**a business suit** 정장

A I bought a suit for the ceremony.
행사에 입을 정장 한 벌을 샀어.

B I think you should dress formally, too.
내 생각에도 네가 옷을 격식 차려서 입는 게 좋을 것 같아.

---

17 stain
[stein]

v 얼룩지다, 더럽히다 **n** 얼룩, 때　　**ink stains** 잉크 얼룩

A I spilled some coffee on my jacket!
나 재킷에 커피를 흘렸어!

B You should wipe it off before it stains.
얼룩이 남기 전에 어서 닦아야겠다.

---

18 tight
[tait]

v tighten 죄다

a (옷·신발 등이) 몸에 꼭 끼는　　**a tight belt** 꽉 죈 벨트

A These pants are too tight for me to wear.
이 바지는 내가 입기에 너무 꼭 껴요.

B Would you like a larger size, sir?
손님, 더 큰 치수로 드릴까요?

---

19 wool
[wul]

n 양모, 모직물

A I don't wear clothes made from wool. Wool
makes me itchy.　　　　　　* itchy : 가려운
난 모직으로 만들어진 옷은 안 입어. 가렵거든.

B But it keeps us warm when it is cold.
하지만, 추울 때 우리를 따뜻하게 해주잖아.

---

20 fur
[fəːr]

n 모피, 모피 제품　　**a fur coat** 모피 코트

A Some people are against making coats out of
fur. 어떤 사람들은 모피로 코트를 만드는 것에 반대해.

B I think it's cruel for the animals, too.
나도 동물들에게 잔인한 짓이라고 생각해.

21 fit
[fit]

ⓥ 적합하다, 어울리다 ⓐ 꼭 맞는, 알맞은 **a fit place** 적당한 장소

A Do the shoes fit on your feet? 신발 네 발에 잘 맞니?

B Yes, they're perfect! 응. 완벽해!

22 loose
[luːs]

ⓐ 헐거운, 매지 않은, 풀린

A Some people prefer wearing loose clothes.
어떤 사람들은 헐렁한 옷을 입는 것을 좋아해.

B I can't stand a tight shirt, either.
나도 꼭 끼는 셔츠를 못 입겠어.

23 striped
[straipt]

ⓝ stripe 줄무늬, 줄

ⓐ 줄무늬가 있는

A Which shirt did you like best, ma'am?
손님, 어떤 셔츠가 가장 마음에 들었나요?

B I liked the striped one. 줄무늬 셔츠가 마음에 들었어요.

24 size
[saiz]

ⓝ (옷 등의) 치수, 크기

A This jacket is too small for my brother.
제 동생이 입기에 이 재킷은 너무 작아요.

B But I'm afraid all the larger sizes are sold out.
죄송하지만, 큰 치수는 모두 품절입니다.

25 shorts
[ʃɔːrts]

ⓝ 반바지

A Is it hot outside, today? 오늘 밖에 더워?

B Yes, you had better wear shorts.
응, 반바지 입는 게 좋을 거야.

Multi-Meaning Word

fit

ⓐ 알맞은, 적당한/건강한, 튼튼한
I have nothing **fit** to wear. 입기에 마땅한 것이 없다.
He was young, good-looking, and **fit**. 그는 젊고 잘 생겼으며 건강했다.

ⓥ ~에 적합하다
This hat does not **fit** me. 이 모자는 내게 맞지 않는다.

Word Search

앞에서 배운 어휘를 기억하며 모두 찾아 보세요.

정답

```
K  S  Z  T  W  D  L  R  J  P  Q  V  B  N  S
X  H  I  J  A  E  E  U  A  T  E  U  L  O  T
A  U  O  S  M  T  A  T  O  K  J  N  O  T  A
S  S  W  C  A  B  C  R  A  W  V  S  U  T  I
T  E  I  E  L  H  T  E  U  H  P  L  S  O  N
R  W  W  S  C  L  N  I  W  B  O  U  E  C  Q
V  S  D  J  H  S  T  P  F  O  T  O  F  O  U
Z  K  A  E  R  O  P  H  S  S  H  S  I  Z  E
U  P  M  W  Q  Q  R  O  E  G  G  C  D  C  G
S  E  E  E  R  U  U  T  L  S  I  H  C  Y  X
Q  S  D  L  G  U  V  S  S  T  T  A  C  Q  I
W  R  D  R  G  Y  F  J  O  W  U  N  H  U  O
W  U  X  Y  S  S  V  V  W  U  H  G  T  J  M
U  P  P  A  M  F  K  S  F  A  E  E  Z  X  J
```

blouse	change	cotton	fit
fur	jewelry	patch	purse
sew	shorts	size	stain
suit	sweater	tight	wear

Word Bubbles

앞에서 배운 어휘를 기억하며 버블을 단어로 채워 보세요.

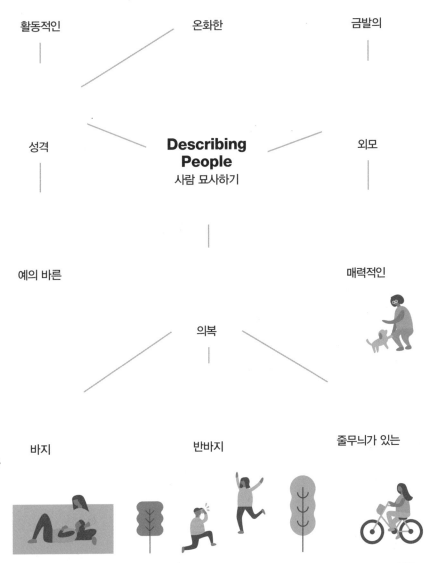

활동적인

온화한

금발의

성격

Describing People
사람 묘사하기

외모

예의 바른

매력적인

의복

바지

반바지

줄무늬가 있는

Review Test

A 우리말을 영어로, 영어를 우리말로 쓰시오.

01 엄격한, 엄한 _____ 08 blouse _____

02 완벽한 _____ 09 cheerful _____

03 옷, 의복 _____ 10 curious _____

04 대머리의 _____ 11 different _____

05 금발인, 금발 _____ 12 cotton _____

06 주의 깊은 _____ 13 fit _____

07 키, 높이 _____ 14 ugly _____

B 빈칸에 알맞은 단어를 쓰시오.

01 스웨터를 뜨다   knit a(n) _____

02 잔혹한 운명   a(n) _____ fate

03 곱슬머리   _____ hair

04 have no doubt   _____ 치 않다

05 ink stains   잉크 _____

06 a charming smile   _____ 미소

C 단어의 관계에 맞게 빈칸을 채우시오.

01 무거운 : 가벼운 = heavy : _____

02 꼭 끼는 : 헐거운 = tight : _____

03 무례한 : 공손한 = rude : _____

04 kind : unkind = 친절한 : _____

05 gracefully : graceful = 우아하게 : _____

06 weight : weigh = 무게, 체중 : _____

D 배운 단어를 사용하여 문장을 완성하시오. (필요하면 형태를 바꾸시오.)

01 The soldiers were _____ and didn't fear death.
군인들은 용감했고 죽음을 두려워하지 않았다.

02 He started growing his _____ when he was thirty.
그는 서른 살 때 턱수염을 기르기 시작했다.

03 The twins have a _____ appearance, so I can't tell the
difference between them.   * tell the difference : 구별하다
그 쌍둥이는 비슷한 외모를 가지고 있어서 나는 그들을 구별할 수 없다.

04 Cindy _____ into pajamas and lay on the bed.
신디는 잠옷으로 갈아입고 침대에 누웠다.

05 The old gentle man put his hand into the _____ and took
out a gold coin.
노신사는 주머니에 손을 넣고는 금화 하나를 꺼냈다.

E 빈칸에 알맞은 말을 보기에서 찾아 쓰시오.

> proud   wonder   size   attractive   trousers

01 A Dad, I won the science contest.
  B Congratulations! I am so _____ of you.

02 A What is so _____ about her?
  B Well, I just feel happy with her.

03 A I _____ why he called me.
  B Why don't you call and ask him?

04 A Do you have these _____ in a larger _____?
  B Let me check, sir.

F 밑줄 친 부분을 우리말로 옮기시오.

01 We had a heavy snow last night. The whole world turned white.

02 The Great Wall is one of the seven wonders of the world.

VOCA Inn!

재미있는 상표 이야기

Nike ★ 그리스 신화에서 승리의 여신인 니케에서 따온 것으로 나이키 로고는 니케의 동상 날개를 형상화한 것으로 열정적인 스포츠 정신과 승리를 의지를 표현한다. 재미있게도 이 나이키 로고는 Carolyn Davidson이 1971년 35달러에 디자인 했으며 1995년에 나이키의 로고가 되었다고 한다.

McDonald's ★ 맥도날드의 로고는 흔히 맥도날드의 M을 따온 것이나, 프렌치 프라이를 연상하도록 디자인되었다고 생각된다. 하지만, 맥도날드의 로고는 1962년 Jim Schindler가 디자인한 것으로 맥도날드 레스토랑 옆 아치 형태의 간판에서 영감을 얻어 아치 모양 두 개를 결합하여 디자인했다.

Apple ★ 애플컴퓨터가 만유인력법칙의 발견만큼 인류의 큰 이슈임을 상징한다는 의미로 초기의 애플사 로고는 나무 아래 앉아 있는 아이작 뉴턴이었다. 1977년 그래픽 디자이너인 Rod Janoff가 애플 2가 최초의 컬러 모니터임을 상징하기 위해 지금의 사과에 무지개 색을 입힌 고로를 디자인하게 되었고 지금까지 색을 달리하면서 사용되고 있다.

Levi's ★ 독일 출신의 리바이스 스트라우스가 갈색 천막 천을 이용하여 리바이의 바지, Levi's Pants를 만들어 팔면서 Levi's라는 상표가 유래하였다. 리바이스 바지 뒷주머니를 보면 말 두 마리가 바지를 잡아당기는 그림을 보게 되는데 이것은 말이 잡아당겨도 찢어지지 않는 튼튼한 바지라는 것을 의미한다.

Starbucks ★ 스타벅스는 허먼 멜빌의 소설 '모비딕'에 등장하는 커피를 좋아하는 일등 항해사의 이름, 스타벅에서 유래되었다. 스타벅스 로고의 여자는 노래로 선원들을 현혹시켜 배를 침몰시키는 세이렌이라는 신화 속의 인물이다. 세이렌을 보면 스타벅스가 연상되도록 로고의 중심이 그려 넣었다고 한다.

Chapter
03

Body & Mind

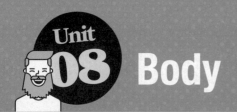

Unit 08 Body

Basic Words

- body 신체
- face 얼굴
- leg 다리
- hair 머리카락
- head 머리
- neck 목
- finger 손가락
- mouth 입
- lip 입술
- shoulder 어깨
- foot 발
- nose 코

01 chest
[tʃest]

ⓝ 가슴   **chest pains** 가슴 통증

A I feel pain in my chest. 나 가슴에 통증이 있어.

B You should see a doctor. It might be because of your heart. 병원에 가봐. 심장 때문일 수도 있어.

02 breathe
[briːð]

ⓝ breath 호흡

ⓥ 숨 쉬다, 호흡하다   **breathe fresh air** 신선한 공기를 마시다

A This dress is too tight to breathe!
이 드레스 너무 조여서 숨을 쉴 수가 없어!

B Take it off. Let's find a different one.
벗어. 다른 걸 찾아보자.

03 cell
[sel]

ⓝ 세포   **a human cell** 인간 세포

A All living things are made of cells.
모든 생물은 세포로 이루어져 있어.

B How many are there in the human body?
사람 몸에는 몇 개나 있니?

04 hand
[hænd]

ⓥ 건네주다 **ⓝ** 손, 일손   **shake one's hand** 악수하다

A Could you hand me the keys on the left?
왼쪽에 있는 열쇠 좀 건네줄래?

B No problem. 물론이지.

05 brain
[brein]

ⓐ brainy 머리가 좋은, 총명한

ⓝ 뇌, 두뇌

A Scientists seem to have brilliant brains.
과학자들은 참 명석한 두뇌를 가진 것 같아.

B Yes, I wish I could be so smart, too.
맞아, 나도 그렇게 똑똑할 수 있으면 좋겠어.

06 skin
[skin]

ⓝ 피부, 가죽   **dry skin** 건성 피부

A You have such wonderful skin! What's your secret? 피부가 참 좋구나! 비법이 뭐니?

B I try to get enough sleep. 잠을 충분히 자려고 노력해.

07 □ toe
[tou]

n 발가락

A Humans are able to walk because we have toes. 사람은 발가락이 있기 때문에 걸을 수 있는 거야.

B I didn't know they were so important.
발가락이 그렇게 중요한 줄 몰랐어.

08 □ knee
[niː]

n 무릎　　　　　　　　**on one's knee** 무릎을 꿇고

A Henry got down on his knee and asked her to marry him. 헨리가 무릎을 꿇고 그녀에게 청혼을 했어.

B Oh, how romantic he is! 오, 정말 로맨틱하다!

09 □ lung
[lʌŋ]

n 허파, 폐

A Smoking can make serious problems in our lungs. 흡연은 우리의 폐에 심각한 문제를 일으킬 수 있어.

B Yes, there are a hundred reasons not to smoke! 맞아, 담배를 피우지 않을 이유가 백 가지는 돼.

10 □ nail
[neil]

n 손톱, 발톱

A How long can we grow our fingernails?
손톱을 얼마나 길게 기를 수 있을까?

B Well, Lee Redmond had the longest nail of 2 feet and 11 inches.
글쎄, 리 레드몬드가 2피트 11인치로 가장 긴 손톱을 가지고 있었어.

11 □ stretch
[stretʃ]

v 쭉 펴다, 잡아 늘이다

A What is the next step? 다음 단계는 뭐야?

B Stretch your arms out to your sides.
네 팔을 양 옆으로 쭉 펴.

12 gesture
[dʒéstʃər]

n 몸짓, 손짓

A Americans use a lot of gestures when they talk. 미국 사람들은 말할 때 몸짓을 많이 사용해.

B Yes, there are different gestures for each situation. 응, 각 상황마다 쓰는 몸짓이 달라.

13 voice
[vɔis]

n 목소리　　**keep one's voice down** 목소리를 낮추다

A I went to the concert yesterday. The voice of the singer was so beautiful.
나 어제 콘서트에 갔었어. 가수의 목소리가 정말 아름다웠어.

B I think I know who you are talking about.
네가 누구 얘기하는지 알 것 같아.

14 step
[step]

n 걸음　**v** 한 걸음 내디디다, 밟다

step forward 앞으로 나아가다

A Watch your step. The floor is very slippery.
걸음 조심해. 바닥이 정말 미끄럽다.

B I'll be careful. 조심할게.

15 bone
[boun]

n 뼈, 골격　　　　　　**a hip bone** 엉덩이 뼈

A What did the doctor say about Peter?
의사가 피터에 대해 뭐라고 했니?

B He said his bones became very weak.
뼈가 매우 약해졌다고 했어.

16 rest
[rest]

n 휴식　**v** 휴식을 취하다　　　**take a rest** 쉬다

A I can't walk any more. I need some rest.
나 더는 못 걸어. 휴식이 필요해.

B But we have so much more to see!
하지만, 우리 아직 볼 게 더 많단 말이야!

17 spirit
[spírit]

ⓐ spiritual 정신의, 정신적인

ⓝ 정신, 영혼

A Do you believe in the afterlife?
너는 사후세계를 믿니?

B Yes, I believe the spirit lives on forever.
응, 나는 영혼이 영원히 산다고 믿어.

18 tongue
[tʌŋ]

ⓝ 혀

A Our tongue makes us speak.
허는 우리가 말할 수 있게 해줘.

B It also allows us to taste different flavors.
여러 맛을 느낄 수 있게 해주기도 하지.

19 tooth
[tuːθ]

pl teeth

ⓝ 이, 치아   **have a tooth pulled out** 이를 빼다

A I think I have to go to the dentist soon.
나 조만간 치과에 가야 할 것 같아.

B Didn't you brush your teeth properly?
이를 제대로 안 닦았니?

20 sweat
[swet]

ⓥ 땀을 흘리다 **ⓝ** 땀

A Why do you hate summer so much?
너는 왜 그렇게 여름을 싫어하니?

B Because I don't like sweating a lot.
땀이 많이 나는 것을 싫어하기 때문이야.

21 fist
[fist]

ⓝ 주먹

A I hurt my hand when I was little. I can't make
a fist. 나 어렸을 때 손을 다쳤어. 주먹을 못 쥐어.

B It must have hurt very much. 많이 아팠겠구나.

22 palm
[pɑːm]

ⓝ 손바닥　　　　**read one's palm** 손금을 보다

A　The baby's hands are so cute! 아기 손이 너무 귀여워!

B　Yes, his hands are smaller than my palm.
응, 아기의 손이 내 손바닥보다도 작아.

23 wrist
[rist]

ⓝ 손목

A　The wrist is important in various sports.
다양한 스포츠에서 손목이 중요해.

B　That's because the wrist controls your
hands. 그것은 손목이 네 손을 통제하기 때문이야.

24 cheek
[tʃiːk]

ⓝ 뺨, 볼　　　　**cheek to cheek** 뺨과 뺨을 맞대고

A　It's very cold today. 오늘 정말 추워.

B　I can tell by your red cheeks.
네 빨간 볼을 보니 그런 것 같았어.

25 balance
[bǽləns]

ⓐ balanced 균형 잡힌

ⓝ 균형, 평형

A　I think I should go on a diet.
다이어트를 해야 할까 봐.

B　You don't have to. It is important to keep a
balance between weight and height.
그럴 필요 없어. 체중과 신장의 균형을 유지하는 게 중요한 거야.

Multi-Meaning Word

hand

ⓝ 손
To prevent a cold, you should wash your **hands** very often.
감기를 예방하려면 손을 자주 씻어야 한다.

ⓝ 일손
Could you give me a **hand**? 나 좀 도와줄래?

ⓝ 박수
Let's give him a big **hand**. 그에게 박수갈채를 보냅시다.

ⓥ 넘겨주다, 건네주다
Please **hand** me the salt. 소금 좀 건네주세요.

Word Search

앞에서 배운 어휘를 기억하며 모두 찾아 보세요.

정답

```
M R F T R E L C X G Z Y L H S
P A L M O L R B C Y K L A N W
C E C T W B R A I N E N A E E
C L U N G P E Y I C D I B N A
G H D H T U U W W X L P D O T
Z J E T T E Z A S K I N B C
C Y S S E O I F I S T T Z M Z
P O S C T S O K N E E R S Q K
M R I U T N R T Z P K J V E K
K O X D C C S S O Q I Q Y E R
V A T Y L L Z P W E B A E L W
H X N N N P I O A F E H U Z A
C L W C A P E B L T C N X T E
D A O J V I U L L A K X S U X
```

bone	brain	cell	cheek
chest	fist	knee	lung
nail	palm	rest	skin
sweat	toe	tooth	voice

Unit 09 Senses

Basic Words

- □ watch 보다
- □ see 보다
- □ listen 듣다
- □ awful 끔찍한

- □ look 보다
- □ hear 듣다
- □ feel 느끼다
- □ enjoy 즐기다

- □ show 보여 주다
- □ touch 만지다
- □ do 하다
- □ soft 부드러운

01 ☑ **sight**
[sait]

v see 보다

n 시야, 시력, 풍경   **at the first sight** 첫눈에

A Stop fooling around! I was so scared at the sight of somebody following me.
장난 그만 쳐 누군가가 날 따라오는 걸 보고 정말 무서웠다고.

B Sorry, I didn't mean to scare you.
미안해, 너를 겁주려고 한 건 아니었어.

---

02 ☑ **imagine**
[imǽdʒin]

n imagination 상상

v 상상하다

A How was your date yesterday?
어제 데이트 어땠어?

B It was great. I can't imagine a better time.
정말 좋았어. 그보다 즐거운 시간을 상상할 수가 없어.

---

03 ☑ **impress**
[imprés]

n impression 감동, 인상

v 감명을 주다

A How was the play, Sammy? 연극 어땠니, 새미?

B I was very impressed by their hard work.
그들의 노력에 크게 감명 받았어.

---

04 ☑ **aware**
[əwέər]

a 깨닫는, 의식하는   **be aware of ~** ~을 깨닫다, 인식하고 있다

A Watch where you're going! 앞을 보고 다녀!

B I'm sorry. I wasn't aware of you.
미안해. 네가 있다고 의식하지 못했어.

---

05 ☑ **sound**
[saund]

v 소리가 나다, 들리다 **n** 소리

A Your English sounds different from Tom's.
네가 쓰는 영어는 톰과 조금 다르게 들려.

B That is because he's American and I'm British. 그건 그는 미국인이고 난 영국인이기 때문이야.

06 smell
[smel]

ⓐ smelly 냄새 나는

ⓝ 냄새 **ⓥ** 냄새 맡다, 냄새가 나다

smell flowers 꽃 냄새를 맡다

A What is that delicious smell?
맛있는 냄새가 무엇이니?

B Mom is cooking. 어머니께서 요리를 하고 계세요.

07 silent
[sáilənt]

ⓝ silence 고요, 침묵

ⓐ 침묵하는, 고요한

A You are silent today. Is something wrong?
너 오늘 조용하다. 무슨 일 있니?

B Because of a sore throat, I have a husky voice. 목이 아파서 목소리가 쉬었거든.

08 noise
[nɔiz]

ⓝ 소음, 잡음 　　　　　　　 **make a noise** 떠들다

A What is all that noise outside?
밖에 저 소음은 다 뭐지?

B I guess the construction finally started.
공사가 드디어 시작됐나 봐.　　　　　 * construction : 공사

09 contact
[kántækt]

ⓝ 접촉, 인접　　**be in contact with ~** ~와 접촉하고 있다

A Americans tend to maintain eye contact when they talk.
미국인들은 이야기할 때 눈을 맞추는 경향이 있어.

B Their culture is quite different from ours.
그들의 문화는 우리와 사뭇 달라.

10 glance
[glæns]

ⓝ 흘긋 봄 **ⓥ** 흘긋 보다, 언뜻 보다

A I thought he was a girl at first glance.
처음에 언뜻 봤을 때 그가 여자인 줄 알았어.

B It must have been because of his long hair.
그의 긴 머리 때문임이 틀림없어.

11 sense
[sens]

ⓥ 알아채다 **ⓝ** 감각, 의식　　　**a sense of smell** 후각

A Why did you go home early last night?
어젯밤에 집에 왜 일찍 갔니?

B I sensed that Fred wanted to be alone.
프레드가 혼자 있고 싶어하는 것을 느꼈어.

12 observe
[əbzə́ːrv]

ⓝ observation 관찰

ⓥ 관찰하다

A The repairman observed the machine carefully. 수리공이 기계를 주의 깊게 관찰했어.

B Did he find what the problem was?
문제가 무엇인지 찾았니?

13 vision
[víʒən]

ⓐ visible 눈에 보이는

ⓝ 시력, 시각

A These glasses will help your vision.
이 안경이 시력에 도움을 줄 것입니다.

B But they don't seem comfortable to wear.
하지만, 쓰기에 편해 보이지 않는데요.

14 smooth
[smuːð]

ⓐ 매끄러운, 부드러운　　　**a smooth surface** 매끄러운 표면

A I like the smooth feeling of this silk shirt.
이 무명 셔츠의 부드러운 감촉이 좋아.

B So do I. 나도 그래.

15 attention
[əténʃən]

ⓝ 주의, 관심　　　**receive attention** 주목을 받다

A You need to pay more attention to class.
수업에 더 집중해야 해.　　　* pay attention to ~: ~에 주의를 기울이다

B I'm sorry. I stayed up late last night.
죄송해요. 어제 늦게까지 깨어 있었어요.

16 stare
[stɛər]

V 응시하다, 빤히 보다

A It's not polite to stare at other people.
다른 사람들을 빤히 보는 것은 무례해.

B Oh, I didn't know I was doing so.
이런, 내가 그러는 줄 몰랐네.

17 notice
[nóutis]

V 알아채다, 인지하다 **N** 통지, 통고
take notice of ~ ~을 알아차리다

A I'm sorry, I didn't notice you standing there.
미안, 거기 네가 서 있는 줄 몰랐어.

B It's okay. Don't worry about it.
괜찮아. 신경 쓰지 마.

18 hearing
[híəriŋ]

N 청각, 청력, 듣기

A My grandfather had poor hearing for a long time. 우리 할아버지께서는 오랫동안 청력이 안 좋으셨어.

B It must have been very uncomfortable for him. 참 불편하셨겠다.

19 deaf
[def]

a 귀먹은

A Don't play your earphones too loud. You will become deaf. 이어폰 너무 크게 틀지 마. 귀가 먹게 될 거야.

B I'll try not to, Mom. 그래 볼게요, 엄마.

20 ignore
[ignɔ́:r]

V 무시하다

A Sometimes my brother annoys me so much.
가끔 내 동생이 나를 너무 성가시게 해.

B Just ignore him when you're busy.
바쁠 때는 그냥 무시해.

21 blind
[blaind]

ⓐ 눈먼, 장님의 **ⓥ** 눈멀게 하다

A Although Helen Keller was blind and deaf, she did many good things.
헬렌 켈러는 시각과 청각 장애인인데도 많은 좋은 일들을 했어.

B Yeah, we should learn something from her.
맞아, 우리는 그녀에게서 뭔가를 배워야 해.

22 hard
[hɑ:rd]

ⓐ 굳은, 단단한

A I feel something hard under my sleeping bag.
침낭 밑에 뭔가 단단한 것이 있는 것 같아.

B See if there are any rocks under it.
밑에 돌멩이가 있는지 한 번 봐.

23 physical
[fízikəl]

ⓐ 육체의, 신체의

A I wonder Mary is recovering soon.
나는 메리가 곧 회복할지 궁금해.

B She is in very poor physical condition.
그녀는 몸 상태가 매우 악화되어 있어.

24 view
[vju:]

ⓝ 광경, 경치, 시력

A My apartment has a great view.
우리 아파트는 전망이 참 좋아.

B I want to live in a high apartment, too.
나도 고층 아파트에 살고 싶어.

25 gaze
[geiz]

ⓥ 주시하다, 응시하다

A How do you feel about this picture?
이 그림을 본 소감이 어때?

B It was so beautiful! I couldn't stop gazing at it. 정말 아름다웠어! 보는 걸 멈출 수 없었어.

Word Search

앞에서 배운 어휘를 기억하며 모두 찾아 보세요.

```
K A Z I H I N S E K E I Q S N
C O N T A C T O V R Z R M U H
S E S I O N H I T G N E A T G
V H P Y U R S A X I L E A T X
W R F E V I I U R L C O S F S
E M L T O D L M O D M E R Y F
I P S N E Q W D P S K P I B L
V Y O I A Z N X S R G U X G J
Z O B G L I E I R B E P M N C
Q S S F L E G G K U G S B I R
P O E B A H M E R A W A S R J
T U R Z T E U T W H K O M A S
R N V L E C D I F R J J R E Z
N D E U D M R W N T X G K H G
```

aware	blind	contact	deaf
hard	hearing	impress	noise
notice	observe	sight	smell
sound	stare	view	vision

Healthful Life

Basic Words

□ cold 감기	□ ill 아픈	□ sick 아픈, 병든
□ doctor 의사	□ nurse 간호사	□ well 건강한
□ strong 튼튼한	□ weak 약한	□ hospital 병원
□ dentist 치과 의사	□ flu 독감	□ health 건강

01 bleed
[bliːd]
🔵 blood 피

🔵 출혈하다

A Your nose is bleeding! 너 코피나!

B What? I must have studied too hard last night. 뭐라고? 어젯밤에 공부를 너무 열심히 했나 보다.

02 medical
[médikəl]

🔵 의학의, 의료의　　　　a medical college 의과 대학

A A new television drama started yesterday.
어제 새로운 텔레비전 드라마가 시작했어.

B Are you talking about the medical drama?
그 의학 드라마 말하는 거니?

03 ache
[eik]
🔵 aching 아픈, 쑤시는

🔵 아프다 🔵 아픔, 통증

A My body is aching everywhere. I think I caught a cold. 나 온몸이 아파. 감기가 든 것 같아.

B Did you go to the doctor, yet? 병원에는 가봤어?

04 prevent
[privént]
🔵 prevention 방해

🔵 막다, 방해하다

A Drinking enough water prevents you from getting sick.
물을 충분히 마시는 건 네가 질병에 걸리는 것을 막아줘.

B How much should I drink a day?
하루에 얼마나 많이 마셔야 할까?

05 cure
[kjuər]

🔵 치료, 치료법 🔵 치료하다, 고치다
　　　　　　cure one's pain ~의 통증을 치료하다

A Is there any cure for the disease?
그 질병에 대한 치료법이 있는 거야?

B The doctors are trying to find one.
의사들이 방법을 찾으려고 애쓰고 있어.

06 cough
[kɔ́ːf]

c.f. sneeze 재채기하다

v 기침을 하다 **n** 기침   **have a cough** 기침을 하다

A My throat hurts, but I can't stop coughing.
나 목이 아픈데 기침을 멈출 수 없어.

B Here, try some tea. 여기, 차 좀 마셔 봐.

07 disease
[dizíːz]

syn sickness 병

n 병, 질병

A Always wash your hands to be safe from diseases. 질병으로부터 안전하려면 항상 손을 씻도록 해.

B Yes, Dr. Greg. 네, 그레그 선생님.

08 drugstore
[drʌ́gstɔ̀ːr]

c.f. drug 약

n 약국

A Silvia, can you get me some aspirin? My head hurts too much.
실비아, 아스피린 좀 사다 주겠니? 머리가 너무 아프구나.

B No problem, Dad. Where's the drugstore?
문제없죠, 아빠. 약국이 어디에 있어요?

09 fever
[fíːvər]

n (몸에서 나는) 열   **have a fever** 열이 있다

A Why didn't David come to school today?
오늘 왜 데이비드는 학교에 안 왔니?

B He said he had a fever. 몸에서 열이 난대.

10 hurt
[həːrt]

v 다치다, 아프다 **n** 상처

hurt one's feeling ~의 마음에 상처를 주다

A I fell down the stairs. My arm hurts so badly.
계단에서 굴렀는데요. 제 팔이 너무 아파요.

B Let's take an X-ray to see if it is broken.
팔이 부러졌는지 엑스레이를 찍어 봅시다.

11 worse

[wəːrs]

(ill/bad-worse-worst)

ant better 더 좋은, 더 나은

ⓐ (병이) 악화된, 보다 나쁜

A I think I caught a cold. 나 감기가 든 것 같아.

B You should take some rest before it gets worse. 악화되기 전에 좀 쉬는 게 좋겠어.

12 headache

[hédèik]

ⓝ 두통

A I have a terrible headache! 나 두통이 너무 심해!

B Take this medicine and have some sleep.
이 약 먹고 좀 자둬.

13 pain

[pein]

ⓐ painful 아픈

ⓝ 아픔, 고통

A Try these pills. They will ease the pain.
이 알약을 먹어봐. 고통이 줄어들 거야.

B I had them before. It worked well then.
전에 먹어봤어. 그때는 효과가 좋았어.

14 bear

[bɛər]

(bear-bore-born)

ⓥ 참다, 낳다

A Are you feeling alright? You don't look so well. 너 괜찮아? 안 좋아 보여.

B I'm okay. I can bear it. 나 괜찮아. 참을 수 있어.

15 poison

[pɔ́izən]

ⓝ 독, 독약

A Medicine can be poison if we use it wrongly.
약은 잘못 쓰면 독이 될 수 있어.

B We always have to be careful. 언제나 조심해야지.

16 alive
[əláiv]

ⓐ 살아있는

A Are you all right? I heard you were in a car accident! 괜찮니? 너 차 사고를 당했다고 들었어!

B It was very dangerous. I'm just happy to be alive. 매우 위험했어. 그저 살아있는 게 다행이야.

17 cancer
[kǽnsər]

ⓝ 암　　　　　　　　　**liver cancer** 간암

A Cancer is one of the most dreadful diseases. 암은 가장 무서운 질병 중 하나야.　　　　* dreadful : 무서운

B I heard it's hard to cure. 치료하기 어렵다고 들었어.

18 suffer
[sʌ́fər]

ⓝ suffering 괴로움, 고통

ⓥ (병을) 앓다, 고통받다　　**suffer from a disease** 병을 앓다

A My mother has suffered from cancer. 저희 어머니께서 암에 걸리셨어요.

B I'm sorry to hear that. 유감이네요.

19 illness
[ílnis]

ⓐ ill 병든

ⓝ 병, 질병

A My grandfather is in the hospital again. 할아버지께서 다시 입원하셨어.

B Is he okay? I thought his illness was cured. 괜찮으셔? 병이 다 나으신 줄 알았는데.

20 healthy
[hélθi]

ⓝ health 건강

ⓐ 건강한, 건강에 좋은　　**healthy food** 건강에 좋은 음식

A How can we stay healthy, Miss Kelly? 켈리 선생님, 어떻게 하면 건강을 유지할 수 있을까요?

B The secret is to be careful before there's trouble. 비법은 문제가 생기기 전에 조심하는 거예요.

21 heal
[hi:l]

ⓥ (병이) 낫다, (병을) 치료하다   **heal a wound** 상처를 치료하다

A Doctor! Will my father get better?
의사 선생님! 저희 아버지 괜찮아지시는 건가요?

B Don't worry. He is already healing.
걱정 마세요. 벌써 회복되고 있어요.

22 injure
[índʒər]
ⓝ injury 부상, 상처

ⓥ 상처를 입히다, 해치다

A How bad was the accident? 사고가 얼마나 심했니?

B The driver was badly injured. 운전자가 크게 다쳤어.

23 medicine
[médəsən]

ⓝ 약, 약물   **take medicine** 약을 먹다

A What did the doctor tell you? 의사가 뭐라고 했니?

B He told me to take my medicine and get
plenty of rest. 약을 먹고 충분히 휴식을 취하라고 했어.

24 death
[deθ]
ⓥ die 죽다

ⓝ 죽음, 사망

A Are you afraid of death? 너 죽음이 두렵니?

B Yes, I am. Even the strongest man will be
afraid, too. 응. 두려워. 가장 강한 사람도 두려워 할 걸.

25 stomachache
[stʌ́məkèik]

ⓝ 복통, 위통

A I have a stomachache. I think I ate too much.
나 복통이 있어. 너무 많이 먹은 것 같아.

B I saw this coming. 이럴 줄 알았어.

Multi-Meaning Word

bear   ⓥ (아이를) 낳다 / 지탱하다 / 참다
He was **born** in America. 그는 미국에서 태어났다.
The ice wasn't thick enough to **bear** his weight.
얼음은 그의 몸무게를 지탱하기에 충분히 두껍지 못하다.
She wouldn't be able to **bear** the pain. 그녀는 고통을 참지 못할 것이다.

ⓝ 곰
Visitors to the park are warned not to feed the **bears**.
공원 방문객들은 곰에게 먹이를 주지 말라고 주의를 받는다.

Word Search

앞에서 배운 어휘를 기억하며 모두 찾아 보세요.

정답

E	K	T	Q	M	A	X	Q	J	U	P	E	M	Y	E
V	O	C	C	A	S	R	A	E	B	N	V	E	R	A
I	C	U	R	E	N	P	X	L	I	O	C	D	X	R
L	Y	Q	P	L	P	H	R	C	A	O	E	I	W	O
A	B	O	E	H	E	E	I	E	U	E	R	C	I	W
H	M	D	Z	A	T	E	B	G	V	F	H	A	N	R
X	A	B	L	A	E	B	G	I	G	E	G	L	J	E
X	O	T	E	M	R	E	F	F	U	S	N	Q	U	V
D	H	S	O	E	V	D	C	A	B	C	K	T	R	E
Y	I	T	E	S	H	A	B	L	E	E	D	E	F
D	B	R	X	P	N	C	V	X	N	T	P	E	T	V
O	E	U	H	C	A	R	A	X	C	V	Z	A	H	D
L	K	H	E	M	I	I	U	S	V	Y	H	T	L	A
E	J	R	F	B	J	B	N	Q	L	J	W	H	D	P

ache	alive	bear	bleed
cancer	cure	death	fever
heal	healthy	hurt	injure
medical	pain	prevent	suffer

Unit 11 Feeling

Basic Words

- □ tired 피곤한
- □ angry 화난
- □ cry 울다
- □ glad 기쁜
- □ excited 신이 난
- □ sad 슬픈
- □ hope 바라다
- □ please 기쁘게 하다
- □ boring 지루한
- □ laugh (소리 내어) 웃다
- □ interesting 흥미로운
- □ surprised 놀란

01 ☑ afraid
[əfréid]

ⓐ 두려워하여, 걱정하여   **be afraid of ~** ~을 두려워하다

A Why don't you go talk to her? You said you like her. 왜 그녀에게 말을 걸지 않니? 좋아한다고 했잖아.

B I'm afraid of her saying no.
그녀가 거절할까 봐 두려워.

02 ☑ worry
[wɔ́:ri]

ⓥ 걱정하다, 괴롭히다   **be worried about ~** ~을 걱정하다

A Has Sally come home, yet? It's getting late.
샐리 집에 왔어? 시간이 늦었어.

B No, she hasn't. I'm starting to get worried.
아니, 오지 않았어. 걱정이 되기 시작해.

03 ☑ mood
[mu:d]

ⓐ moody 침울한, 변덕스러운

ⓝ 기분, 마음, 분위기   **in a good mood** 기분이 좋은

A Can you play a different song, please?
혹시 다른 노래 틀어줄 수 있니?

B I guess you're not in the mood for dance music. 댄스 음악 들을 기분이 아닌 모양이구나.

04 ☑ depressed
[diprést]

ⓥ depress 우울하게 하다

ⓐ 우울한, 의기소침한

A You look so depressed. What happened?
너 우울해 보여. 무슨 일 있었어?

B Bad things keep happening to me over and over again. 나에게 자꾸 안 좋은 일이 생겨.

05 ☑ disappointed
[dìsəpɔ́intid]

ⓥ disappoint 실망시키다

ⓐ 실망한, 좌절된

A What did your father say about your grades?
너희 아버지께서 네 성적에 대해 뭐라고 하셨니?

B Nothing. He just looked disappointed.
아무 말씀 없으셔. 그냥 실망하신 눈치야.

06 surprise
[sərpráiz]

ⓥ 놀라게 하다 ⓝ 놀람, 놀라운 일

a surprised party 깜짝 파티

A I was surprised when he asked me on a date. 그가 내게 데이트 신청을 했을 때 놀랐어.

B Where did he say he would take you?
너를 어디로 데려간다고 했어?

07 nervous
[nə́:rvəs]

ⓝ nerve 신경

ⓐ 초조한, 신경질적인　　　　　**get nervous** 긴장하다

A What do you do when you feel nervous?
초조한 느낌이 들 때 어떻게 하니?

B I close my eyes and breathe deeply.
눈을 감고 심호흡을 해.

08 pleasant
[pléznt]

ⓝ pleasure 즐거움, 기쁨

ⓐ 즐거운, 기분 좋은, 유쾌한

A What a pleasant surprise, Henry! What brought you here?
갑자기 만나다니 기분이 정말 좋아, 헨리! 여긴 뭐 하러 왔니?

B I had some business in the area.
근처에 일이 좀 있었어요.

09 terrible
[térəbəl]

ⓐ 끔찍한, 소름 끼치는　　　　**terrible news** 끔찍한 소식

A I had an accident on my way home.
집에 오는 길에 사고를 당했어.

B That's terrible! 끔찍한 일이구나!

10 lonely
[lóunli]

ⓐ 고독한, 외로운

A To tell you the truth, I was an orphan.
사실을 말씀드리면, 저는 고아였어요.

B Oh, I'm so sorry. You must have been lonely.
오, 유감이네요. 외로웠겠어요.

11 ☑ tear
[tiər]

ⓝ 눈물 **ⓥ** 눈물을 흘리다　　　　　　　　**tears of joy** 기쁨의 눈물

A Sarah seems depressed, doesn't she?
사라가 우울해 보인다. 그렇지 않니?

B Yes, I saw her shed tears yesterday.
응, 나는 그녀가 어제 눈물 흘리는 것을 봤어.

12 ☑ fear
[fiər]
ⓐ fearful 무서운, 두려운

ⓝ 두려움, 공포 **ⓥ** 무서워하다, 겁내다

fear to die 죽는 것을 두려워하다

A What is your worst fear, Jessica?
제시카, 너의 가장 큰 두려움이 무엇이니?

B I am afraid of heights. 나는 높은 곳이 무서워.

13 ☑ eager
[íːgər]

ⓐ 열망하는, 간절히 바라는

be eager to meet 몹시 만나고 싶어하다

A I'm so eager to see her again!
나는 그녀를 다시 보고 싶은 마음이 간절해.

B Why don't you try calling her?
전화 한 번 해보는 것은 어때?

14 ☑ sadness
[sǽdnis]
ⓐ sad 슬픈

ⓝ 슬픔

A It is important to express your feelings.
네 감정을 표현하는 것이 중요해.

B But I am bad at expressing sadness.
하지만, 나는 슬픔을 표현하는 것이 서툴러.

15 ☑ delight
[diláit]
ⓐ delightful 기쁜

ⓝ 기쁨, 즐거움 **ⓥ** 기쁘게 하다

A What is your dream for your future?
네 미래의 꿈은 무엇이니?

B I want to be a singer. Singing is my delight.
가수가 되고 싶어. 노래하는 것이 나의 기쁨이야.

16 desire
[dizáiər]

V 바라다 **n** 욕구, 욕망

A Everyone desires to be happy.
모든 사람은 행복해지길 바라.

B I do, too. I wish we all could be.
나도 그래. 우리 모두 그렇게 됐으면 좋겠어.

17 satisfy
[sǽtisfài]

a satisfied 만족한
n satisfaction 만족

V 만족시키다

A I don't think an artist will ever be satisfied with his work. 예술가는 항상 자기 작품에 만족하지 못하는 것 같아.

B Maybe or maybe not. 그럴 수도 있고, 아닐 수도 있고.

18 joy
[dʒɔi]

a joyful 즐거운, 기쁜

n 기쁨

A Thank you for sharing your joy with me.
기쁨을 저와 함께 해주셔서 감사합니다.

B The pleasure is all mine. 오히려 제가 감사하죠.

19 hide
[haid]

V 숨기다, 감추다

A You're not hiding anything from me, are you?
나한테 뭔가 숨기는 거 아니지, 그렇지?

B Of course not, Mr. Phillip. 물론입니다. 필립 선생님.

20 regret
[rigrét]

a regretful 후회하는

V 후회하다 **n** 유감, 후회

A I regret that I said bad things to you.
너에게 나쁜 것을 말한 걸 후회하고 있어.

B It's okay. I forgive you. 괜찮아. 용서해 줄게.

21 upset
[ʌpsét]

a 혼란한, 당황한 **V** 뒤집어엎다, 당황케 하다

A Why are you so upset, Susan?
수잔, 기분이 왜 언짢니?

B My mom read my diary and spoke to me about it. 엄마가 내 일기장을 보고는 그것에 대해 내게 얘기를 했어.

22 emotion

[imóuʃən]

ⓐ emotional 감정의, 감정적인

ⓝ 감정

A Don't be angry with the police.
경찰에게 화를 내지는 마.

B Don't worry! I can control my emotion.
걱정하지 매! 내 감정은 조절할 수 있어.

23 ashamed

[əʃéimd]

ⓐ 부끄러운, 수줍어하는

A I'm ashamed of what I did in the past.
과거에 내가 한 일이 부끄러워.

B Cheer up! Forget the past and focus on the future. 힘내! 과거는 잊고 미래에 집중해.

24 anger

[ǽŋgər]

ⓐ angry 화난

ⓝ 화, 노여움

A Did you see her screaming and crying in anger last night?
어젯밤 그녀가 화가 나서 소리 지르며 우는 거 봤어?

B Yes, I didn't think she could control herself.
응. 그녀는 감정을 억제하지 못했던 것 같아.

25 because

[bikɔ́:z]

ⓒⓞⓝⓙ 왜냐하면 ~이므로

A Why are you so happy today, Angela?
안젤라, 오늘 왜 그렇게 기분이 좋아요?

B Because my husband gave me a nice gift last night. 왜냐하면 어젯밤에 남편이 멋진 선물을 줬거든요.

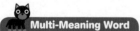 **Multi-Meaning Word**

tear

ⓝ 눈물 [tiər]

The good news brought a **tear** of joy to my eyes.
그 좋은 소식이 내게 기쁨의 눈물을 흘리게 했다.

ⓥ 찢다 [tɛər]

You can **tear** a sheet of paper in two pieces.
종이를 둘로 찢을 수 있다.

Word Search

앞에서 배운 어휘를 기억하며 모두 찾아 보세요.

정답

```
D L E M M N S T P E E L I X M
C R D M H G F G D S S R P N H
I N M E O Q Z Q W I E J O Y J
I D C V P T S W G R A I L E I
N Z M S Q P I W N P C C K R T
G P G V J G E O O R E N A H T
S U O V R E N S N U B E G Y D
W A N G E R Y H S S T I C I T
O D W G O Y W F C E L E A F E
R O V U L E S D S A D R V U R
R O S E P V D A D O F Q P F G
Y M N N B P I I J A T S Z E E
T O D E S I R E H O E A V A R
L E A G E R G V O T G V S R V
```

afraid	anger	desire	eager
emotion	fear	hide	joy
lonely	mood	nervous	regret
surprise	tear	upset	worry

Unit 12 Thoughts

Basic Words

- □ find 찾다
- □ know 알다
- □ remember 기억하다
- □ creative 창의적인
- □ think 생각하다
- □ forget 잊다
- □ image 이미지, 인상
- □ educate 교육하다
- □ catch 알아채다
- □ idea 생각, 계획
- □ correct 올바른, 옳은
- □ expect 예상하다

01 knowledge
[nálidʒ]

V know 알다

n 지식, 학식

A Why do you want to be a scientist?
너는 왜 과학자가 되고 싶니?

B It's because I want to explore knowledge about the universe.
우주에 대한 지식을 탐구하고 싶기 때문이야.

02 understand
[ʌndərstǽnd]

V 이해하다, 알다

A How could a nine-year-old girl understand French perfectly?
어떻게 아홉 살짜리 소녀가 프랑스어를 완벽하게 이해할 수 있지?

B Don't you know her father is French?
그녀의 아버지가 프랑스인이라는 거 몰랐니?

03 realize
[ríːəlàiz]

n realization 깨달음

V 깨닫다, 인식하다

A I came to say I'm sorry. I realized it was my fault. 사과하러 왔어. 내 잘못이라는 것을 깨닫게 되었어.

B I forgive you. 용서해줄게.

04 ability
[əbíləti]

a able 능력이 있는

n 능력　　　　　　　**a language ability** 언어 능력

A Sean shows a great ability in mathematics.
션은 수학에 대단한 재능을 가지고 있어.

B I so envy him. I am always poor with numbers.
정말 그가 부럽다. 난 항상 숫자에 약한데.

05 wisdom
[wízdəm]

a wise 현명한

n 지혜

A People used to stay in this temple in search of true wisdom.
사람들은 진정한 지혜를 찾아 이 사찰에 머무르곤 했어.

B That's an interesting story. Did anybody find it? 흥미로운 이야기구나. 그걸 찾은 사람은 있니?

06 judge
[dʒʌdʒ]

ⓥ 판단하다, 재판하다 **ⓝ** 재판관

A I didn't know John was such a nice guy.
존이 그렇게 착한 사람인 줄 몰랐어.

B Me, neither. We should never judge a book by its cover.
나도 마찬가지야. 절대 겉만 보고 판단하면 안 되는 것 같아.

07 decide
[disáid]
ⓝ decision 결정

ⓥ 결정하다, 결심하다

decide what to do 무엇을 할지 결정하다

A So what do you want to eat? 그래, 무엇을 먹을래?

B I can't decide! They all look good.
결정을 못 하겠어! 다 맛있어 보여.

08 intelligent
[intélədʒənt]
ⓝ intelligence 지성

ⓐ 지적인, 영리한

A Jamey is a very intelligent student.
제이미는 참 영리한 학생이에요.

B I'm happy she's doing well.
그녀가 잘하고 있어서 기쁘네요.

09 reason
[ríːzən]
ⓐ reasonable 이성적인

ⓝ 이유, 이성

A Why did you ask me to come early?
나보고 왜 일찍 오라고 했어?

B There is no reason. I just wanted to see you.
아무 이유 없어. 그냥 네가 보고 싶었어.

10 intend
[inténd]
ⓝ intention 의도

ⓥ ~할 작정이다, 의도하다

A How could you say that to me?
너 어떻게 나에게 그렇게 말할 수 있니?

B I am sorry, I didn't intend to hurt your feelings.
미안해. 네 감정을 상하게 할 의도는 아니었어.

11 conclude
[kənklúːd]

ⓝ conclusion 결론

ⓥ 결론을 내리다

A How did the meeting go? 회의는 어떻게 됐니?

B They concluded to change the plan.
계획을 바꾸기로 결론을 내렸어.

12 guess
[ges]

ⓥ 추측하다 ⓝ 추측

A How did you know what I like?
내가 무엇을 좋아하는지 어떻게 알았어?

B I just guessed. I was lucky.
그냥 추측했어. 운이 좋았지.

13 remind
[rimáind]

ⓥ 생각나게 하다, 상기시키다

A This book reminds me of my youth.
이 책은 내 어렸을 때를 생각나게 해.

B I really liked it, too. 나도 그 책 정말 좋아했었어.

14 seem
[siːm]

ⓥ ~인 것 같다, ~인 듯하다

A I heard the scientists are preparing an experiment again.
과학자들이 다시 실험을 준비한대.

B It seems that they never get tired.
그들은 지치지 않는가 봐.

15 memorize
[méməràiz]

ⓝ memory 기억, 추억

ⓥ 기억하다, 암기하다

A Did you study a lot for the midterms?
중간고사 공부 많이 했니?

B Yes. I memorized everything I need.
응. 필요한 건 전부 암기했어.

16 determine
[ditə́:rmin]

ⓥ 결심하다, 결정하다

A Think carefully and make a decision. Your decision determines your future.
잘 생각해 보고 결정해. 네 결정이 너의 미래를 정하니깐.

B I have thought enough. 충분히 생각했어.

17 mind
[maind]

ⓝ 마음, 정신　　　　　　　　　　　**mind and body** 심신

A My mind is full of thoughts about the concert. 내 마음이 공연에 대한 생각으로 가득 차 있어.

B I'm looking forward to it, too. 나도 정말 기대 돼.

18 consider
[kənsídər]

ⓝ consideration
생각, 고려

ⓥ 생각하다, 고려하다

A What should we do now? 우리 이제 어떻게 하지?

B Let's consider other options.
다른 사항들도 생각해보자.

19 regard
[rigá:rd]

ⓥ 간주하다, 생각하다　　　　　　**regard A as B** A를 B로 여기다

A I don't believe you anymore. Do you regard me as a fool? 난 더 이상 너를 믿지 않아. 날 바보로 생각하니?

B Please believe me. I've never told you a lie.
제발 날 믿어. 난 너에게 거짓말한 적 없어.

20 thought
[θɔːt]

ⓥ think 생각하다

ⓝ 생각, 사고　　　　　　　　**read one's thoughts** 생각을 읽다

A We all are free to express our thoughts.
우리 모두 자신의 생각을 표현할 자유가 있어.

B Yes, it's wrong to stop us from doing so.
맞아, 우리가 그렇게 못하게 막는 것은 잘못된 일이야.

21 control
[kəntróul]

Ⓥ 지배하다, 억제하다   **control oneself** 자제하다

A Our brain is divided into two parts. The left part controls language and logic. 우리의 뇌는 두 부분으로 나누어져 있어. 왼쪽 부분은 언어와 논리를 통제해.

B Then what about the right side? 그럼 오른쪽은?

22 research
[risə́:rtʃ / rí:sə:rtʃ]

Ⓥ 연구하다 **Ⓝ** 연구, 조사

A He spent 40 years in doing cancer research and he died of liver cancer. 그는 암 연구를 하면서 40년을 보내고 간암으로 세상을 떠났어.

B What an irony it was! 정말 아이러니하다!

23 suppose
[səpóuz]

Ⓥ 가정하다, 상상하다

A Oh, it's all my fault that we lost! 아, 우리가 진 건 다 내 잘못이야!

B I suppose you're right. 네 말이 맞다고 생각해.

24 organize
[ɔ́:rɡənàiz]
Ⓝ organization 구성, 조직

Ⓥ 조직하다, 구성하다

A I find it difficult to write down my thoughts. 내 생각을 글로 쓰는 것이 어려워.

B Try organizing your thoughts again before you write. 쓰기 전에 생각을 다시 한 번 정리해봐.

25 while
[hwail]

conj ~하는 동안

A Can you do two things at once? 한 번에 두 가지 일을 할 수 있어?

B I can read a book while speaking on the phone. 나는 전화를 하는 동안 책을 읽을 수 있어.

Word Search

앞에서 배운 어휘를 기억하며 모두 찾아 보세요.

정답

```
Y  R  I  N  T  E  N  D  T  Y  E  L  D  E  T
I  E  S  H  K  G  M  E  Y  T  Z  O  N  L  Y
A  D  A  S  E  J  A  A  B  I  I  R  I  I  X
H  I  W  S  E  L  T  R  F  L  R  T  M  H  V
B  S  K  I  I  U  A  N  Q  I  O  N  E  W  W
P  N  O  Z  S  G  G  X  X  B  N  O  R  X  L
A  O  E  O  E  D  K  C  T  A  E  C  R  V  E
P  C  B  R  L  I  O  H  O  F  M  E  D  G  W
E  D  I  C  E  D  O  M  M  N  S  S  D  V  Z
M  I  N  D  C  U  R  B  K  E  C  U  E  X  H
B  B  H  L  G  D  H  G  E  P  J  L  N  E  X
N  Q  C  H  I  W  B  R  W  B  X  Q  U  G  M
D  L  T  Z  S  H  C  R  E  A  S  O  N  D  L
U  Z  V  Z  W  H  S  U  P  P  O  S  E  Z  E
```

ability	conclude	consider	control
decide	guess	intend	judge
mind	reason	remind	seem
suppose	thought	while	wisdom

Word Bubbles

앞에서 배운 어휘를 기억하며 버블을 단어로 채워 보세요.

정답

Chapter 3

시야, 시력

손바닥

뺨, 볼

Body & Mind
몸과 마음

감각

뼈, 골격

감정

사고, 생각

의학의, 의료의

기쁨

고려하다

치료, 치료하다

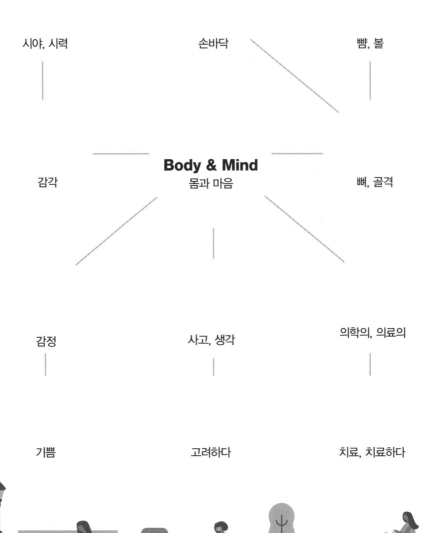

Review Test

A 우리말을 영어로, 영어를 우리말로 쓰시오.

01 피부, 가죽 _____

02 소음 _____

03 실망한, 좌절한 _____

04 기침을 하다 _____

05 이해하다 _____

06 뼈 _____

07 감각, 의식 _____

08 emotion _____

09 ashamed _____

10 guess _____

11 sweat _____

12 observe _____

13 control _____

14 poison _____

B 빈칸에 알맞은 단어를 쓰시오.

01 가슴 통증 _____ pains

02 발자국 소리 the _____ of footsteps

03 상처를 치료하다 _____ a wound

04 in a good mood _____ 이/가 좋은

05 decide what to do 무엇을 할지 _____

06 take medicine _____ 을/를 먹다

C 단어의 관계에 맞게 빈칸을 채우시오.

01 숨 쉬다 : 숨 = breathe : _____

02 귀가 먹은 : 눈이 먼 = deaf : _____

03 피 : 출혈하다 = blood : _____

04 silence : silent = 침묵 : _____

05 joy : joyful = 기쁨 : _____

06 body : mind = 몸 : _____

D 배운 단어를 사용하여 문장을 완성하시오. (필요하면 형태를 바꾸시오.)

01 Her two _____ turned red like a tomato with shame.

그녀의 두 빰은 부끄러워서 토마토처럼 빨개졌다.

02 People were not _____ of the danger of the disease.

사람들은 그 병의 위험을 인식하지 못했다.

03 Rosalie gave birth to a(n) _____ baby girl.

로잘리는 건강한 여자 아이를 출산했다.

04 She started to _____ telling her secret to him.

그녀는 자신의 비밀을 그에게 말한 것을 후회하기 시작했다.

05 I didn't _____ to leave early.

일찍 떠나려고 의도하지는 않았다.

E 빈칸에 알맞은 말을 보기에서 찾아 쓰시오.

rest	worry	imagine	nervous	voice

01 **A** I am so _____ about my job interview.

   B Don't _____. Everything will be fine.

02 **A** You love watching TV, don't you?

   B Yes, TV is so much fun. I can't _____ my life without it.

03 **A** I thought your mother was you.

   B Yeah, she has a similar _____ with me.

04 **A** Are you sick? You look terrible.

   B I am just tired. I need some _____.

F 밑줄 친 부분을 우리말로 옮기시오.

01 Would you mind handing me the potato chips?

02 I think that making money is hard work.

VOCA Inn!

The Story of Calendar 달력 이야기

고대 로마인들이 사용하던 최초의 달력은 March로 시작하여 December까지 1년이 10개월이었다. 기원전 8세기경 로마의 왕 누마 폼필리우스가 두 달을 넣어 1년을 12개월 355일로 하는 태양력이 만들어졌다. 하지만, 기원전 46년 율리우스가 평년을 365일, 4년에 한 번씩 윤년으로 366일로 하는 율리우스력을 만들었다. 율리우스의 생일인 7월의 명칭을 5를 뜻하는 퀸틸리스에서 자신의 이름을 따서 율리(July)로 바꾸었다. 율리우스 이후 황제가 된 아우구스투스(Augustus)는 자신의 생일과 대전투를 기념하기 위해 8월의 명칭을 6을 뜻하는 섹스틸리스에서 아우구스투스(Augustus)로 개칭하였다.

1월★January
과거와 미래를 보는 두 개의 얼굴을 가진 야누스(Janus-문을 수호하는 신)에서 유래되어 신년과 구년을 앞뒤로 내다보는 달을 의미한다.

2월★February
2월은 고대 로마에서 결실의 신인 루페르쿠스(lupercus)를 모시는 제전이 있는 달로 Februarius(부정 방지의 달)이라 부른 것에서 유래했다.

3월★March
곡식의 종자를 심는 달이기 때문에 군신이며 농업의 신인 마르스(Mars)에서 따 온 라틴어인 Martius에서 유래했다.

4월★April
자연계의 만물이 열리는 달이기 때문에 'Aperire'는 '열리다'의 라틴어에서 유래했다.

5월★May
성장과 번식의 여신인 Maia에게 드리는 달이라는 뜻의 단어 Maius에서 유래했다.

6월★June
결혼과 출산의 여신 Juno의 이름에서 유래되었다.

7월★July
현재 쓰이는 태양력을 정리한 쥴리어스 시저(Julius)에서 유래되었다.

8월★August
로마제국의 초대 황제 Caesar Augustus의 이름에서 유래되었다. 당시의 8월은 30일이었으나 2월에서 1일을 빼서 7월과 같은 일수로 하기 위해서 8월을 31일로 하였다.

9월★September
'7'을 의미하는 라틴어인 septem에서 유래되었다. 고대 로마 시대에는 3월이 지금의 1월이었고 September가 7월이었는데, 두 달을 추가해 달력을 수정하면서 두 달이 늦춰진 지금의 9월이 되었다.

10월★October
라틴어에서 octo는 '8'의 뜻이다.

11월★November
라틴어에서 novem은 '9'를 나타낸다.

12월★December
라틴어에서 decem은 '10'을 의미한다.

Chapter
04

Daily Life

Unit 13 Food

Basic Words

- bread 빵
- drink 음료
- breakfast 아침
- lunch 점심
- dinner 저녁
- milk 우유
- pepper 후추
- curry 카레
- tea 차
- water 물
- fish 생선
- rice 밥

01 ☑ **meal**
[mi:l]

ⓝ 식사, 한 끼니   **skip a meal** 식사를 거르다

A That was a wonderful meal! 정말 훌륭한 식사였어!

B Thank you. I made it myself.
고마워. 내가 직접 만든 거야.

02 ☑ **flavor**
[fléivər]

ⓝ 맛, 풍미   **add flavor to ~** ~에 맛을 더하다

A What flavor is this candy? 이 사탕은 무슨 맛이니?

B It is apple flavor. 사과 맛이야.

03 ☑ **dish**
[diʃ]

ⓝ 요리, 접시

A What is your favorite Korean dish, Emma?
엠마, 네가 가장 좋아하는 한국 요리는 무엇이야?

B My favorite Korean dish is samgyupsal.
내가 가장 좋아하는 요리는 삼겹살이야.

04 ☑ **sweet**
[swi:t]

ⓐ 달콤한 **ⓝ** 단것, 사탕   **eat sweets** 단것을 먹다

A Do you want sugar in your coffee?
커피에 설탕을 넣어 드릴까요?

B Yes, I'd like it very sweet, please.
네, 매우 달게 해주세요.

05 ☑ **chopstick**
[tʃápstìk]

ⓝ 젓가락

A Wow! You are very good with chopsticks!
우와! 젓가락을 굉장히 잘 쓰는구나!

B Thank you. This is my third visit to Korea.
고마워. 한국에 세 번째 오는 거야.

06 ☑ **dessert**
[dizə́:rt]

ⓝ 디저트, 후식

A What would you like for dessert, sir?
후식으로 무엇을 드시겠습니까, 손님?

B A cup of coffee will do. 커피 한 잔이면 돼요.

07 ☑ **taste**

[teist]

ⓐ **tasty**
맛있는, 식욕을 돋우는

ⓝ 맛, 미각 ⓥ 맛을 보다, 맛이 나다

A Won't you have a taste of this wine?
이 포도주를 맛보시지 않겠습니까?

B No thanks. 사양하겠습니다.

---

08 ☑ **seafood**

[síːfùːd]

ⓝ 해산물, 해산 식품

A James, do you eat seafood? 제임스, 너 해산물 먹니?

B I couldn't at first, but now I love it.
처음에는 못 먹었는데, 지금은 엄청 좋아해.

---

09 ☑ **spicy**

[spáisi]

ⓝ **spice** 양념, 향신료

ⓐ 양념을 넣은, 향긋한   **spicy food** 양념을 많이 한(매운) 음식

A This curry is really spicy. 이 카레 정말 향긋해.

B I'm glad you like it. 네가 그것을 좋아하니 기뻐.

---

10 ☑ **noodle**

[núːdl]

ⓝ 면, 국수

A Mom, I'm hungry. Can I have something?
엄마, 저 배고파요. 뭐 좀 먹을 수 있을까요?

B Let's see. How about some noodles?
어디 보자. 국수 어때?

---

11 ☑ **order**

[ɔ́ːrdər]

ⓝ 주문, 명령 ⓥ 주문하다, 명령하다   **give orders** 명령하다

A May I take your order? 주문하시겠습니까?

B Yes, I'll have a tuna salad sandwich and
coke. 네, 참치 샐러드 샌드위치와 콜라로 할게요.

---

12 ☑ **bitter**

[bítər]

ⓐ (맛이) 쓴, (추위가) 혹독한

A Mom, this medicine is too bitter to get down.
엄마, 이 약 너무 써서 삼킬 수가 없어요.

B You know a good medicine tastes bitter.
좋은 약은 쓰다는 거 너도 알잖니.

13 delicious
[dilíʃəs]

ⓐ 맛있는, 맛 좋은   **smell delicious** 맛있는 냄새가 나다

A That store serves the most delicious pies in town. 저 가게는 동네에서 가장 맛있는 파이를 팔아.

B Yes, I see people wait in line every day.
응, 매일 사람들이 줄 서서 기다리는 것을 볼 수 있어.

14 thirsty
[θə́ːrsti]
ⓝ thirst 목마름

ⓐ 목마른

A Do you need something to drink, John?
존, 뭐 마실 것 필요하니?

B No, I'm okay. I'm not thirsty.
아니, 괜찮아. 목마르지 않아.

15 food
[fuːd]

ⓝ 음식, 식량   **food and drink** 음식물

A Our company decided to send food aid.
우리 회사는 식량 원조를 보내기로 했습니다.

B That sounds like a good idea.
좋은 생각인 것 같습니다.

16 diet
[dáiət]

ⓝ 규정식, 식이 요법   **a low-calorie diet** 저칼로리식

A My doctor recommended that I control my diet. 의사가 나보고 식이 요법을 권장했어.

B What did he tell you to eat?
무엇을 먹으라고 이야기했어?

17 restaurant
[réstərənt]

ⓝ 음식점, 레스토랑   **Japanese restaurant** 일식당

A A new Chinese restaurant opened near my house. 우리 집 근처에 새 중식당이 개업했어.

B Would you like to go there tonight?
오늘 저녁에 거기 가볼래?

18 ☑ **salty**

[sɔ́:lti]

n salt 소금

a 짠, 소금기가 있는

A French fries are too salty for me.

감자튀김이 내겐 너무 짜.

B But that is why people like me love them.

하지만, 짠맛 때문에 나 같은 사람이 감자튀김을 좋아하는 거야.

---

19 ☑ **bite**

[bait]

(bite-bit-bitten)

v 물다, 물어뜯다 **n** 한 입의 음식, 한 입 거리

grab a bite to eat 간단히 먹다

A I bit my tongue and now it is bleeding.

혀를 씹어서 지금 피가 나.

B I'll go get some cold water.

내가 가서 찬물 좀 가져다줄게.

---

20 ☑ **chew**

[tʃuː]

v 씹다

chewing gum 씹는 껌

A It's important to chew your food well.

음식을 꼭꼭 잘 씹는 것은 중요해.

B I'll make sure I do. 그렇게 하도록 할게요.

---

21 ☑ **appetite**

[ǽpitàit]

n 식욕

lose one's appetite 식욕을 잃다

A You really eat a lot of food for one meal.

한 끼 식사로 음식을 엄청 많이 먹는구나.

B Yes, people say I have a big appetite.

응, 사람들이 나보고 식욕이 왕성하다고 이야기해.

---

22 ☑ **snack**

[snæk]

n 가벼운 식사, 간식

have a snack 간식을 먹다

A Do you want to go get something to eat?

뭐 좀 먹으러 갈래?

B Okay. I wanted a snack, too.

그래. 나도 군것질하고 싶었어.

23 supper
[sʌ́pər]

n 저녁식사

A Will you be back before supper?
저녁 먹기 전에 돌아오시나요?

B I'm sorry, but I don't think so. Don't wait for me. 미안하지만, 못 그럴 것 같아요. 기다리지 마세요.

24 menu
[ménjuː]

n 식단, 메뉴

A Is there any salad on the menu?
메뉴에 샐러드는 없나요?

B Yes. Our salads are on the last page.
네. 샐러드는 마지막 페이지에 있습니다.

25 cafeteria
[kæ̀fətíəriə]

n 카페테리아(간이 식당)

A Where do you want to go for lunch?
점심을 어디서 먹을래?

B Let's go to the school cafeteria.
학교 카페테리아로 가자.

Multi-Meaning Word

taste

n 미각, 맛
Won't you have a **taste** of this coffee?
이 커피 맛보시지 않겠습니까?

n 취미, 기호, 취향
My **taste** for music is just different from others'.
음악에 대한 내 취향이 다른 사람과 단지 다를 뿐이다.

v 맛을 느끼다
Can you **taste** anything strange in this soup?
이 수프엔 뭔가 이상한 맛이 나지 않습니까?

Word Search

앞에서 배운 어휘를 기억하며 모두 찾아 보세요.

정답

T	D	P	W	J	L	D	B	H	K	T	M	D	F	B
T	A	T	M	T	A	P	S	W	T	A	O	D	L	I
M	R	S	Z	Q	E	I	M	A	Q	O	Z	Y	A	T
E	R	E	T	T	D	A	R	B	F	E	C	D	V	T
A	G	J	Z	E	E	S	F	A	U	I	X	I	O	E
L	F	W	J	S	T	A	E	T	P	P	S	E	R	R
K	O	E	X	Y	E	S	Z	S	O	J	P	T	T	Y
R	O	H	H	R	U	E	V	S	X	R	O	E	T	A
E	D	C	L	H	A	P	H	W	M	X	D	L	R	O
E	T	L	B	Y	D	T	A	S	I	V	B	E	B	A
M	P	I	T	B	F	D	Y	R	E	D	I	O	R	J
V	A	L	I	M	E	N	U	V	G	P	T	O	O	A
R	A	I	R	V	E	L	D	O	O	N	E	D	J	C
S	S	N	A	C	K	V	J	L	C	O	K	Q	P	B

bite	bitter	chew	diet
dish	flavor	food	meal
menu	noodle	order	salty
seafood	snack	spicy	taste

Unit 14 Cooking & Recipe

□ cup 컵
□ knife 칼
□ pan 냄비
□ glass 한 잔(의 양)

□ put 넣다
□ chop 다지다
□ bake 굽다
□ slice (얇게 썬) 조각

□ cut 자르다
□ fry 튀기다
□ oven 오븐
□ spoon 숟가락

01 spoil
[spɔil]
(spoil-spoiled-spoiled)

ⓥ 망치다, 더럽히다

A Cindy, is the steamed rice ready?
신디야, 밥 준비 다 됐어?

B Don't open the pot! You'll spoil it!
냄비 열지 매 밥을 망치게 될 거야!

02 bowl
[boul]

ⓝ 사발, 공기   **a bowl of cereal** 시리얼 한 그릇

A What is in the bowl? 사발에 든 것이 무엇이니?

B It is sugar. I am going to make apple jam.
설탕이야. 사과 잼을 만들려고.

03 cook
[kuk]

ⓝ cooker 요리 기구

ⓝ 요리사 **ⓥ** 요리하다

A What do you want for dinner, Ally?
앨리, 저녁에 뭐 먹고 싶니?

B Are you tonight's cook? 네가 오늘 밤 요리사니?

04 recipe
[résəpì:]

ⓝ 요리법, 조리법   **a recipe book** 요리책

A How is the soup, Nancy? 낸시야, 수프 어때?

B It's great! Can I have the recipe?
맛있어! 요리법 좀 알려줄래?

05 boil
[bɔil]

ⓥ 끓이다   **boil eggs** 계란을 삶다

A That smells nice. What is it? 냄새 좋다. 무슨 요리니?

B I'm boiling chicken soup. 치킨 수프를 끓이고 있어.

06 fruit
[fruːt]

ⓝ 과일   **a fruit salad** 과일 샐러드

A Fruit is very healthy for your body.
과일은 몸에 매우 좋아.

B Yes, and very tasty, too. 맞아, 그리고 정말 맛있어.

07 fridge
[fridʒ]

syn refrigerator 냉장고

n 냉장고 **inside a fridge** 냉장고 안에

A What's for dinner? 저녁에 우리 뭐 먹어?

B Let's eat out. The fridge is empty.
외식하자. 냉장고가 비어 있네.

08 overcook
[òuvərkúk]

v 너무 익히다

A Waiter, I said I wanted my steak well done,
not overcooked! 웨이터, 스테이크를 충분히 익혀달라고 했지,
너무 익히라고 한 게 아니잖아요!

B I am so sorry. I'll get you a new one.
정말 죄송합니다. 새것으로 다시 준비해 드리지요.

09 vegetable
[védʒətəbəl]

n 야채 **green vegetables** 녹색 채소

A I don't like eating vegetables.
나 야채 먹는 것을 좋아하지 않아.

B But they are good for you! Eat up your beans!
하지만, 네 몸에 좋아! 어서 콩을 모두 먹어!

10 sauce
[sɔːs]

n 소스, 양념

A I like the sauce they give you with fried
chicken in Korea.
나는 한국에서 후라이드 치킨하고 같이 주는 소스를 좋아해.

B They don't have that in America?
미국에는 그런 것이 없니?

11 add
[æd]

v 더하다, 추가하다 **add sugar to coffee** 커피에 설탕을 타다

A Can I add something to my order?
주문에 무얼 추가해도 될까요?

B Of course. What will it be?
물론입니다. 무엇을 추가하시겠어요?

12 rotten
[rátn]

ⓐ 썩은, 부패한   **rotten bananas** 썩은 바나나

A You have to be careful when you buy fish.
생선을 살 때는 조심해야 해.

B Yes, it's easy for fish to become rotten.
맞아, 생선은 쉽게 썩지.

13 mix
[miks]

ⓝ mixture 혼합, 섞기

ⓥ 섞다, 혼합하다

A Five different fruits are mixed in this juice.
이 주스에는 다섯 가지의 과일이 섞여 있어.

B That is why it is delicious.
맛있는 이유가 그거였구나.

14 fresh
[freʃ]

ⓐ 신선한, 생생한   **fresh fruit juice** 생 과일 주스

A How did that store become a big success?
저 가게는 어떻게 크게 성공하게 되었니?

B The owner tried to use the freshest
ingredients. 주인이 늘 가장 신선한 재료를 사용하려고 했거든.

                              * ingredient : 재료

15 serve
[sə:rv]

ⓥ 음식을 차리다, 시중을 들다, (음식을) 제공하다

A What kind of food does the restaurant serve?
그 음식점은 어떤 음식을 파니?

B They mainly serve Italian dishes.
주로 이탈리아 요리를 팔아.

16 raw
[rɔː]

ⓐ 날것의, 가공하지 않은   **raw fish** 날 생선

A Some people are not comfortable with eating
raw food. 어떤 사람들은 음식을 날것으로 먹는 것을 불편해 해.

B I think it's important to accept each other's
differences. 각자의 차이를 받아들이는 것이 중요하다고 생각해.

17 burn
[bə:rn]
(burn-burnt/ed-burnt/ed)

Ⓥ 음식을 태우다, 타다   **burn black** 검게 타다

A Be careful not to burn the steak.
스테이크 태우지 않게 조심해.

B Don't worry, honey. I can handle it.
걱정하지 마, 여보. 잘할 수 있어.

18 chef
[ʃef]

Ⓝ 주방장, 요리사

A The food in this restaurant tastes different from before. 이 음식점의 음식 맛이 예전과 달라.

B Maybe they changed the chef.
주방장이 바뀌었나 봐.

19 stir
[stə:r]

Ⓥ 휘젓다, 움직이다   **stir one's tea** 차를 젓다

A Mom, do I have to keep on stirring? My arm hurts. 엄마, 계속 저어야 하는 거예요? 팔이 아프단 말이에요.

B If you stop, you will eat burnt stew.
네가 멈추면 넌 탄 스튜를 먹게 될 걸.

20 steam
[sti:m]

Ⓥ 찌다 **Ⓝ** 증기   **a steamed sweet potato** 찐 고구마

A What is Cecil doing in the kitchen?
세실이 부엌에서 무엇을 하고 있니?

B He is steaming some potatoes to make salad. 샐러드를 만든다고 감자를 찌고 있어.

21 medium
[mí:diəm]

ⓐ 중간 정도로 구워진, 중간의

A Give me a course A and I want my steak medium please.
A 코스로 주시고, 스테이크는 중간 정도 구워 주세요.

B Thank you. Anything else?
감사합니다. 다른 주문 있으세요?

22 flour
[flauər]

ⓝ 밀가루

A We don't have enough flour to make the cake. 케이크 만드는 데 밀가루가 부족해.

B I'll go buy some. 내가 가서 좀 사올게.

23 stove
[stouv]

ⓝ (요리용) 레인지, 난로

A What's on the stove? 가스레인지 위에 있는 것이 뭐니?

B I am making spaghetti. It smells delicious, doesn't it? 스파게티를 만들고 있어. 냄새 좋지, 그렇지 않니?

24 meat
[miːt]

ⓝ 육류, 고기

A My sister is a vegetarian. 우리 누나는 채식주의자야.　　　* vegetarian : 채식주의자

B How can she stand not eating meat? 고기 안 먹는 것을 어떻게 견딜까?

25 nut
[nʌt]

ⓝ 견과류, (호두 등) 나무 열매

A What kind of snack do you like? 너는 어떤 군것질 거리를 좋아하니?

B I usually have some nuts. 주로 견과류를 먹어.

Multi-Meaning Word

fruit

ⓝ 과일

Jim's grocery store only sells fresh **fruit** and vegetables.
짐 씨네 식료품 가게는 신선한 과일과 채소만을 판매합니다.

ⓝ 성과, 결과

I have worked really hard for ten years. Now, it's time to enjoy the **fruits** of my labor.
나는 십년 동안 매우 열심히 일했다. 이제는 내 노동의 결과를 즐길 시간이다.

Word Search

앞에서 배운 어휘를 기억하며 모두 찾아 보세요.

정답

```
E  V  O  K  D  J  S  T  F  E  P  H  N  U  T
A  C  B  X  B  D  M  E  P  F  S  Y  U  E  S
C  B  U  U  U  I  A  I  D  E  U  I  T  V  T
H  H  R  A  M  B  C  M  R  Z  K  I  T  R  O
E  N  Q  Y  T  E  J  F  Q  W  U  L  T  E  B
F  T  R  J  R  R  G  D  M  O  A  U  R  S  E
Q  H  D  S  J  A  N  B  L  I  S  X  L  C  A
O  F  U  D  T  W  Y  O  B  I  T  O  C  J  B
Z  S  U  N  F  E  U  W  Q  I  O  A  X  V  S
B  P  G  I  S  U  A  L  E  N  O  B  E  Z  G
I  O  E  L  H  I  F  M  J  S  Q  C  E  M  L
V  I  E  X  C  J  L  Y  T  R  U  O  V  Y  U
P  L  F  L  O  U  R  I  E  Z  M  O  A  R  L
O  W  Y  H  K  M  R  G  M  U  P  K  E  A  H
```

add	boil	bowl	burn
chef	cook	flour	fresh
meat	nut	raw	recipe
serve	spoil	steam	stir

Word Search 125

Unit 15 Daily Activities

Basic Words

- [ ] get up 일어나다
- [ ] wash 씻다
- [ ] clean 청소하다
- [ ] wake up 잠에서 깨다
- [ ] eat 먹다
- [ ] sleep 자다
- [ ] drive 운전하다
- [ ] go to school 학교에 가다
- [ ] work 일하다
- [ ] get dressed 옷을 입다
- [ ] chat 수다를 떨다
- [ ] study 공부하다

01 bathe
[beið]

n bath 목욕

v 목욕하다

A Honey, Sam called when you were bathing.
여보, 당신이 목욕하고 있을 때 샘이 전화했어.

B Okay. I'll call him back. 알았어. 다시 전화할게.

02 diary
[dáiəri]

n 일기, 일기장

A I've kept a diary since I was in the second grade. I never missed a day.
난 2학년 때부터 일기를 썼어. 하루도 거른 적이 없어.

B Wow, how many diaries do you have now?
우와, 지금 일기장을 몇 개나 가지고 있니?

03 skip
[skip]

v 건너뛰다   **skip a class** 수업을 빼먹다

A I'm hungry. Let's go get something to eat.
나 배고파. 뭐 먹으러 가자.

B Me, too. I woke up late this morning, so I had to skip breakfast.
나도 배고파. 오늘 아침에 늦게 일어나서 아침을 걸러야 했거든.

04 activity
[æktívəti]

n 활동   **after-school activities** 방과 후 활동

A I need to get more exercise.
나는 운동을 좀 더 해야 할 것 같아.

B Let's do more outdoor activities.
우리 야외 활동을 더 하자.

05 dream
[driːm]

n 꿈 **v** 꿈꾸다   **dream of success** 성공을 꿈꾸다

A You look very tired. Is everything okay with you? 너 정말 피곤해 보인다. 괜찮아?

B I'm fine. I just had a bad dream last night.
괜찮아. 어젯밤에 나쁜 꿈을 꿨을 뿐이야.

06 borrow

[bɔ́ːrou]

ant lend 빌려주다

ⓥ 빌리다

A Where did you get that bicycle, Joe?
조, 그 자전거 어디서 났니?

B I borrowed it from my friend, Mom.
친구에게서 빌렸어요, 엄마.

07 happen

[hǽpən]

ⓥ 일어나다, 생기다

A Hey, Jimmy's already here!
이봐, 지미가 벌써 와 있어!

B Really? That seldom happens!
정말? 그건 좀처럼 일어나지 않는 일인데!

08 clean-up

[kliːnʌp]

ⓝ 청소, 정화

A Your house is very clean! 집이 참 깨끗하네요!

B Thank you. We had a clean-up just one hour ago. 고마워요. 바로 한 시간 전에 청소를 했거든요.

09 act

[ækt]

ⓝ action 행동

ⓥ 행하다, 활동하다

A Can't you act like a gentleman?
신사답게 행동하면 안 되겠니?

B Why should I do that? 내가 왜 그래야 되는데?

10 schedule

[skédʒu(ː)l]

ⓝ 계획, 일정   **be behind schedule** 예정보다 늦다

A Could you attend the meeting instead of me, Clark? 나 대신 그 회의에 참석해 줄래, 클라크?

B Hmm, let me check my schedule first.
음, 먼저 내 일정을 확인해 볼게.

11 haircut
[hέərkʌt]

ⓝ 이발

A Your hair is too long and messy.
네 머리가 너무 길고 지저분하구나.

B I am planning to get a haircut today, Mom.
오늘 머리를 자르려고 했어요, 엄마.

12 greet
[griːt]
ⓝ greeting 인사, 절

ⓥ 인사하다

A Is Susan still angry with you?
수잔은 아직도 너에게 화가 났니?

B No, she's not. She greeted me happily this morning. 아니, 그렇지 않아. 오늘 아침에 반갑게 인사했어.

13 behave
[bihéiv]
ⓝ behavior 행동

ⓥ 행동하다

A What do you think about the new student?
전학생에 대해 어떻게 생각해?

B I think he's nice. I like how he behaves.
괜찮은 아이 같아. 행동하는 게 마음에 들어.

14 brush
[brʌʃ]

ⓝ 솔, 솔질 **ⓥ** 솔질하다　　**brush one's teeth** 이를 닦다

A I try to brush my teeth three times a day for three minutes.
나는 하루에 세 번 삼 분 동안 이를 닦으려고 노력해.

B I should do the same, but sometimes it gets so annoying! 나도 그래야 할 텐데, 가끔 너무 귀찮아!

15 habit
[hǽbit]

ⓝ 습관

A Pick the habit you want to change the most.
네가 가장 고치고 싶은 습관 하나 골라 봐.

B As you know, biting fingernails.
네가 알다시피, 손톱 물어뜯기.

16 ☑ **garbage**
[gáːrbidʒ]

n 쓰레기, 폐기물　　　　　　**a garbage can** 쓰레기통

A Tom, did you take out the garbage?
톰, 쓰레기 내다 버렸니?

B Oh, I forgot! I'll do it now, Mom.
앗, 잊고 있었어요. 지금 할게요, 엄마.

17 ☑ **awake**
[əwéik]

a 깨어있는, 자지 않고　　　　**keep awake** 깨어 있다

A What time did you go to bed last night?
어젯밤 몇 시에 잤어?

B I was awake until 5 o'clock a.m.
새벽 5시까지 깨어 있었어.

18 ☑ **daily**
[déili]
n day 날, 하루

ad 매일, 날마다　**a** 매일의, 일상의
a daily newspaper 일간 신문

A I decided to exercise daily starting today.
오늘부터 매일 운동하기로 결심했어.

B I hope that decision lasts. 그 결심이 오래가면 좋겠다.

19 ☑ **usually**
[júːʒuəli]
a usual 보통의, 일상의

ad 보통, 일반적으로

A What do you usually do after school?
방과 후엔 주로 무엇을 하니?

B I usually play basketball with my friends.
보통 친구들과 농구를 해.

20 ☑ **exercise**
[éksərsàiz]

v 운동하다　**n** 운동, 연습　　**regular exercise** 규칙적인 운동

A I think I have gained weight. 나 체중이 는 것 같아.

B I think so, too. You need to exercise more.
내 생각에도 그래. 너 운동을 좀 더 해야 할 것 같아.

21 **comb**
[koum]

ⓝ 빗, 빗질하는 기구 ⓥ 빗다

A Why don't you comb your tangled hair?
네 엉킨 머리 좀 빗지 그래?   * tangled : 뒤얽힌

B I tried, but I can't get a comb through. I think
I should cut it.
해봤는데, 머리가 잘 안 빗겨져. 그냥 잘라야 할까 봐.

---

22 **wipe**
[waip]

ⓥ 가볍게 문지르다, 닦다

A Jacob, will you come and wipe the table?
제이콥, 와서 식탁 좀 닦아줄래?

B Yes, Mom. 네, 엄마.

---

23 **regular**
[régjələːr]

ⓐ 규칙적인, 정기적인

A I try to volunteer on a regular basis.
나는 정기적으로 봉사활동을 하려고 해.

B Can I go with you next time?
다음에 나도 같이 가도 되니?

---

24 **weekday**
[wíːkdèi]

ⓝ 주중, 평일

A Sally, can you help me out on Tuesday?
샐리, 나 화요일에 도와줄 수 있니?

B Sorry, I don't think I'll have time on
weekdays. 미안한데, 평일에는 시간이 안 될 것 같아.

---

25 **accident**
[ǽksidənt]

ⓝ 사고, 우연

A There was a car accident on the highway.
고속도로에서 자동차 사고가 일어났어.

B Was anybody hurt? 다친 사람 있었어?

Word Search

앞에서 배운 어휘를 기억하며 모두 찾아 보세요.

정답

E	R	E	P	Z	Z	V	O	Y	R	A	I	D	H	H
B	G	A	H	L	L	X	A	I	T	G	L	Y	S	T
E	O	A	L	T	A	D	K	S	B	T	G	U	Y	Y
V	O	R	P	O	A	W	A	I	M	H	T	Y	L	E
A	W	A	R	R	G	B	A	W	O	B	Q	I	P	U
H	X	A	T	O	A	E	J	K	C	N	A	I	S	N
E	E	R	J	D	W	G	R	T	E	D	W	U	E	G
B	O	L	A	C	C	I	D	E	N	T	E	P	F	R
T	C	A	U	T	J	E	M	E	L	L	P	M	F	E
S	V	U	I	D	R	J	C	P	L	A	M	A	D	E
D	N	B	U	I	E	N	Y	Y	H	D	X	E	N	T
Z	A	X	A	X	O	H	P	I	K	S	H	R	W	S
H	P	D	I	I	V	J	C	L	D	I	G	D	R	X
X	L	U	S	D	V	R	H	S	E	V	O	C	L	Y

accident	act	awake	bathe
behave	borrow	comb	daily
diary	dream	greet	habit
happen	schedule	skip	wipe

Unit 16 House

Basic Words

□ bedroom 침실	□ bathroom 욕실	□ kitchen 주방
□ living room 거실	□ wall 벽	□ door 문
□ table 식탁	□ lamp 등, 램프	□ clock 시계
□ room 방	□ key 열쇠	□ house 집

01 **furniture**
[fə́ːrnitʃər]

n 가구   **wooden furniture** 목재 가구

A Is there a good furniture store near the new house? 새집 근처에 괜찮은 가구점 있어?

B Yes, I was planning to buy our new bed there. 응, 거기서 우리 새 침대를 사려고 했어.

---

02 **yard**
[jɑːrd]

n 마당, 안뜰

A What are you doing, Dad? 아빠, 뭐하고 계세요?

B I'm trying to grow grass on our front yard. 우리집 앞뜰에 잔디를 기르려고 해.

---

03 **arrange**
[əréindʒ]

n arrangement 정리, 배열

v 가지런히 하다, 정리하다

A How do you arrange your books on your shelves? 책장에 책을 어떻게 정리하니?

B I arrange them in alphabetical order. 난 알파벳순으로 정리해.   * alphabetical : 알파벳순의

---

04 **floor**
[flɔːr]

n 바닥, 층

A Why is the cup broken? 컵이 왜 깨져 있어?

B I dropped it on the floor. I'm sorry. 내가 바닥에 떨어뜨렸어. 미안해.

---

05 **rent**
[rent]

n 임대료, 집세, 방세   **pay the rent** 집세를 내다

A Do you like the house, sir? 집은 마음에 드시나요, 손님?

B Yes, I do. How much is the rent? 네, 마음에 들어요. 집세는 얼마죠?

---

06 **garage**
[gərɑ́ːʒ]

n 차고, 자동차 수리소

A Where did you park the car? The garage is empty. 차 어디에 주차했어? 차고가 비었어.

B I took it outside to wash it. 세차하려고 꺼냈어.

07 roof
[ru:f]

ⓝ 지붕, 꼭대기   **the roof of the mouth** 입천장

A I can't reach the ball on the roof.
지붕 위에 있는 공에 손이 닿지 않아.

B I'll go get a ladder. 가서 사다리 가져올게.

08 remain
[riméin]

ⓥ 남다, ~인 채로 있다   **remain silent** 침묵을 지키다

A I think the traditional buildings in Korea are very beautiful.
한국에 있는 전통 건물들이 매우 아름다운 것 같아.

B Yes, there remain many in the city, too.
응, 도시에도 많은 건물이 남아있어.

09 nearby
[níərbài]

prep 가까이에 ⓐ 바로 이웃의, 가까운

a nearby village 바로 이웃 마을

A Is there a post office nearby the house?
집 근처에 우체국 있니?

B I saw one just around the corner.
모퉁이 지나서 하나 봤어.

10 brick
[brik]

ⓝ 벽돌   **a brick wall** 벽돌담

A That red brick building gives warmth to the cold city. 저 빨간 벽돌 건물이 차가운 도시에 온기를 주는구나.

B Yes, it's a treasure to the neighborhood.
네, 이 동네의 보물이에요.

11 garden
[gá:rdn]

ⓝ 정원   **a roof garden** 옥상 정원

A Dad, do you know where Mom is?
아빠, 엄마 어디 계신지 아세요?

B Yes, she is watering the flowers in the garden. 응, 정원에서 꽃에 물을 주고 있어.

12 basement
[béismənt]

n 지하실, 지하층   **basement garage** 지하 주차장

A Where should we keep our old couch?
오래된 소파는 어디에 둘까요?

B Let's keep it in the basement. 지하실에 두자.

13 toilet
[tɔ́ilit]

n 화장실, 변기

A Mrs. Potter, can I use your toilet?
포터 아주머니, 화장실 좀 써도 될까요?

B Of course. It's the first door to your right.
물론이지. 오른쪽으로 첫 번째 문이다.

14 grass
[græs]

n 풀, 잔디   **lie down on the grass** 잔디밭에 눕다

A It's been a long time since we went on a picnic. 우리 소풍 다녀온 지 오래됐어.

B Yes. I miss the smell of grass. 맞아. 풀 냄새가 그립다.

15 bill
[bil]

n 청구서, 계산서   **electricity bill** 전기 요금

A Have you paid the phone bill? 전화 요금 냈어?

B Oh, I totally forgot about it. When is the due date? 아, 나 까맣게 잊고 있었어. 언제까지야?

16 stair
[stɛəːr]

n 계단   **fall down the stairs** 계단에서 굴러 떨어지다

A Where is your room, Joseph? 조셉, 네 방은 어디니?

B We have to go up the stairs. 계단으로 올라가야 해.

17 build
[bild]
(build-built-built)

n (건물을) 짓다, 건축하다

A Look at the beautiful temple!
저 아름다운 사원을 봐!

B Yes, I heard it was built in the early 15th century. 응, 저 사원은 15세기 초에 지어졌다고 들었어.

18 curtain
[kə́ːrtən]

① 커튼, 휘장   **draw a curtain** 커튼을 치다

A The carpet and curtain are a good match.
카펫과 커튼이 잘 어울린다.

B Thanks a lot. My mother helped me choose the color. 정말 고마워. 어머니가 색 고르는 것을 도와주셨어.

19 address
[ǽdres / ədrés]

① 주소, 연설 **Ⓥ** 연설하다

A How can I find your house?
너희 집을 어떻게 찾아갈 수 있지?

B I'll give you my address. 우리 집 주소를 가르쳐줄게.

20 around
[əráund]

prep 주변에, 둘레에

A Where were you, Jenny?
제니, 어디에 있었니?

B I was taking a walk around the park.
공원 주변을 산책하고 있었어요.

21 apartment
[əpáːrtmənt]
c.f. flat 〈영국〉 아파트

① 아파트

A Living in an apartment is very convenient.
아파트에 사는 것은 참 편해.

B Houses have advantages of their own, too.
주택도 그 나름의 장점이 있어.

22 messy
[mési]

ⓐ 엉망인, 어질러진

A I'm sorry that my room is a bit messy.
방이 좀 지저분해서 미안해요.

B It's all right. I don't mind at all.
괜찮아요. 전혀 신경 안 써요.

23 ceiling
[síːliŋ]

n 천장

A Honey, there's water dropping from the ceiling. 여보, 천장에서 물이 떨어져요.

B We should have fixed the roof earlier.
지붕을 일찍 수리해 놓았어야 했는데.

24 decorate
[dékərèit]

n decoration 장식

v 장식하다

A How do you want to decorate the house?
집을 어떻게 장식하고 싶어?

B First of all, I want to have pink wallpaper.
우선, 분홍색 벽지를 붙이고 싶어.

25 attic
[ǽtik]

n 다락방

A Mom, I've been looking for my yearbook for two hours. Have you seen it?
엄마, 저 두 시간째 졸업앨범을 찾고 있어요. 그거 보신 적 있으세요?

B I think I saw it somewhere in the attic.
다락방 어디선가 그것을 본 거 같구나.

Multi-Meaning Word

floor

n 마루, 마루방
His little kids are playing on the kitchen **floor**.
그의 어린 아이들이 부엌 마루에서 놀고 있다.

n (건물의) 층
Our office is on the top **floor**, so it has a nice view.
우리 사무실은 꼭대기 층에 있어서 전망이 좋아.

n 밑바닥, 바닥
What life forms live on the ocean **floor**?
어떤 형태의 생물체가 바다 밑바닥에 살까?

Word Search

앞에서 배운 어휘를 기억하며 모두 찾아 보세요.

정답

E	X	Y	T	C	B	L	C	Z	T	E	A	W	Y	B
Z	B	E	A	E	B	R	L	U	C	G	D	D	S	X
B	Z	H	L	I	J	E	I	I	Z	A	D	N	S	M
C	B	P	I	L	R	Z	S	C	B	R	R	U	E	Q
J	O	M	O	I	I	Z	Z	E	K	A	E	O	M	T
J	N	R	T	N	A	C	N	A	M	G	S	R	U	N
S	M	Z	T	G	T	U	F	A	P	E	S	T	E	A
R	E	N	T	A	S	U	Y	R	R	E	N	D	F	F
A	T	T	I	C	I	A	Y	O	Z	R	R	T	G	L
J	N	L	L	G	R	N	W	O	M	A	A	G	F	O
X	W	Q	Q	D	E	S	P	F	G	M	R	N	I	O
O	R	K	L	N	B	R	S	Y	L	X	I	M	G	R
S	S	A	R	G	V	R	B	F	G	C	K	X	G	E
N	I	A	M	E	R	A	A	V	F	E	O	M	R	X

address	arrange	attic	bill
brick	ceiling	floor	garage
garden	grass	messy	remain
rent	roof	stair	yard

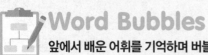

Word Bubbles

앞에서 배운 어휘를 기억하며 버블을 단어로 채워 보세요.

정답

Chapter 4

해산물

맛, 풍미

끓이다

음식

Daily Life
일상 생활

조리법

행동하다

가구

임대료

규칙적인

장식하다

다락방

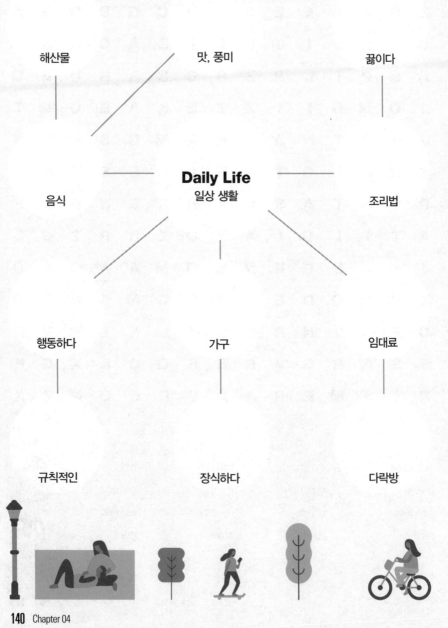

A 우리말을 영어로, 영어를 우리말로 쓰시오.

01 음식점, 요리점 _____ 08 fruit _____

02 지붕 _____ 09 chew _____

03 인사하다 _____ 10 messy _____

04 신선한, 생생한 _____ 11 habit _____

05 정리하다 _____ 12 stir _____

06 후식 _____ 13 rent _____

07 보통, 일반적으로 _____ 14 meal _____

B 빈칸에 알맞은 단어를 쓰시오.

01 음식물 _____ and drink

02 요리책 a(n) _____ book

03 방과 후 활동 after-school _____

04 a garbage can _____통

05 draw a curtain _____을/를 치다

06 lose one's appetite _____을/를 잃다

C 단어의 관계에 맞게 빈칸을 채우시오.

01 빌려주다 : 빌리다 = lend : _____

02 소금 : 짠 = salt : _____

03 장식 : 장식하다 = decoration : _____

04 taste : tasty = 맛이 나다 : _____

05 meat : vegetable = 고기 : _____

06 bathe : bath = 목욕하다 : _____

D 배운 단어를 사용하여 문장을 완성하시오. (필요하면 형태를 바꾸시오.)

01 I always become _____ after eating ice cream.
아이스크림을 먹고 나면 항상 나는 목이 마르다.

02 The watermelon looked fresh, but it was _____ inside.
수박이 싱싱해 보였지만, 안은 썩어 있었다.

03 My childhood _____ was to be a superhero.
내 어릴 적 꿈은 슈퍼 히어로가 되는 것이었다.

04 David wrote her _____ on an envelope carefully and put the
letter into it.
데이비드는 그녀의 주소를 봉투에 조심스럽게 써서 편지를 그 안에 넣었다.

05 Sophia _____ as if she were a princess.
소피아는 마치 그가 공주라도 되는 듯이 행동한다.

E 빈칸에 알맞은 말을 보기에서 찾아 쓰시오.

habit	toilet	boil	weekdays	wiping

01 **A** I have a bad _____ of biting my fingernails.
   B You should keep your nails short so you can't bite them.

02 **A** How many hours do you sleep on _____?
   B Almost every day, I go to bed at 11 and get up at 6.

03 **A** I feel like having a cup of coffee. Could you _____ some
   water?
   B Okay, I will go and make some coffee for you.

04 **A** Guys, have you finished cleaning?
   B I am _____ the floor and Johnny is cleaning the
   _____.

F 밑줄 친 부분을 우리말로 옮기시오.

01 There is nothing wrong with the bag. It is just not <u>my taste</u>.

02 A young lady got on and asked me to push the button for <u>the fourth
floor</u>.

Chapter
05

Studies

Unit 17 School

- □ class 수업
- □ classroom 교실
- □ desk 책상
- □ chair 의자
- □ teacher 선생님
- □ school 학교
- □ student 학생
- □ library 도서관
- □ teach 가르치다
- □ middle school 중학교
- □ high school 고등학교
- □ pencil 연필

01 absent
[ǽbsənt]

ⓝ absence 결석

ⓐ 부재의, 결석한   **be absent** 결석하다

A Is anybody absent today? 오늘 결석한 사람 있니?

B Jenny said she was sick, Ms. Marge.
마지 선생님, 제니가 아프다고 했어요.

02 exam
[igzǽm]

ⓝ 시험(= examination)   **take an exam** 시험을 보다

A You know what? I passed the exam.
너 그거 알아? 나 그 시험 통과했어.

B Wow! Congratulations! 와! 축하해!

03 lesson
[lésn]

ⓝ 수업, 교훈   **give a lesson** 교훈을 주다

A We're going to have a party today. Will you join us? 오늘 파티를 열려고 해. 너도 올래?

B I'd love to, but I have a piano lesson today.
그러고 싶은데 오늘 피아노 수업이 있어.

04 advise
[ædváiz]

ⓝ advice 충고, 조언
[ədváis]

ⓥ 충고하다, 조언하다

A Jane was lazy during the vacation.
제인은 방학 동안 게으른 생활을 했어.

B She needs someone to advise her.
그녀는 그녀를 충고해 줄 사람이 필요해.

05 break
[breik]

ⓝ 중단, 잠시의 휴식   **take a break** 휴식을 취하다

A I often have a coffee break when I'm studying. 나는 공부할 때 자주 커피 마시며 휴식을 가져.

B I usually have some green tea.
난 주로 녹차를 마셔.

06 □ homework
[hóumwə̀rk]

ⓝ 숙제   **do one's homework** 숙제를 하다

A What are you doing now? 지금 뭐해?

B I'm doing my math homework. 수학 숙제 하고 있어.

07 □ classmate
[klǽsmèit]

ⓝ 학급 친구

A Do you know the girl wearing a red skirt?
빨간 치마를 입고 있는 소녀 아니?

B Sure. She's my classmate, Rachel.
그럼. 그녀는 같은 반 친구, 레이첼이야.

08 □ grade
[greid]

ⓝ 학년, 성적, 등급   **get a good grade** 좋은 점수를 얻다

A What grade are you in? 몇 학년이니?

B I'm in the first grade of middle school.
난 중학교 1학년이야.

09 □ subject
[sʌ́bdʒikt]

ⓝ 과목, 주제   **a favorite subject** 좋아하는 과목

A What subject are you studying? 무슨 과목 공부해?

B I'm studying history. 역사 공부 하고 있어.

10 □ report
[ripɔ́ːrt]

ⓝ reporter
보도 기자, 보고자

ⓝ 성적표, 보고서 **ⓥ** 보고하다   **a report card** 성적표

A Did you show your report card to your
parents? 너 성적표를 부모님께 보여드렸니?

B No, not yet. 아니, 아직.

11 □ playground
[pléigràund]

ⓝ 운동장

A Where is Charlie? I can't find him.
찰리는 어디 있어? 그를 찾을 수가 없어.

B He's on the playground. 운동장에 있어.

12 university
[jùːnəvə́ːrsəti]

① (종합)대학교

A Did you apply to the university?
그 대학교에 지원 했니?

B Yes, I did. I am waiting for an answer now.
응, 했어. 지금 답변을 기다리고 있어.

13 college
[kálidʒ]

① 대학, 단과대학

a college student 대학생

A What are you going to do after graduating from college? 대학 졸업 후에 뭐 할 거니?

B I think I'll be a teacher. 선생님이 될 것 같아.

14 course
[kɔːrs]

① 강의, (학교의) 교육과정

A The English course was very useful.
그 영어 강좌는 참 유익했어.

B Right. I'm going to take the course again next year. 맞아. 나는 내년에 또 그 강좌를 들으려고 해.

15 principal
[prínsəpəl]

① 교장

A Mr. Smith is the principal of my school.
스미스 선생님이 우리 교장 선생님이세요.

B Is he? He used to be my teacher.
정말이니? 내 예전에 선생님이셨는데.

16 textbook
[tékstbùk]

① 교과서

A Where is your English textbook?
너 영어 교과서 어디 있어?

B Oops! I forgot to bring it.
앗! 나 가져오는 걸 깜박했어.

17 elementary
[èləméntəri]

ⓐ 초등학교의, 초보의

A How old is your younger brother?
너의 남동생은 몇 살이니?

B He's ten. He's in elementary school.
열 살이야. 초등학생이지.

18 education
[èdʒukéiʃən]
ⓥ educate 교육하다

ⓝ 교육, 훈련　　　　　　school education 학교 교육

A Why is education so important?
왜 그렇게 교육이 중요한 거죠?

B Because it gives people the necessary knowledge.
그것이 사람들에게 필요한 지식을 제공하기 때문이야.

19 continue
[kəntínjuː]

ⓥ 계속하다, 지속하다

A Have you decided what to do after your graduation? 졸업 후에 무엇을 할지 결정했어?

B I will go to graduate school and continue my studies. 대학원에 가서 공부를 계속할 거야.
* graduate school : 대학원

20 attend
[əténd]

ⓥ 출석하다

A Will you be attending the meeting?
오늘 회의에 출석하십니까?

B Yes, I'll be there on time. 네, 시간 맞춰서 갈게요.

21 praise
[preiz]

ⓥ 칭찬하다 ⓝ 칭찬, 찬양　　the highest praise 최고의 찬사

A The teacher praised Jenny during class.
선생님이 수업 중에 제니를 칭찬했어.

B I think she is a good student, too.
나도 그녀가 좋은 학생인 것 같아.

22 enter
[éntər]

n entrance 입학, 입장

v 입학하다, 들어가다   **enter a college** 대학에 들어가다

A My sister will enter middle school next year.
여동생이 내년에 중학교 입학해.

B Time really flies, doesn't it?
시간 참 빠르지, 그렇지 않니?

23 uniform
[júːnəfɔ̀ːrm]

n 교복, 제복   **out of uniform** 사복으로

A People say our school uniform looks good.
사람들이 우리 교복이 예뻐 보인대.

B Yes, our uniform is very stylish.
우리 유니폼이 세련됐지.

24 average
[ǽvəridʒ]

n 평균, 보통   **below the average** 평균 이하

A Did you do well on the test? 시험 잘 봤니?

B I think I'm above average.
평균 점수다는 높을 것 같아.

25 even though

conj 비록 ~할지라도

A I was too tired to finish my homework.
너무 피곤해서 숙제를 마칠 수가 없었어.

B James did it even though he had to prepare
for a test. 제임스는 시험 준비를 했어야 했는데도 그것을 했어.

Multi-Meaning Word

grade

n 등급
Top-**grade** teas are expensive.
최고 등급의 차는 매우 비싸다.

n 학점, 점수
He got a **grade** B in math.
그는 수학에서 B 학점을 받았다.

n 학년
My brother is in the sixth **grade**.
내 남동생은 6학년이다.

Word Search

앞에서 배운 어휘를 기억하며 모두 찾아 보세요.

정답

W	T	U	N	E	K	R	A	E	K	N	U	W	E	Z
O	R	O	Y	O	D	R	E	T	D	W	J	U	U	V
E	N	T	E	R	I	U	O	P	T	D	W	P	N	E
N	O	S	S	E	L	T	C	E	O	E	R	R	I	S
M	R	O	T	I	N	U	A	A	E	R	N	G	T	I
P	R	A	I	S	E	N	A	N	T	M	T	D	N	V
C	L	A	S	S	M	A	T	E	I	I	O	R	O	D
T	E	X	T	B	O	O	K	S	A	M	O	H	C	A
B	T	A	V	E	R	A	G	E	U	B	E	N	E	Z
K	A	E	R	B	G	C	Q	E	V	B	S	X	B	B
L	Y	L	Y	V	T	C	Y	H	E	R	J	E	E	C
C	O	L	L	E	G	E	N	S	V	M	D	E	N	V
C	O	U	R	S	E	Q	W	N	F	G	B	F	C	T
Q	R	Z	E	V	A	J	Z	S	V	R	G	W	T	T

absent	advise	attend	average
break	classmate	college	continue
course	education	enter	lesson
praise	report	subject	textbook

- □ pass 합격
- □ read 읽다
- □ wrong 틀린
- □ must ~해야 한다
- □ fail 불합격
- □ write 쓰다
- □ play 놀다
- □ should ~해야 한다
- □ test 시험
- □ sing 노래하다
- □ learn 배우다
- □ can ~할 수 있다

01 ☑ excellent
[éksələnt]

ⓝ excellence 우수함

ⓐ 우수한, 훌륭한

A My son is excellent at math and science.
제 아들은 수학과 과학에 뛰어나요.

B You must be very proud of him.
아들이 정말 자랑스러우시겠어요.

02 ☑ question
[kwéstʃən]

ⓝ 질문, 문제, 의제   **question and answer** 질의응답

A Sir, can I ask you a question about today's class? 선생님, 오늘 수업에 대해 질문해도 되나요?

B Sure, go ahead. 물론이지. 어서 해 보아라.

03 ☑ equal
[íːkwəl]

ad equally 똑같이, 동등하게

ⓐ 같은, 동등한   **an equal amount** 같은 양

A What is ten times ten? 십 곱하기 십이 뭐지?

B Ten times ten is equal to one hundred.
십 곱하기 십은 백이야.

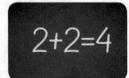

04 ☑ simple
[símpəl]

ad simply 간단히, 알기 쉽게

ⓐ 단순한, 간단한   **a simple question** 간단한 문제

A Science tries to explain things in a simple way. 과학은 사물을 단순하게 설명하려고 한단다.

B Yes, but why is it still hard?
네, 하지만 왜 여전히 어려운가요?

05 ☑ prepare
[pripέər]

ⓝ preparation 준비

ⓥ 준비하다

A Your band is practicing a lot these days.
너희 밴드 요즘 연습을 많이 하는구나.

B Yes, we're preparing for a contest.
응, 대회 준비하고 있거든.

06 review
[rivjú:]

ⓥ 복습하다, 재검토하다 **ⓝ** 복습, 재검토

A I'm not good at mathematics. 나는 수학을 잘 못해.

B It is necessary to review math every day.
수학은 매일 복습을 해야 해.

07 difficult
[dífikʌlt]

ⓝ difficulty 어려움

ⓐ 어려운

A This question is difficult for me. Can you help me? 이 질문은 나한테 어려워. 도와줄래?

B Sure. 물론이지.

08 achieve
[ətʃíːv]

ⓝ achievement 성취

ⓥ (목적을) 이루다, 달성하다

A We finally achieved victory! 드디어 승리를 이루어냈어!

B Yes, I knew we could do it.
응, 난 우리가 해낼 수 있을 줄 알았어.

09 result
[rizʌ́lt]

ⓝ 결과, 결말, 성과   **as a result of ~** ~의 결과로

A Did you see the test results? 시험 결과 봤니?

B No. I'm too nervous! 아니. 너무 긴장 돼!

10 explain
[ikspléin]

ⓝ explanation 설명

ⓥ 설명하다

A Tom, can you explain this problem to me?
톰, 이 문제 나한테 설명해줄 수 있니?

B Sure, let me see it. 물론이지. 한 번 보자.

11 mean
[miːn]

ⓥ 의미하다, 의도하다   **mean nothing** 아무런 의미가 없다

A Do you know what the word "correct"
means? correct라는 단어가 무슨 뜻인지 아니?

B Oh, that means "right." 아, 그 단어는 '옳은'이라는 뜻이야.

12 complete
☑

[kəmplíːt]

ad completely
완전히, 철저히

⑦ 완성하다 **ⓐ** 완전한   **complete darkness** 암흑

A You look happy today. 너 오늘 기분이 좋아 보여.

B It's because I finally completed my essay.
드디어 내 에세이를 완성했거든.

13 exact
☑

[igzǽkt]

ad exactly 정확하게

ⓐ 정확한

A What is the exact number of the students in
your class? 너희 반 학생들의 정확한 수가 어떻게 되니?

B My class has 33 students.
우리 반에는 33명의 학생이 있어.

14 attempt
☑

[ətémpt]

ⓝ 시도 **⑦** 시도하다   **attempt an escape** 탈출을 시도하다

A I heard Freddy failed the experiment again.
프레디가 그 실험에서 또 실패했다고 들었어.

B Poor Freddy! Is he going to make another
attempt? 불쌍한 프레디! 그가 다시 시도할까?

15 solve
☑

[sɑlv]

ⓝ solution 해결책

⑦ 풀다, 해결하다

A How was the test? Wasn't it hard?
시험 어땠어? 어렵지 않았니?

B I solved all the questions, but question 5 was
quite difficult.
문제를 다 풀긴 했는데 5번 문제가 꽤 어려웠어.

16 dictionary
☑

[díkʃənèri]

ⓝ 사전   **a walking dictionary** 만물박사

A I bought a new English-English dictionary
today. 오늘 영영사전을 새로 샀어.

B I need to buy one, too. 나도 하나 사야 하는데.

17 divide
[diváid]

n division 나누기

v 나누다

A How much does each of us have to pay?
우리 각자 얼마씩 내야 해?

B Well, divide 30 dollars by 4.
음. 30달러를 4로 나눠 봐.

18 minus
[máinəs]

ant plus 플러스의,
~을 더하여

prep 마이너스한, ~을 뺀 **a** 마이너스의

A What does the minus sign mean?
마이너스 부호가 무엇을 의미하나요?

B It means that the number is below zero.
그 숫자가 0보다 작다는 뜻이야.

19 trouble
[trʌbəl]

n 고생, 어려움 **v** 괴롭히다　**family troubles** 가족 불화

A I have trouble solving these problems.
이 문제들을 푸는 게 어려워.

B Let me help you. 내가 도와줄게.

20 count
[kaunt]

v 세다, 계산하다　**count down** 수를 거꾸로 읽다

A Are you sure you counted everybody?
모두 다 센 것이 확실하니?

B Yes, I didn't leave anybody out.
네, 아무도 빠뜨리지 않았어요.

21 finish
[fíniʃ]

v 끝내다, 마치다, 완료하다　**finish school** 학업을 끝마치다

A What do you want to do after you graduate?
졸업한 다음에 무엇을 하고 싶니?

B I want to go to college after I finish high
school. 고등학교를 마치면 대학에 가고 싶어.

22 □ calculate
[kǽlkjəlèit]

Ⓥ 계산하다

A Many people tried to calculate the speed of light. 많은 사람이 빛의 속도를 계산하려고 시도했어.

B Who was the first to succeed?
처음으로 성공한 것이 누구였어?

23 □ repeat
[ripíːt]

Ⓥ 되풀이하다, 반복하다

A Sir, these words are hard to pronounce.
선생님, 이 단어들은 발음하기 어려워요.

B Then repeat each word after me.
그렇다면, 나를 따라 각 단어를 반복해 보아라.

24 □ mistake
[mistéik]

Ⓝ 잘못, 착각　　　　　　**by mistake** 잘못하여, 실수로

A I try not to make a mistake.
나는 실수를 하지 않으려고 노력해.

B Don't be so hard on yourself.
너무 너 자신을 심하게 몰아대지 마.

25 □ although
[ɔːlðóu]

conj ~일지라도, ~이기는 하지만

A Although I worked hard, I failed the test.
공부를 열심히 했지만, 시험에는 떨어졌어.

B Cheer up! There's always next time.
힘내! 언제나 다음 기회가 있는 법이야.

Multi-Meaning Word

question
Ⓝ 질문, 물음

May I ask you a **question**?
한 가지 질문을 해도 될까요?

Ⓝ 문제

Answer two out of the five **questions**.
다섯 문제 중 두 문제에 답하시오.

Ⓝ 의심, 의문

There is no **question** that parents are the best teachers.
부모님이 가장 훌륭한 선생님이라는 것은 의심의 여지가 없다.

Word Search

앞에서 배운 어휘를 기억하며 모두 찾아 보세요.

정답

W	G	F	Q	I	W	L	N	E	T	M	U	J	T	N
N	B	S	W	C	S	E	D	O	I	L	W	F	E	U
S	I	M	P	L	E	I	I	N	I	T	U	A	M	I
Z	Y	H	W	L	V	C	U	V	M	P	L	S	V	O
U	Q	S	T	I	A	S	O	R	E	P	S	I	E	O
K	Q	I	D	E	D	U	W	U	X	R	X	E	P	R
I	B	N	U	E	E	I	Q	E	N	V	B	V	U	X
K	B	I	H	Q	V	P	F	E	T	T	I	C	U	Q
J	Y	F	L	P	S	E	E	I	J	C	M	Q	S	P
E	L	B	U	O	R	T	I	R	I	E	A	N	D	Q
E	R	A	P	E	R	P	V	H	A	C	D	X	S	W
E	K	A	T	S	I	M	M	N	C	G	U	H	E	J
J	E	X	C	E	L	L	E	N	T	A	V	L	E	F
Q	P	D	E	V	L	O	S	U	X	G	E	W	T	F

achieve   count   divide   equal

exact   excellent   finish   mean

minus   mistake   prepare   result

review   simple   solve   trouble

Word Bubbles

앞에서 배운 어휘를 기억하며 버블을 단어로 채워 보세요.

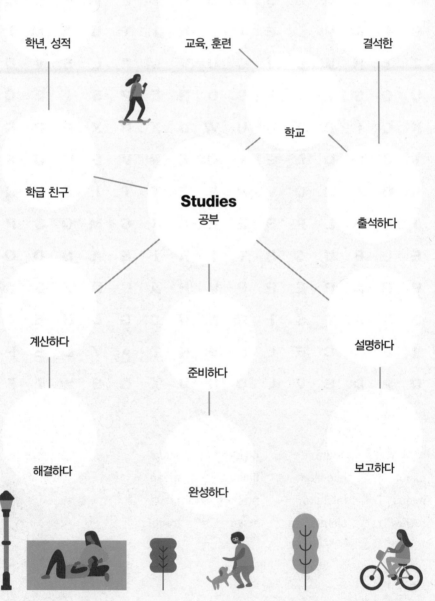

학년, 성적

교육, 훈련

결석한

학교

학급 친구

Studies
공부

출석하다

계산하다

설명하다

준비하다

해결하다

보고하다

완성하다

Review Test

A 우리말을 영어로, 영어를 우리말로 쓰시오.

01 성적표, 보고서 _____   08 textbook _____

02 교복, 제복 _____   09 result _____

03 시도, 시도하다 _____   10 divide _____

04 의미하다 _____   11 average _____

05 수업, 교훈 _____   12 calculate _____

06 숙제 _____   13 review _____

07 풀다 _____   14 continue _____

B 빈칸에 알맞은 단어를 쓰시오.

01 수를 거꾸로 세다 _____ down

02 초등학교 _____ school

03 휴식을 취하다 take a(n) _____

04 school education 학교 _____

05 finish school 학업을 _____

06 pass the exam _____에 통과하다

C 단어의 관계에 맞게 빈칸을 채우시오.

01 설명하다 : 설명 = explain : _____

02 어려운 : 어려움 = difficult : _____

03 질문 : 대답 = question : _____

04 exact : exactly = 정확한 : _____

05 entrance : enter = 입학, 입장 : _____

06 plus : minus = ~을 더하여 : _____

D 배운 단어를 사용하여 문장을 완성하시오. (필요하면 형태를 바꾸시오.)

01 Jina is my _____, and she gets along well with me.

지나는 내 반 친구이고 그녀는 나와 사이좋게 지낸다.

02 Chemistry is a difficult _____, so I should study it harder.

화학은 어려운 과목이어서 나는 더 열심히 공부해야 한다.

03 Sue is a(n) _____ student, so every teacher likes her.

수는 우수한 학생이어서 모든 선생님이 그녀를 좋아한다.

04 Parents should _____ their children more often.

부모들은 자신들의 자녀를 더 자주 칭찬해 주어야 한다.

05 _____ I passed the test, I wasn't happy at all.

나는 그 시험을 통과했지만, 전혀 기쁘지 않았다.

E 빈칸에 알맞은 말을 보기에서 찾아 쓰시오.

absent	advise	playground	mistakes	college

01 **A** I can't decide what to study in _____.

B I think Mr. Matthew can _____ you on that.

02 **A** Where are we going to play soccer tomorrow?

B I think we can play on the _____.

03 **A** I made lots of _____ on my math exam.

B What? You studied very hard.

04 **A** Why was Sarah _____ yesterday?

B She got cavities, so she went to the dentist.

F 밑줄 친 부분을 우리말로 옮기시오.

01 I could answer only three out of <u>ten questions</u>.

02 Even though Tina didn't study at all, she got <u>a high grade</u> in science.

Chapter
06

Leisure

Unit 19 Sports & Hobbies

Let's play!

Basic Words

- □ sport 운동
- □ win 이기다
- □ music 음악
- □ baseball 야구
- □ bat 방망이
- □ lose 패하다
- □ hiking 도보 여행
- □ dance 춤, 춤추다
- □ ball 공
- □ paint 그리다
- □ basketball 농구
- □ football 축구

01 climb
[klaim]

ⓥ 오르다, 기어오르다

A What is the secret to your health?
네 건강 비법이 뭐야?

B I climb a mountain every weekend.
난 주말마다 산에 올라.

02 hobby
[hábi]

ⓝ 취미

A I play the guitar in my free time.
나는 한가한 시간에 기타를 연주해.

B Really? What a nice hobby!
정말이니? 정말 좋은 취미구나!

03 favorite
[féivərit]

ⓐ 마음에 드는, 아주 좋아하는

A Do you have a favorite painting?
네가 특히 좋아하는 그림 있니?

B Yes, it's the Mona Lisa. 응, 그건 모나리자야.

04 collect
[kəlékt]
ⓝ collection 수집

ⓥ 수집하다, 모으다

A I see you like to buy music albums.
너는 음반 사는 것을 좋아하는구나.

B Yes, I do. I have collected them since I was twelve. 응, 맞아. 열두 살 때부터 음반을 수집해 왔어.

05 hunt
[hʌnt]

ⓥ 사냥하다 **ⓝ** 사냥   **go on a hunt** 사냥하러 가다

A I saw an eagle hunt a hare on television.
텔레비전에서 독수리가 산토끼를 사냥하는 걸 봤어.

B Oh, that poor thing! 아, 불쌍한 토끼!

06 score
[skɔːr]

ⓝ (경기에서의) 득점, 점수

A I'm sorry I'm late! What's the score?
늦어서 미안해! 지금 점수가 몇 대 몇이니?

B It's 3 to 2 right now. 지금 3 대 2야.

07 ☑ **compete**
[kəmpíːt]

ⓝ competition 경쟁

ⓥ 경쟁하다, 겨루다

compete in the contest 대회에서 경쟁하다

A Who are we competing against next in the school basketball tournament?
학교 농구 대회에서 우리가 겨룰 다음 상대는 누구야?

B We play against Class 5. 5반하고 경기할 거야.

---

08 ☑ **champion**
[tʃǽmpiən]

ⓝ 챔피언, 우승자

A Who was the figure skating champion?
피겨 스케이팅 경기 우승자가 누구였니?

B It was Kim Yuna. She was so wonderful!
김연아 선수였어. 정말 멋졌어!

---

09 ☑ **prefer**
[prifə́ːr]

ⓥ ~을 더 좋아하다

A Which do you prefer to play, baseball or basketball? 야구와 농구 중 어떤 경기를 하는 걸 더 좋아하니?

B I prefer to play basketball.
농구 경기하는 것을 더 좋아해.

---

10 ☑ **fair**
[fɛər]

ad fairly 공정히

ⓐ 공평한, 공정한   **a fair play** 정정당당한 시합

A I am really angry that our team lost the game.
우리 팀이 게임에 져서 무척 화가 나.

B Me too. But the play was fair.
나도 그래. 하지만, 시합은 공정했어.

---

11 ☑ **coach**
[koutʃ]

ⓝ 코치, 지도자

A There is always a good coach behind a good player. 훌륭한 선수 뒤에는 반드시 훌륭한 코치가 있어.

B I agree. Leadership is very important in sports. 내 생각도 그래. 스포츠에서 리더십은 굉장히 중요해.

12 interest
[íntərist]

Ⓥ 관심을 끌다 Ⓝ 관심, 흥미

A People these days are greatly interested in health. 사람들은 요즘 건강에 관심이 많아.

B Yes, they all wish for well-being.
응, 모두 웰빙을 원하고 있어.

13 challenge
[tʃǽlindʒ]

Ⓥ 도전하다 Ⓝ 도전　　**accept a challenge** 도전에 응하다

A Fred, I challenge you to this game.
프레드, 이 게임에서 너에게 도전하겠어.

B Are you sure? I'm the champion of this one.
진심이야? 이 게임은 내가 챔피언이야.

14 match
[mætʃ]

Ⓝ 경기, 시합

A I'm looking forward to the soccer match tonight. 나는 오늘 밤 축구 경기가 기대 돼.

B Me, too! Let's watch it together.
나도 그래! 경기 같이 보자.

15 record
[rékərd/rikɔ́ːrd]

Ⓝ 기록 Ⓥ 기록하다　　**set a record** 기록을 세우다

A Who holds the men's 400 meter swimming world record?
누가 400미터 남자 수영 세계 기록을 보유하고 있니?

B Michael Phelps set the world record in 2008.
마이클 펠프스가 2008년에 세계 기록을 세웠어.

16 practice
[prǽktis]

Ⓝ 연습 Ⓥ 연습하다　　**practice the cello** 첼로를 연습하다

A You need a lot of practice to become a pitcher. 투수가 되려면 많은 연습이 필요해.

B Yes, hard work is very important in all sports.
맞아, 모든 스포츠에서 연습은 매우 중요해.

17 ☑ gym
[dʒim]

ⓝ 체육관(=gymnasium)

A Where do you exercise mostly, Helen?
헬렌, 넌 주로 어디서 운동하니?

B I usually go to the gym. 대개 체육관에 가.

18 ☑ victory
[víktəri]

ant defeat 패배

ⓝ 승리, 승전

A Cheer up! We are very close to victory!
힘내! 조금만 더 하면 승리할 거야!

B Yes, sir! 네, 알겠습니다!

19 ☑ final
[fáinəl]

ⓐ 마지막의, 최종의 ⓝ 결승전

the tennis finals 테니스 결승전

A This weekend is the final chance for a ski
trip. 이번 주말이 스키 여행을 갈 마지막 기회야.

B Let's all go together! 모두 함께 가자!

20 ☑ foul
[faul]

ⓝ 반칙

A It's a foul to push someone during the game.
경기 중에 누군가를 미는 것은 반칙이야.

B Okay. I'll keep that in mind. 알았어. 기억하고 있을게.

21 ☑ goal
[goul]

ⓝ 득점, 결승점   **get a goal** 득점하다

A I'm sorry. I couldn't make the goal.
미안해. 득점하지 못했어.

B That's alright. Keep trying! 괜찮아. 계속 노력해 봐!

22 rival
[ráivəl]

ⓝ 경쟁자, 라이벌, 적수

A In sports, a rival can help you improve your skills.
스포츠에서 경쟁자는 네 기술을 향상시키는 데 도움을 줄 수 있어.

B That can be true in other fields as well.
그건 다른 분야에서도 마찬가지야.

23 stadium
[stéidiəm]

ⓝ 스타디움, 경기장

A Were there a lot of people at the game?
경기에 사람들 많았니?

B Yes, the stadium was crowded with people.
응, 경기장이 사람들로 붐볐어.

24 cheer
[tʃiər]

ⓐ cheerful 기분 좋은

ⓥ 환호하다 ⓝ 환호, 갈채　　**words of cheer** 격려의 말

A I can still hear the crowds cheer!
관객들이 환호하는 소리가 아직도 생생해!

B Me too. It was a great game. 나도 그래. 멋진 경기였어.

25 excite
[iksáit]

ⓐ excited 흥분된
ⓝ excitement 흥분, 자극

ⓥ 흥분시키다

A How was the movie yesterday? 어제 영화 어땠어?

B The movie was okay, but it didn't excite me.
영화는 괜찮았는데 내 흥미를 끌지는 못했어.

Multi-Meaning Word

fair

ⓐ 공평한, 공정한/상당한/금발의

We need more time to make a **fair** decision.
공정한 결정을 내리려면 시간이 더 필요하다.

Collins earns a **fair** income from his writing.
콜린스는 집필을 해서 상당한 소득을 번다.

She tied her **fair** hair back with a blue ribbon.
그녀는 파란 리본으로 자신의 금발을 뒤로 묶었다.

ⓝ 박람회, 장

A book **fair** will be held at the library this weekend.
책 박람회가 이번 주에 도서관에서 열릴 것이다.

Word Search

앞에서 배운 어휘를 기억하며 모두 찾아 보세요.

정답

U	Z	V	P	B	H	X	B	X	D	F	Z	C	B	G
M	P	C	R	I	M	O	H	C	T	A	M	H	V	D
X	V	U	E	N	O	I	D	Q	T	Y	Y	E	Y	H
F	O	K	F	T	B	R	K	B	H	N	T	E	C	E
M	A	F	E	E	Q	F	W	C	Y	X	U	R	O	R
I	C	I	R	R	V	I	C	T	O	R	Y	H	M	O
L	R	L	R	E	F	L	B	K	E	A	Z	E	P	C
L	A	A	O	S	R	E	C	O	R	D	X	N	E	S
P	A	N	U	T	R	N	C	Y	T	C	C	M	T	U
X	U	O	I	S	W	I	F	S	E	U	O	Y	E	C
K	S	I	G	F	H	S	V	T	N	M	A	G	Y	K
T	C	E	L	L	O	C	E	A	Q	U	C	V	U	S
E	E	I	X	T	L	W	Q	V	L	O	H	M	V	J
R	C	E	J	B	Y	Q	X	T	F	F	Y	V	U	C

cheer	coach	collect	compete
fair	final	goal	gym
hunt	interest	match	prefer
record	rival	score	victory

Shopping

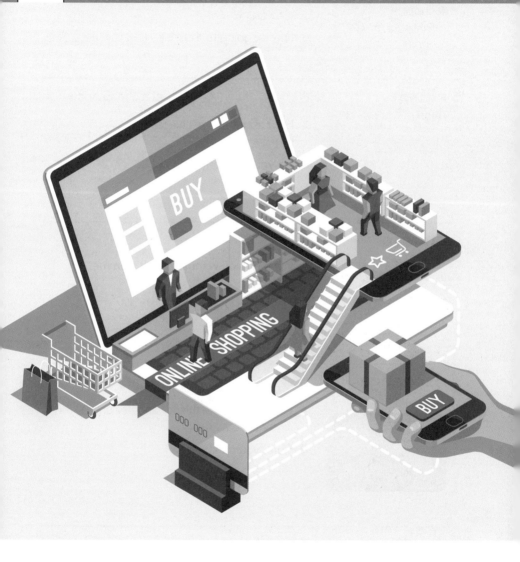

Basic Words

□ store 상점	□ coin 동전	□ need 필요로 하다
□ sell 팔다	□ buy 사다	□ pay 지불하다
□ look for 찾다	□ try on ~을 입어보다	□ shop 쇼핑하다
□ pick 고르다	□ basket 바구니	□ supermarket 슈퍼마켓

01 shopping
[ʃápiŋ]

ⓥ shop
(가게에서)물건을 사다

ⓝ 쇼핑, 물건사기   **go shopping** 쇼핑하다

A Where do you usually go shopping?
주로 쇼핑하러 어디로 가니?

B I prefer going to the mall. 나는 쇼핑몰에 가는 걸 좋아해.

02 cheap
[tʃíːp]

ⓐ 값이 싼   **at a cheap price** 싼 값에

A How about this necklace, sir?
이 목걸이는 어떤가요, 손님?

B Do you have anything cheaper?
값이 더 싼 건 없나요?

03 choose
[tʃuːz]
(choose-chose-chosen)

ⓝ choice 선택

ⓥ 고르다, 선택하다

A What do you want to eat? It's on me.
무엇을 먹을래? 내가 낼게.

B Oh, it's so hard to choose!
아, 선택하기 너무 어렵다!

04 exchange
[ikstʃéindʒ]

ⓥ 교환하다   **exchange gifts** 선물을 주고받다

A Can I exchange this for another one?
이것을 다른 것으로 교환할 수 있을까요?

B Sure, you can.
물론입니다.

05 spend
[spend]
(spend-spent-spent)

ⓥ 돈을 쓰다, 소비하다

A I think I spend too much money on clothes.
나 옷에 돈을 너무 많이 쓰는 것 같아.

B I think so, too. 나도 그렇게 생각해.

06 expensive
[ikspénsiv]

ⓐ 값비싼, 비용이 많이 드는

A I like this hat, but it's too expensive. Can you cut the price?
이 모자가 마음에 드는데. 너무 비싸요. 깎아 주실 수 있나요?

B Sorry, I can't do that. 죄송한데 깎아 드릴 수 없습니다.

07 sale
[seil]
ⓥ sell 팔다

ⓝ 판매, 할인판매　　　　　　on sale (할인)판매 중

A Concert tickets go on sale from August 15.
콘서트 티켓이 8월 15일부터 판매가 된데.

B I am so excited that I can't wait.
너무 흥분돼서 기다릴 수가 없어.

08 price
[prais]

ⓝ 값, 가격, 대가　　　　the lowest price 최저가

A Did you buy the guitar you wanted?
네가 가지고 싶어했던 기타 샀니?

B Yes, I did. The price was expensive, but it was worth it.
응, 샀어. 가격은 비쌌지만, 그만한 가치가 있었어.

09 bargain
[bá:rgən]

ⓝ 매매, 싼 물건　ⓥ 흥정을 하다

at a bargain price 싼 값으로

A What a nice sweater! 참 예쁜 스웨터구나!

B Thanks. It was a real bargain.
고마워. 진짜 싸게 산 거야.

10 waste
[weist]
ⓐ wasteful 낭비하는

ⓥ 낭비하다　ⓝ 낭비, 쓰레기　waste of time 시간 낭비

A I keep buying things I don't really need.
나는 필요하지 않은 물건을 자꾸만 사게 돼.

B You shouldn't waste your money like that.
돈을 그렇게 낭비하면 안 돼.

11 ☑ cash
[kæʃ]

ⓝ 현금　　　　　　　　　　**pay in cash** 현금으로 지불하다

A　Do you have any cash? 너 혹시 현금 좀 있니?

B　Why? This store doesn't take credit cards?
　　왜? 이 가게 신용카드는 안 받니?

12 ☑ consumer
[kənsúːmər]

ⓥ consume 소비하다

ⓝ 소비자

A　Consumers are very important in the economy. 경제에서 소비자는 매우 중요해.

B　What are their roles? 그들의 역할이 무엇인데?

13 ☑ item
[áitəm]

ⓝ 항목, 물건, 상품

A　Some items in the shop are on sale.
　　매장의 일부 상품들은 세일을 하고 있습니다.

B　Do you have a list of them?
　　세일 품목 목록이 있나요?

14 ☑ cost
[kɔːst]

ⓥ (비용이) 들다, 청구하다 **ⓝ** 비용, 값　　**free of cost** 무료로

A　How much does this phone cost?
　　이 전화기는 값이 어떻게 되나요?

B　It's 100 dollars, Miss. 백 달러입니다, 손님.

15 ☑ brand
[brǽnd]

ⓝ 상표, 품질

A　This is my favorite brand of clothes.
　　이게 내가 가장 좋아하는 의류 브랜드야.

B　It does look like your style. 네 취향처럼 보이네.

16 ☑ grocery
[gróusəri]

ⓝ 식료품, 식품점　　　　**a grocery store** 식료품점

A　Groceries are getting quite expensive.
　　식료품들이 꽤 비싸지고 있어.

B　I hope it gets better soon. 상황이 곧 나아지면 좋겠다.

17 deliver
[dilívər]

ⓝ delivery 배달

ⓥ 배달하다, 전하다

A Can you deliver the washing machine by 8 tonight? 세탁기를 오늘 밤 8시까지 배달해 줄 수 있나요?

B No problem, Sir. We will deliver it on time.
문제없습니다. 손님. 제시간에 배달해 드리겠습니다.

18 department
[dipá:rtmənt]

ⓝ 백화점, 부(部), 부문

A The department store has a sale on shoes.
백화점에서 신발 세일을 해.

B That's good! I think I am going to buy a pair of sneakers.
잘됐다! 나 운동화 한 켤레 사려고.

19 package
[pǽkidʒ]

ⓝ 꾸러미, 포장

A Can I get a refund on this item?
이 제품을 반품할 수 있나요?

B Yes, you may, as long as you didn't open the package.
네, 포장을 뜯지 않으셨다면 반품하실 수 있습니다..

20 charge
[tʃɑ:rdʒ]

ⓝ 대가, 값 ⓥ 청구하다

A How much is the ribbon?
리본은 얼마예요?

B It is free of charge if you buy this hat.
이 모자를 사시면 무료입니다.

21 discount
[dískaunt]

ⓝ 할인 ⓥ 할인하다

A I got a 50% discount on this shirt!
이 셔츠 50% 할인해서 샀어!

B Wow, tell me where you bought it.
우와, 어디서 샀는지 얘기해 줘.

22 ☑ wrap
[ræp]

ⓥ 싸다, 포장하다   **wrap a gift** 선물을 포장하다

A Do you want me to wrap up this ring, sir?
손님, 이 반지 포장해 드릴까요?

B Yes, please. 네, 그렇게 해주세요.

23 ☑ clerk
[klə:rk]

ⓝ 판매원, 점원

A The clerk recommended this smart phone to me. 판매점원이 내게 이 스마트폰을 추천해 주었어.

B What was the reason for that? 그 이유가 뭐였니?

24 ☑ bring
[briŋ]
(bring-brought-brought)

ⓥ 가져오다

A Don't forget to bring your camera.
네 카메라 가져오는 것을 잊지 마.

B Of course. See you tomorrow.
물론이지. 내일 봐.

25 ☑ both A and B

A, B 둘 다

A What color do you want? 무슨 색깔을 원하니?

B I can't choose one. I like both black and red.
하나를 고를 수가 없어. 검정과 빨강 둘 다 마음에 들어.

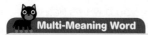

Multi-Meaning Word

charge

ⓝ 책임
The police take **charge** of the public safety.
경찰은 공공의 안전을 책임진다.

ⓝ 부담, 요금
There will be no **charge** for the repair service.
수리 서비스는 무료입니다.

ⓥ (전지에) 충전하다
I need to **charge** my cell phone.
내 휴대전화를 충전시켜야 해.

Word Search

앞에서 배운 어휘를 기억하며 모두 찾아 보세요.

정답

```
E Y Q R P D T H D N C L G P S
C G Z I E R Y Y S O L N O A A
Y O E C N V Z V S A I B X C L
D A N A I G I T X P C X I K E
I C I S H N P L T A B M T A B
S A H H U C Z O E A L Z N G N
C E V E G M H L R D M U B E E
O C B W A S E R G R O C E R Y
U I P Q W P A R C H O O S E J
N R E Q A I L P H D N P P S P
T P T K N D N A R B C L E R K
Y Z S I T E M W R A P P H R T
M E A R V G G O F I Q X W J Q
Y Z W N Z K H Z S J D L U Y E
```

brand	cash	cheap	choose
clerk	consumer	cost	deliver
discount	grocery	item	package
price	sale	waste	wrap

Unit 21 Travel

TAIPEI CITY

Basic Words

- □ visit 방문하다
- □ stay 머무르다
- □ picture 사진
- □ via 경유하여

- □ camp 야영지
- □ plan 계획
- □ camera 카메라
- □ airline 항공사

- □ hotel 호텔
- □ free 자유로운
- □ fly 비행하다
- □ board 승선하다

01 travel
[trǽvəl]

n 여행 **v** 여행하다

a travel agency 여행사

A Travel safely, Tom! 톰. 여행 안전하게 다녀와!

B Yes, Mom. Don't worry. 네, 엄마. 걱정 마세요.

02 experience
[ikspíəriəns]

a experienced 경험 있는

n 경험, 체험 **v** 경험하다

experience difficulties 역경을 경험하다

A How was your trip to Turkey? 터키 여행 어땠어?

B It was a very special experience.
참 특별한 경험이었어.

03 vacation
[veikéiʃən]

n 휴가, 방학

take a vacation 휴가를 얻다

A I am going to travel during the summer
vacation. 나는 여름방학에 여행을 가려고 해.

B Have you decided where to go, yet?
어디로 갈지 결정했어?

04 flight
[flait]

v fly 날다

n 비행, 항공편

book a flight 항공편을 예약하다

A How long does it take to go to America?
미국에 가는 데 얼마나 걸리니?

B The flight usually takes over ten hours.
비행은 대체로 열 시간이 넘게 걸려.

05 tour
[tuə:r]

n 여행

a tour guide 여행 안내원

A Do you have any plans for weekend?
주말에 무슨 계획 있니?

B I'm planning to go on a walking tour.
도보 여행을 가려고 계획 중이야.

06 ☑ airport
[έərpɔ̀ːrt]

ⓝ 공항   **an international airport** 국제공항

A How can I go to the hotel from the airport?
공항에서 호텔까지 어떻게 갑니까?

B We will send somebody to pick you up, sir.
손님을 모실 사람을 보내겠습니다.

07 ☑ safe
[seif]
ⓝ safety 안전

ⓐ 안전한   **a safe place** 안전한 장소

A Did you check whether the country is safe?
그 나라가 안전한지 확인하셨나요?

B Yes. My uncle lives there, so I don't worry.
네. 삼촌 거기 사셔서 걱정 안 해요.

08 ☑ journey
[dʒə́ːrni]

ⓝ (육상의) 긴 여행   **take a journey** 여행하다

A How long will we ride this train, Dad?
아빠, 우리 이 기차 얼마나 오래 타요?

B About ten hours. It is going to be a long
journey. 열 시간 정도. 긴 여행이 될 거야.

09 ☑ photograph
[fóutəgræf]

ⓝ 사진   **take a photograph** 사진을 찍다

A I took this photograph when I was in France.
프랑스에 있을 때 이 사진을 찍었어.

B All the buildings are so beautiful.
모든 건물들이 정말 아름다워.

10 ☑ pack
[pæk]

ⓥ (짐을) 싸다 **ⓝ** 꾸러미, 보따리

A Did you pack all your things? 짐 다 쌌니?

B Yes, I'm ready to go. 응. 출발할 준비 다 됐어.

11 baggage
[bǽgidʒ]

ⓝ (여행용) 수화물   **carry-on baggage** 기내 반입 수하물

A Would you like to load this baggage into the plane, sir? 이 수화물을 비행기에 실으실 건가요, 손님?

B Yes, please. 네, 그렇게 할게요.

12 except
[iksépt]

prep ~을 제외하고는

A Was the hotel you stayed in nice, Jimmy?
네가 투숙한 호텔은 괜찮았어, 지미?

B It was good. Everything was great except the food. 괜찮았어. 음식을 제외하고는 다 좋았어.

13 trip
[trip]

ⓝ (비교적 짧은) 여행   **go on a trip** 여행을 떠나다

A Where did you spend your vacation?
휴가 어디서 보냈어?

B I took a trip to China. 중국으로 여행 갔었어.

14 leisure
[líːʒəːr]

ⓝ 여가, 여가 시간   **leisure activities** 여가 활동

A What is your hobby? 당신은 취미가 무엇입니까?

B I go traveling for leisure. 여가로 여행을 다닙니다.

15 backpack
[bǽkpæk]

ⓝ 가방, 배낭

A Excuse me. Your backpack is open.
실례합니다. 배낭이 열려 있어요.

B Oops, thank you! 앗, 고맙습니다!

16 picnic
[píknik]

ⓝ 소풍, 피크닉   **go on a picnic** 소풍 가다

A The trees are green, and the sun is shining.
나무들은 푸르고 태양은 빛나고 있어.

B Yeah, it's the perfect weather for a picnic.
응, 소풍 가기 완벽한 날씨야.

17 return
[ritə́ːrn]

V 되돌아가다, 돌아가다

A When do you plan to return to Korea?
한국에 언제 되돌아오실 계획이세요?

B I'm not really sure, yet. 아직 확실하지 않아요.

18 check-in
[tʃékin]

n 체크인, 기록

A What is the check-in time?
체크인 시간이 언제인가요?

B Check-in is at 2 p.m. You are welcome to arrive earlier if you wish.
체크인 시간은 오후 2시입니다. 원하시면 일찍 도착하셔도 좋습니다.

19 postcard
[póustkàːrd]

n 우편엽서

A Jack sent me a postcard from Japan.
잭이 일본에서 엽서를 보냈어.

B I miss him. I will reply to him.
그가 보고 싶어. 내가 답장을 보낼게.

20 danger
[déindʒər]

a dangerous 위험한

n 위험　　　　**be in danger of ~** ~할 위험이 있다

A Drivers need to know their cars can be a great danger.
운전사들은 자동차가 큰 위험이 될 수도 있다는 것을 알아야 해.

B Yes, drivers always have to be careful.
맞아, 운전사들은 언제나 조심해야 돼.

21 freedom
[fríːdəm]

a free 자유로운

n 자유

A Why do you like traveling so much, Peter?
피터, 너는 여행이 왜 그렇게 좋니?

B Because of the freedom it gives me.
여행이 주는 자유 때문이야.

22 passport
[pǽspɔ̀ːrt]

ⓝ 여권, 통행증

A May I see your passport, sir?
손님, 여권 좀 보여주시겠습니까?

B Sure. Here you are. 물론이죠. 여기 있습니다.

23 honeymoon
[hʌ́nimùːn]

ⓝ 신혼여행

A Where do you plan to go on your honeymoon? 신혼여행을 어디로 갈 계획인가요?

B I'm planning to go to Fiji. 피지로 갈 생각입니다.

24 guide
[gaid]

ⓝ 안내자, 가이드 **ⓥ** 안내하다

A The guide showed me around the old village.
가이드가 오래된 마을을 구경시켜 주었어.

B Did you see anything special?
특별한 거 뭐 본 것 있니?

25 either A or B

A, B 둘 중의 하나

A You can't go there by yourself. You should go with either your brother or your friend.
너 혼자 그곳에 갈 수는 없단다. 형이나 친구와 함께 가야 해.

B Mom, I am old enough to travel alone.
엄마, 전 혼자 여행할 만큼 나이를 먹었다고요.

Multi-Meaning Word

pack

ⓝ 꾸러미
He hid the book into his **pack**.
그는 그 책을 그의 꾸러미 안에 숨겼다.

ⓝ 팩, 상자
She gave me three **packs** of chocolate.
그녀는 나에게 세 상자의 초콜릿을 주었다.

ⓥ 가방을 꾸리다, 싸다
Have you finished **packing** for a trip?
여행 가방 다 쌌니?

Word Search

앞에서 배운 어휘를 기억하며 모두 찾아 보세요.

정답

V	T	T	A	M	B	E	K	T	B	E	Z	U	N	H
N	V	P	V	F	R	I	R	W	A	S	Y	X	J	M
P	E	G	E	O	W	A	V	P	G	M	E	A	D	R
W	C	C	S	C	V	Z	A	U	G	M	N	I	R	E
K	L	I	M	E	X	S	Z	R	A	D	R	R	E	T
Y	E	M	L	E	S	E	O	Y	G	I	U	P	C	U
L	M	X	P	I	G	T	N	E	T	O	O	C	R
J	N	P	O	G	N	R	O	G	O	E	J	R	F	N
Q	V	R	U	A	R	I	E	S	C	I	J	T	L	G
Y	T	I	D	U	T	O	T	P	E	V	T	C	I	I
X	D	R	O	A	I	C	B	R	X	F	S	G	G	M
E	D	T	C	C	A	K	C	A	P	E	A	A	H	O
Z	U	A	O	R	C	I	N	C	I	P	D	S	T	T
E	V	S	D	M	O	D	E	E	R	F	T	R	I	P

airport	baggage	except	flight
freedom	guide	journey	pack
passport	picnic	return	safe
tour	travel	trip	vacation

Unit 22 Art & Media

□ title 제목	□ ticket 표, 티켓	□ book 책
□ movie 영화	□ radio 라디오	□ concert 콘서트
□ famous 유명한	□ art 미술, 예술	□ television 텔레비전
□ cinema 영화관	□ canvas 화폭	□ comedy 코미디, 희극

01 ☑ **well-known**
[wélnóun]
syn famous 유명한

- **ⓐ** 유명한, 잘 알려진　　**a well-known fact** 잘 알려진 사실

A Who should we cast for this movie?
이 영화에 누구를 캐스팅할까?

B We should look for someone well-known.
잘 알려진 사람을 찾아야겠지요.

---

02 ☑ **amazing**
[əméiziŋ]
ⓥ amaze 놀라게 하다
ⓐ amazed 놀란

- **ⓐ** 놀랄 만한, 굉장한

A The man is an amazing magician.
저 남자는 굉장한 마술사야.

B I think he's the best. 그가 최고인 것 같아.

---

03 ☑ **museum**
[mjuːzíːəm]

- **ⓝ** 박물관　　**a folk museum** 민속 박물관

A I want to know how Korean people lived in the past.
나는 과거에 한국 사람들이 어떻게 살았는지 알고 싶어.

B I know a good museum. Let's meet up at six.
나 좋은 박물관 알아. 여섯 시에 만나자.

---

04 ☑ **artist**
[áːrtist]
ⓝ art 예술, 미술

- **ⓝ** 예술가, 화가

A Please tell me how to draw.
그림을 어떻게 그리는지 말해줘.

B I'm not an artist, but I'll try to.
내가 예술가는 아니지만, 해볼게.

---

05 ☑ **popular**
[pápjələr]
ⓝ popularity 인기

- **ⓐ** 인기 있는

A He has become popular since he played as James Bond in the 007 series.
그가 007시리즈에서 제임스 본드 역할을 한 이후로 인기를 끌고 있어.

B Yes, he looks so cool in the movies.
맞아. 영화에서 그는 정말 멋있어.

06 stage
[steidʒ]

n 무대, 단계

A I'm so happy when I'm on stage.
난 무대에 서면 너무 행복해.

B You were born to be an actor, Damon.
데이먼, 너는 타고난 배우야.

07 orchestra
[ɔ́ːrkəstrə]

n 오케스트라, 관현악단

A It must be very hard to enter an orchestra.
관현악단에 들어가는 건 아주 어려운 게 분명해.

B Yes, they choose the best from the best.
응, 최고 중의 최고만 골라.

08 admire
[ædmàiər]

n admiration 감탄

v 감탄하다

A This painter is a real genius. 이 화가는 진정한 천재야.

B I admire his work, too. 나도 그 사람 작품에 감탄해.

09 reporter
[ripɔ́ːrtər]

v report 보도하다

n 보고자, 기자

A Reporters should not express their own opinions. 기자들은 자신들의 의견을 표현해서는 안 돼.

B They also need to write only the truth.
그들은 또한 사실만을 써야 해.

10 gallery
[gǽləri]

n 화랑, 미술관

A I saw a beautiful drawing at the gallery yesterday. 나 어제 화랑에서 정말 아름다운 그림을 봤어.

B What was in the picture? 무엇을 그린 그림이었는데?

11 classical
[klǽsikəl]

a 고전의, 고전적인   classical literature 고전 문학

A What kind of music do you like?
너는 어떤 음악을 좋아하니?

B I really like classical music.
나는 고전 음악을 정말 좋아해.

12 ballet
☑

[bǽlei]

ⓝ ballerina 발레리나

ⓝ 발레

A I have wanted to learn ballet since I was little.

나는 어렸을 때부터 발레를 배우고 싶었어.

B Why not try now? It's never too late!

지금부터 해보는 건 어때? 너무 늦은 때는 없는 거야!

13 violent
☑

[váiələnt]

ⓝ violence 폭력

ⓐ 격렬한, 폭력적인

A People often say that movies these days are too violent.

사람들은 요즘 영화들이 너무 폭력적이라고 흔히 말해.

B I understand why they think so.

그들이 왜 그렇게 생각하는지 이해가 돼.

14 series
☑

[síəri:z]

ⓝ 일련, 연속, 시리즈   **a series of stamps** 연속 발행의 우표

A A new TV series will be starting tonight.

오늘 밤부터 새로운 TV 시리즈가 시작할 거야.

B I heard many people are looking forward to it.

많은 사람이 기대하고 있다고 들었어.

15 modern
☑

[mάdərn]

ⓐ 현대의, 근대의   **modern history** 근대사

A What do you want to study in college?

대학에서 무엇을 공부하고 싶니?

B I would like to study modern art.

현대 미술을 공부하고 싶어.

16 role
☑

[roul]

ⓝ 배우의 배역, 역할   **a leading role** 주역

A My favorite actor was in this movie.

내가 좋아하는 배우가 이 영화에 나왔어.

B Really? What was his role? 정말? 어떤 역할이었는데?

17 magazine
[mǽgəzíːn]

ⓝ 잡지

A What are you reading so eagerly, Sam?
샘, 뭘 그렇게 열심히 읽는 거야?

B Oh, it is just a magazine about culture and art. 아, 그냥 문화와 예술에 관한 잡지야.

18 newspaper
[njúːzpèipəːr]

ⓝ 신문　　　　　　**a weekly newspaper** 주간 신문

A Have you read today's newspaper, yet?
오늘 신문 읽었니?

B I only went through the headlines. Why?
머리기사만 대충 봤어. 왜?

19 character
[kǽríktər]

ⓐ characteristic
독특한, 특유의

ⓝ 등장인물, 성격

A This movie was pretty good.
이 영화 꽤 괜찮았어.

B Yes, the characters felt real.
응, 등장인물들이 실감 났어.

20 theater
[θíːətər]

ⓝ 극장, 야외극장　　　　**a movie theater** 영화관

A When was the last time you went to a theater? 마지막으로 극장에 간 게 언제였니?

B It was about a month ago. 대략 한 달 전이었어.

21 publish
[pʌ́bliʃ]

ⓝ publication 출판

ⓥ 출판하다, 발표하다　　**a publishing company** 출판사

A Many writers are looking for a chance to publish their book.
많은 작가가 자신의 책을 출판할 기회를 찾고 있어.

B It is important for publishers to pick the right one. 출판업자들은 제대로 된 것을 고르는 것이 중요하지.

22 broadcast
[brɔ́:dkæst]

ⓥ 방송하다, 알리다

A How can we let people know about this news? 어떻게 하면 이 소식을 여러 사람에게 알릴 수 있을까?

B I'll broadcast it throughout the building.
제가 건물 전체에 방송하겠습니다.

23 proper
[prɑ́pər]

ⓐ 적당한, 타당한

A Someday people will know the proper value of your art.
언젠가 사람들이 당신 예술의 제대로 된 가치를 알게 될 거예요.

B I hope so. 나도 그러길 바라요.

24 scene
[si:n]

ⓝ 장면, 경치   **a scene of beauty** 아름다운 광경

A How did you like the play? 연극 어땠니?

B It was great! I cried during the last scene.
정말 좋았어! 마지막 장면에서 울었어.

25 neither A nor B

A, B 둘 다 아닌

A Which movie do you prefer? Action or horror? 어떤 영화가 좋나요? 액션 아니면 공포?

B Neither action nor horror. What about melodrama? 둘 다 싫어요. 멜로드라마는 어때요?

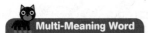
Multi-Meaning Word

character   **ⓝ** 특성, 성격

He has a cheerful but quiet **character**.
그는 명랑하고 조용한 성격이다.

ⓝ 등장인물

Ted is the central **character** in the movie.
테드는 그 영화에서 중심 등장인물이다.

ⓝ 문자

I have studied Chinese **characters** since 12 years old.
나는 12살 때부터 한자를 공부했다.

Word Search

앞에서 배운 어휘를 기억하며 모두 찾아 보세요.

정답

R	B	E	Z	G	U	T	S	E	M	O	W	O	C	R
G	E	R	N	C	A	E	N	O	G	P	E	H	A	E
B	J	T	O	I	I	L	D	E	U	A	T	Z	D	P
F	A	R	A	R	Z	E	L	B	L	R	T	Y	M	O
E	J	L	E	P	R	A	L	E	A	O	A	S	I	R
C	N	S	L	N	S	I	G	C	R	R	I	T	R	T
G	L	E	R	E	S	W	T	A	T	Y	S	V	E	E
G	K	A	C	H	T	E	E	I	M	R	O	L	E	R
L	C	H	S	S	R	M	S	N	R	E	P	O	R	P
B	O	P	K	S	U	T	G	N	I	Z	A	M	A	Z
E	V	P	V	E	I	R	A	L	U	P	O	P	R	V
S	P	F	S	Y	G	C	K	T	M	I	L	D	A	Z
D	M	U	H	S	N	S	A	J	F	E	S	W	J	W
F	M	P	O	C	I	L	F	L	F	A	E	K	K	I

admire	amazing	artist	ballet
classical	gallery	modern	museum
popular	proper	publish	reporter
role	scene	stage	violent

Word Bubbles

앞에서 배운 어휘를 기억하며 버블을 단어로 채워 보세요.

정답

Chapter 6

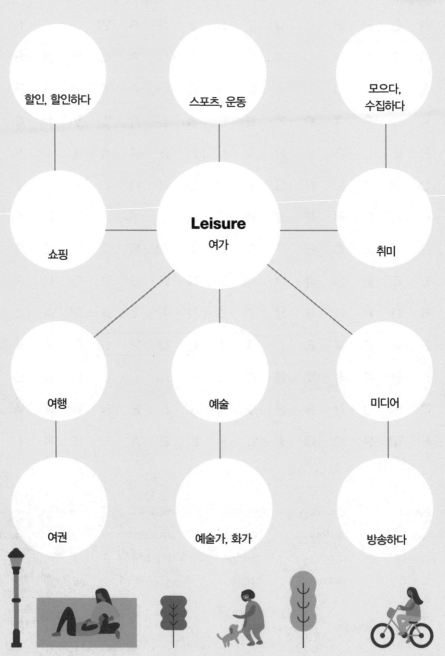

할인, 할인하다

스포츠, 운동

모으다,
수집하다

쇼핑

Leisure
여가

취미

여행

예술

미디어

여권

예술가, 화가

방송하다

Review Test

A 우리말을 영어로, 영어를 우리말로 쓰시오.

01 경기, 시합 _____ 08 clerk _____

02 배달하다 _____ 09 danger _____

03 인기 있는 _____ 10 cost _____

04 여행하다 _____ 11 modern _____

05 환호하다 _____ 12 score _____

06 적당한, 타당한 _____ 13 amazing _____

07 판매 _____ 14 airport _____

B 빈칸에 알맞은 단어를 쓰시오.

01 선물을 포장하다 _____ a gift

02 민속 박물관 a folk _____

03 싼 값에 at a(n) _____ price

04 practice the cello 첼로를 _____

05 go on a trip _____을/를 떠나다

06 take a photograph _____을/를 찍다

C 단어의 관계에 맞게 빈칸을 채우시오.

01 수집 : 수집하다 = collection : _____

02 안전한 : 안전 = safe : _____

03 선택하다 : 선택 = choose : _____

04 art : artist = 예술 : _____

05 freedom : free = 자유 : _____

06 victory : defeat = 승리 : _____

D 배운 단어를 사용하여 문장을 완성하시오. (필요하면 형태를 바꾸시오.)

01 We _____ about 200 dollars at a grocery store every week.

우리는 매주 식료품점에서 약 200달러를 소비한다.

02 _____ Sam and Johnny enjoy going to an art gallery.

샘과 조니 둘 다 미술관에 가는 것을 즐긴다.

03 Her _____ are reading English storybooks and painting.

그녀의 취미는 영어 이야기책을 읽고 그림을 그리는 것이다.

04 People _____ chocolate, cards, and gifts on Valentine's Day.

사람들은 밸런타인데이에 초콜릿, 카드, 그리고 선물을 교환한다.

05 James reads the _____ every morning.

제임스는 매일 아침 신문을 읽는다.

E 빈칸에 알맞은 말을 보기에서 찾아 쓰시오.

cash	ballet	well-known	favorite	passport

01 **A** I think I have lost my _____. What should I do?

   B When was the last time you used it?

02 **A** What did you do last weekend?

   B I went to see a _____ with Sean.

03 **A** Chicago is my _____ city in the U.S.

   B I have been there, too. It is _____ as the Windy City.

04 **A** Will you pay in _____ or by card?

   B I will pay by card.

F 밑줄 친 부분을 우리말로 옮기시오.

01 Where can I charge my mobile phone?

02 It's not hard to see South Koreans compete for the gold medal in short track speed skating.

Chapter
07

Things

Unit 23 Objects

Basic Words

- □ large 대형의
- □ big 큰
- □ small 작은
- □ new 새
- □ same 같은
- □ long 긴, 길이
- □ thing 물건
- □ this 이것
- □ that 저것
- □ these 이것들
- □ those 저것들
- □ keep 가지고 있다

01 another
[ənʌ́ðər]

ⓐ 다른, 또 하나의

A What are they building here?
여기에 무엇을 짓는 거야?

B They said it's another skyscraper.
고층 빌딩을 하나 더 짓는대.

02 belong
[bilɔ́(:)ŋ]
ⓝ belongings 소유물

ⓥ ~에 속하다, 소유이다   **belong to** ~에 속하다

A Whose jacket is this? 이 재킷은 누구 것이니?

B I think it belongs to Mark. 마크 것인 것 같아.

03 valuable
[vǽljuːəbəl]
ⓝ value 가치

ⓐ 값진, 귀한

A A computer virus wiped out all my data last night. 간밤에 컴퓨터 바이러스가 내 자료를 몽땅 지워버렸어.

B You should have kept a backup for the valuable ones. 귀중한 자료는 백업을 해 놓지 그랬어.

04 edge
[edʒ]

ⓝ 끝, 가장자리

A I had a paper cut this morning.
나 오늘 아침에 종이에 베였어.

B Be careful. Paper can have sharp edges.
조심해. 종이도 가장자리가 날카로울 수 있어.

05 piece
[piːs]

ⓝ 조각, 단편

A I think I lost a piece of the jigsaw puzzle.
퍼즐조각을 하나 잃어버린 것 같아.

B Let's find it together. 같이 찾아보자.

06 fill
[fil]

ⓥ 채우다, 가득 차다

A You need help with the garden?
정원에 도움이 필요하시다고요?

B Yes, Tom. Can you fill this bucket with water?
응. 톰. 이 양동이에 물을 채워줄래?

07 flat
[flæt]

ⓐ 평평한, 납작한　　　　**flat shoes** 굽이 낮은 신발

A People thought the world was flat a long time ago. 옛날에 사람들은 세상이 납작하다고 생각했어.

B Yes, they were afraid of falling off the edges.
응. 가장자리에서 떨어지는 것을 무서워했어.

08 feature
[fíːtʃər]

ⓝ 특징, 모습　　　　**a typical feature** 전형적인 모습

A What feature of Korea do you remember most? 한국의 어떤 특징이 가장 기억에 남니?

B I don't think I will forget Korean food.
한국 음식은 잊을 수 없을 거야.

09 nothing
[nʌ́θiŋ]

ⓝ 무(無) **pron** 아무 것도 ~아님

A There is nothing in this bag.
이 가방에는 아무것도 없어요.

B Our X-ray scanner shows something strange in your bag. 엑스레이에서는 가방 속에 이상한 것이 보여서요.

10 tiny
[tàini]

ⓐ 작은, 조그마한　　　　**tiny fingers** 조그마한 손가락

A Watch out! There are tiny pieces of glass around here. 조심해! 이 주위에 작은 유리 조각들이 있어.

B Did someone drop a mirror?
누가 거울을 떨어뜨렸어?

11 rough
[rʌf]
ant smooth 매끄러운

ⓐ 거친

A Why is the car bumping so much?
차가 왜 심하게 흔들리지?

B Because we entered a rough dirt road.
울퉁불퉁한 비포장도로에 들어왔기 때문이지.

12 stiff
[stif]

ⓐ 뻣뻣한, 경직된   **a stiff neck** 뻣뻣한 목

A My computer's power button became a little
stiff. 컴퓨터 전원 스위치가 조금 뻣뻣해졌어.

B Do you think it needs to be repaired?
수리를 해야 할 것 같니?

13 helpful
[hélpfəl]
ⓥ help 돕다

ⓐ 도움이 되는, 유용한   **a helpful tip** 도움이 되는 조언

A The program will be helpful to your children's
education. 이 프로그램은 당신 아이들의 교육에 유용할 것입니다.

B How does it help? 어떻게 도움이 되나요?

14 precious
[préʃəs]

ⓐ 비싼, 귀중한   **precious memories** 소중한 추억

A This gate is a precious treasure to Koreans.
이 대문은 한국인들에게 있어 귀중한 보물이야.

B There must be a lot of history in it.
그 안에 많은 역사가 담겨있는 모양이구나.

15 huge
[hju:dʒ]
ad hugely 크게, 엄청나게

ⓐ 거대한, 막대한

A A huge truck is blocking the road.
거대한 트럭이 길을 막고 있어.

B Do we have to go around it?
그 주변으로 돌아가야 하나요?

16 necessary
[nésəsèri]

n necessity 필수

ⓐ 필요한, 필수의

A Do I have to bring my toolbox?
내 공구함을 가져와야 할까?

B No, it's not necessary to do so .
아니, 그럴 필요는 없어.

---

17 object
[ábdʒikt]

n 물건, 물체

A What is that round object in the sky?
하늘에 저 둥근 물체가 무엇이니?

B It's too far to tell what it is.
그게 무엇인지 구분하기에 너무 멀리 있어.

---

18 shape
[ʃeip]

n 모양, 형상

A I think I lost my bag.
나 내 가방을 잃어버린 것 같아.

B What shape is it? 무슨 모양이야?

---

19 narrow
[nǽrou]

ⓐ 폭이 좁은, 한정된　**a narrow space** 좁은 장소

A A vase has a narrow opening. 꽃병은 입구가 좁아.

B That is used to hold the flower up.
그것은 꽃을 지지하기 위해서야.

---

20 color
[kʌ́lər]

ⓐ colorful 화려한

n 색, 빛깔

A What is the color of your bag? 네 가방 무슨 색이니?

B My bag is dark brown. 내 가방은 어두운 갈색이야.

---

21 form
[fɔːrm]

ⓐ formal
형식을 갖춘, 정식의

n 형식, 형태, 모양

A I bought a cake in the form of a heart.
하트 모양 케이크를 샀어.

B How lovely! 참 예쁘다!

---

22 ☑ **sharp**
[ʃɑːrp]

ⓐ 날카로운, 뾰족한, 예민한　　**a sharp point** 뾰족한 끝

A Be careful not to cut yourself. The knife is very sharp. 베지 않게 조심해라. 칼이 아주 날카로워.

B Okay, Mom. 알았어요, 엄마.

---

23 ☑ **broad**
[brɔːd]

ⓐ 폭이 넓은, 광대한

A This river is too broad to swim across.
수영해서 건너기엔 이 강은 너무 폭이 넓어.

B Let's see if we can ride that boat.
저 배를 탈 수 있는지 보자.

---

24 ☑ **sort**
[sɔːrt]

syn kind 종류

ⓝ 종류, 부류　　**a sort of** 일종의

A What are those pills in your hand?
손안에 있는 그 알약은 무엇인가요?

B You can say they're a sort of vitamin.
비타민의 일종이라고 할 수 있어요.

---

25 ☑ **against**
[əgénst]

prep ~에 기대어서

A Have you seen my umbrella? 내 우산 못 봤어?

B I leaned it against the wall. 벽에 기대어 놓았어.

Multi-Meaning Word

sharp

ⓐ 예리한, 날카로운

I pricked myself with the **sharp** needle while sewing a shirt.
셔츠를 꿰매다가 예리한 바늘에 찔렸다.

ⓐ 급격한

There is a **sharp** increase in the number of jobless people.
실직자의 수가 급격히 증가했다.

ⓐ 뚜렷한, 선명한

They have a **sharp** difference in opinion.
그들은 뚜렷한 의견 차이를 보인다.

Word Search

앞에서 배운 어휘를 기억하며 모두 찾아 보세요.

정답

R	V	N	K	M	P	Q	H	Z	K	N	V	H	C	U
H	E	F	E	R	R	O	N	N	O	T	H	I	N	G
G	J	H	A	R	L	O	E	G	G	F	F	B	L	Y
U	S	H	T	P	R	G	F	Z	X	I	F	R	F	N
O	S	Q	F	A	D	O	F	T	W	L	I	O	R	I
R	U	U	S	E	N	L	W	B	C	L	T	A	E	T
W	L	B	M	Y	K	A	T	E	P	E	S	D	L	S
E	C	E	I	P	U	A	M	L	N	E	J	E	O	O
E	P	A	H	S	L	E	E	O	I	W	V	B	C	R
G	D	L	H	F	P	I	O	N	E	D	Q	P	O	T
Y	U	Q	E	S	L	C	Q	G	G	U	U	J	C	V
P	N	K	B	P	L	U	R	X	U	K	P	H	E	O
N	S	O	U	V	Y	O	Z	Z	H	N	E	K	J	Y
L	D	N	M	D	I	I	E	S	Y	T	D	K	N	N

belong	broad	edge	fill
flat	form	huge	nothing
object	piece	rough	shape
sharp	sort	stiff	tiny

Number & Quantity

- few 약간의
- much 많은
- number 숫자
- amount 총액

- little 작은
- some 몇몇의
- all 모든
- only 오직

- many 많은
- any 어느, 어떤
- none 아무도 ~않다
- have 소유하다

01 ☑ **century**
[séntʃuri]

ⓝ 1세기, 100년　　**the twenty-first century** 21세기

A Human life was very different centuries ago.
수세기 전에 인간의 삶은 매우 달랐어.

B Think how different it will become centuries
later. 수세기 후에는 얼마나 다를지 생각해 봐.

---

02 ☑ **empty**
[émpti]

ant full 가득 찬

ⓐ 빈, 공허한

A How much water do we have left, Susan?
수잔, 우리 물 얼마나 남았어?

B I'm afraid the bottle is empty.
안타깝지만 물병이 비었어.

---

03 ☑ **decade**
[dékeid]

ⓝ 10년간　　**in a few decades** 몇 십 년 안에

A The IT industry is growing fast.
IT산업이 빠르게 성장하고 있어.

B Yes. Especially in the last decade.
맞아, 특히 지난 10년간.

---

04 ☑ **major**
[méidʒəːr]

ⓝ majority 다수

ⓐ 주요한, 다수의

A What is the major problem for the project?
프로젝트에 주요한 문제가 무엇인가요?

B The biggest problem is that we don't have
enough time.
가장 큰 문제는 시간이 충분하지 않다는 겁니다.

---

05 ☑ **dozen**
[dʌzən]

ⓝ 한 다스, 12개　　**a half dozen** 6개

A Mom, how many eggs do we need for the
cake? 엄마, 케이크 만들려면 달걀이 몇 개 필요하나요?

B I'll say about a dozen of them.
내 생각에는 한 12개 정도면 될 것 같아.

06 plenty
[plénti]
ⓐ plentiful 풍부한, 많은

ⓝ 많음, 풍부

A There is so much to study! 공부할 게 너무 많아!

B Don't worry, Jenny. We have plenty of time.
걱정하지 마, 제니야. 우리 시간이 많아.

07 almost
[ɔ́:lmoust]

ad 거의

A Honey, how long will your work take?
여보, 일하는 거 얼마나 걸려?

B Just a minute. I'm almost finished.
잠깐만. 거의 끝났어.

08 million
[míljən]
c.f. billion 십억

ⓝ 100만 **ⓐ** 100만의

A How many zeros are in one million?
백만에 '0'이 몇 개나 있니?

B There are six zeros. 여섯 개야.

09 increase
[inkríːs]

ⓥ 늘어나다, 증가하다 **ⓝ** 증가

A The number of members greatly increased
recently. 최근에 회원 수가 크게 늘었어.

B That's good news for our club.
우리 동아리에 좋은 소식인데.

10 twice
[twais]
c.f. once 한 번

ad 두 번, 2회 **ⓝ** 두 번, 두 배

A How did you like the movie? 영화 어땠어요?

B It was wonderful. I think I could see it twice.
재미있었어. 두 번도 볼 수 있을 것 같아.

11 **bit**
[bit]

ⓝ 작은 조각, 조금, 소량   **a tiny bit of hope** 실낱같은 희망

A Are you hungry? 너 배고프니?

B Only a bit. I had a large breakfast.
조금. 아침을 많이 먹었거든.

12 **whole**
[houl]

ⓐ 전부의, 모든   **the whole year** 일 년 중 내내

A I spent a whole month on this project.
나는 이 프로젝트에 꼬박 한 달을 보냈어.

B Don't worry. I'm sure it will succeed.
걱정 마. 난 그것이 성공할 거라 믿어.

13 **degree**
[digríː]

ⓝ 정도, (온도, 각도 등의) 도
    ten degrees below zero 영하 10도

A Is it cold today? 오늘 날씨 추워?

B The weather report said it is five degrees Celsius. 일기예보에서는 지금 섭씨 5도라고 했어.

14 **extra**
[ékstrə]

ⓐ 여분의, 규정 외의   **extra time** 여분의 시간

A The teacher gave us ten extra minutes for the test. 선생님이 시험에 추가로 십 분을 더 주셨어.

B Were you able to write a satisfying answer?
만족스러운 답안을 썼니?

15 **decrease**
[dikríːs]

ⓥ 감소하다, 줄이다 **ⓝ** 감소
    decrease in population 인구의 감소

A What can we do for our company?
우리가 회사를 위해 무엇을 할 수 있을까요?

B We need to decrease the costs, sir.
사장님, 비용을 감소해야 합니다.

16 mass
[mæs]

ⓐ massive 큰 덩어리의, 대량의

ⓝ 덩어리, 다량

A How can the products be so cheap?
어떻게 상품들이 이렇게 값이 쌀 수 있나요?

B It's because most of them are made in mass production. 왜냐하면 대부분 대량 생산하기 때문입니다.

17 quarter
[kwɔ́ːrtər]

ⓝ 4분의 1, 15분　　　　　　**a quarter of an hour** 15분

A Sam finished up a quarter of the cake.
샘이 케이크의 4분의 1을 먹어 치웠어.

B Wasn't the cake pretty big?
그 케이크 꽤 크지 않았니?

18 double
[dʌ́bəl]

ⓐ 두 배의, 이중의

A If you work on holidays, you get double pay.
휴일에 근무하면 두 배의 급료를 받게 됩니다.

B How about overtime pay?
초과 근무 수당은 어떻게 됩니까?

19 enough
[inʌ́f]

ⓐ 충분한 **ad** 충분히

A Did you have enough time to think it over?
그것을 충분히 생각할 시간이 있었니?

B I'm sorry, but can you give me another hour?
죄송한데, 한 시간 더 주실 수 있나요?

20 several
[sévərəl]

ⓐ 몇몇의, 몇 개의

A I met Janis several weeks ago.
몇 주 전에 제니스를 만났어.

B Was she doing well? 그녀는 잘 지내고 있었니?

21 total
[tóutl]

ad totally 완전히, 모두

ⓐ 전체의, 합계의

A Did anybody record the total score?
점수 총계를 기록하는 사람이 있나요?

B Yes, it was 34 to 58. 네, 34 대 58이었습니다.

²² ☑ **scale**
[skeil]

ⓝ 규모, 저울

A Why do you wish to find a new job?
새 직업을 찾고 싶은 이유가 무엇이니?

B I want to work for a company of a larger
scale. 규모가 더 큰 회사에서 일하고 싶어.

---

²³ ☑ **quantity**
[kwɑ́ntəti]

c.f. quality 질, 품질

ⓝ 양, 다량

a huge quantity of garbage 엄청난 양의 쓰레기

A I prefer quantity over quality. 나는 질보다 양이 좋아.

B I don't agree with you. 나는 너와 생각이 달라.

---

²⁴ ☑ **half**
[hǽf]

pl. halves

ⓝ 반, 절반

cut in half 반으로 자르다

A When did Amy leave? 에이미가 언제 떠났니?

B I think it was about half an hour ago.
30분 전쯤이었던 것 같아.

---

²⁵ ☑ **about**
[əbáut]

prep ~에 대하여, ~의 주위에

a movie about a war 전쟁에 관한 영화

A How many people were at the meeting?
회의에 몇 명이 사람들이 있었니?

B About fifteen. 열다섯 명 정도.

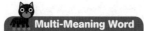
Multi-Meaning Word

major

ⓐ 다수의
What is the **major** opinion about the plan?
그 계획에 대한 다수의 의견은 무엇입니까?

ⓐ 주요한
Making money is not my **major** concern.
돈을 버는 것이 내 주요 관심사는 아니다.

ⓥ 전공하다
He **majored** in economics at college.
그는 대학에서 경제학을 전공했다.

Word Search

앞에서 배운 어휘를 기억하며 모두 찾아 보세요.

정답

Y	L	L	H	E	E	T	E	R	O	J	A	M	S	T
Y	J	A	L	D	E	V	E	Z	S	X	N	Y	E	I
X	L	O	A	T	M	S	R	M	Y	U	J	E	V	B
F	T	C	A	E	S	T	G	H	A	F	L	K	E	R
W	E	L	Z	A	P	S	E	H	X	A	X	E	R	V
D	P	O	M	C	G	O	D	C	C	B	N	E	A	X
S	D	L	N	T	R	M	Q	S	U	O	B	V	L	L
Q	C	C	E	O	P	L	O	U	U	E	C	I	W	T
Q	C	C	X	N	I	A	M	G	A	Y	C	S	N	E
F	H	K	D	V	T	L	H	K	T	R	M	W	Y	X
E	L	B	U	O	D	Y	L	P	K	O	T	G	B	T
Q	L	G	E	V	G	W	M	I	R	X	Y	E	M	R
D	N	Y	A	C	G	E	G	X	N	G	S	M	R	A
O	K	E	L	Y	R	H	S	P	P	C	S	Q	X	J

almost	bit	decade	degree
double	empty	enough	extra
half	major	mass	plenty
quarter	scale	several	twice

Word Search **207**

Unit 25 Time & Space

- morning 아침
- noon 정오
- evening 저녁
- night 밤
- minute (시간 단위의) 분
- hour 시간
- day 하루
- week 주
- month 달, 월
- year 연
- today 오늘
- tomorrow 내일

01 **youth**
[ju:θ]

ⓐ young 젊은

ⓝ 젊음　　　　　**the secret of youth** 젊음의 비결

A Sophia, you should spend your youth wisely.
소피아, 너의 젊음을 현명하게 보내야 한단다.

B I'm trying my best, Mr. Wilson.
최선을 다하고 있어요, 월슨 선생님.

02 **future**
[fjúːtʃər]

ⓝ 미래 ⓐ 미래의　　　　**a future husband** 미래의 남편

A How do you think the future will be?
미래는 어떨 것 같니?

B I think it will be like science fiction movies.
내 생각에 공상과학 영화처럼 될 것 같아.

03 **adult**
[ədʌ́lt]

ⓝ 어른, 성인 ⓐ 성장한

A What kind of adult do you want to be?
넌 어떤 어른이 되고 싶니?

B I want to be like my father.
저는 저희 아버지처럼 되고 싶습니다.

04 **period**
[píəriəd]

ⓝ 기간, 시기　　　　**the short period** 짧은 기간

A How long is the period for the exam?
시험 기간이 얼마나 되나요?

B The period will be about three days.
시험 기간은 3일 정도입니다.

05 **monthly**
[mʌ́nθli]

ⓝ month 달

ⓐ 월간의, 달마다의

A Is Susan getting better? 수잔은 건강이 나아지고 있니?

B The doctor said she was better on her
monthly check-up.
매달 받는 검진에서 의사가 나아졌다고 했어.

06 ancient
☑
[éinʃənt]

ⓐ 옛날의, 고대의   **the ancient Greeks** 고대 그리스인

A The Pyramids were built in ancient Egypt.
피라미드는 고대 이집트에 건설되었어.

B They remain a mystery to this day.
오늘날까지도 수수께끼로 남아있어.

---

07 dawn
☑
[dɔːn]

ⓢⓨⓝ day-break 새벽

ⓝ 새벽, 동틀 녘   **from dawn till dust** 새벽부터 해질 때까지

A Helen couldn't come back until after dawn.
헬렌은 새벽이 지난 다음에야 돌아왔어.

B She must be very busy these days.
그녀는 요즘 많이 바쁜 모양이구나.

---

08 recently
☑
[ríːsəntli]

ⓐ recent 최근의

ⓐⓓ 최근에

A Wasn't there a bookstore here before?
전에 여기에 서점이 있지 않았어?

B They recently moved to a bigger store.
최근에 더 큰 가게로 이사했어.

---

09 tonight
☑
[tənáit]

ⓐⓓ 오늘밤에 **ⓝ** 오늘밤

   tonight's TV program 오늘밤의 텔레비전 프로그램

A The moon is shining so bright tonight.
오늘 밤 달이 참 밝게 빛나네.

B Yes, it's so pretty. 응. 참 예뻐.

---

10 midnight
☑
[mídnàit]

ⓝ 한밤중, 자정   **after midnight** 자정이 지나서

A James called me at midnight.
제임스가 한밤중에 전화를 했어.

B It must have been important.
중요한 일이었나 보다.

11 ☑ **teenager**
[tíːnèidʒəːr]

ⓝ 십대

A How old is your daughter now, Mr. Thomas?
토머스 선생님, 따님은 이제 몇 살인가요?

B She's fifteen. I can't believe she is already a teenager! 열다섯 살이에요. 벌써 십대라는 게 믿기지 않아요!

12 ☑ **universe**
[júːnəvèːrs]

ⓐ universal 전 세계의, 우주의

ⓝ 우주, 전 세계

A Someday, I'm going to solve the mysteries of the universe. 언젠가 나는 우주의 신비들을 파헤칠 거야.

B I hope you succeed! 성공하길 바라!

13 ☑ **always**
[ɔ́ːlweiz]

ⓐⁿᵗ never 한 번도 …않다

ⓐᵈ 항상, 언제나

A I can't see Jimmy. Where is he?
지미가 안 보이네. 어디에 있어?

B Oh, he's always late. 아, 걔는 항상 늦어.

14 ☑ **already**
[ɔːlrédi]

ⓐᵈ 벌써, 이미

A Stop playing around on the computer. Why don't you clean your room?
컴퓨터를 가지고 그만 놀아라. 가서 방 청소 좀 하지 그래?

B I already cleaned it, Mom. 이미 청소했어요, 엄마.

15 ☑ **moment**
[móumənt]

ⓝ 순간   **in a few moments** 곧

A I wish I could see her again for just one moment. 한 순간만이라도 그녀를 다시 볼 수 있으면 좋겠어.

B I miss her, too. 나도 그녀가 그리워.

16 elder
[éldər]

ⓐ elderly 나이가 지긋한

ⓝ 연장자

A I find Koreans are very kind to their elders.
내가 보기에 한국 사람들은 연장자에게 매우 친절한 것 같아.

B Yes, that is our tradition. 응, 그게 우리 전통이야.

17 often
[ɔ́ːfən]

ad 종종, 자주

A This is such a nice restaurant.
여긴 참 좋은 식당이네요.

B I don't come here often. I only come with someone special.
여기 자주 오지는 않아요. 특별한 사람하고만 오죠.

18 delay
[diléi]

ⓥ 미루다, 연기하다 **ⓝ** 지연, 지체

without delay 지체 없이, 곧

A They decided to delay the project for a month. 그들이 프로젝트를 한 달간 미루기로 결정했어.

B So what are you going to do now?
그래서 너는 이제 뭘 할 거니?

19 space
[speis]

ⓝ 공간, 우주

time and space 시간과 공간

A Is there enough space in the room for the bed? 방에 침대를 넣을 충분한 공간이 있니?

B That depends on how big the bed is.
그거야 침대 크기에 따라 다르지.

20 far
[fɑːr]

ad 멀리 **ⓐ** 먼, 먼 길의

a far country 먼 나라

A How far is it from your school to your home?
학교에서 집까지 얼마나 머니?

B My school is within walking distance from my home. 학교는 집에서 걸어 다닐 수 있을 거리에 있어.

21 length
[leŋkθ]
ⓐ long 긴

ⓝ 길이, 기간

A How was the movie? Was it fun?
영화 어땠어? 재미있었니?

B The movie was quite interesting, but its length was too short.
영화는 꽤 재미있었는데 영화 시간이 너무 짧았어.

---

22 former
[fɔ́ːrməːr]

ⓐ 앞의, 전자의　　　**a former President** 전 대통령

A Did you feel anything after you read the book? 그 책을 읽은 다음에 느낀 거 있니?

B I changed my former ideas of the world.
세계에 대해 가졌던 이전의 내 생각을 바꾸게 되었어.

---

23 weekend
[wíːkènd]

ⓝ 주말

A Do you have any plans for the weekend?
주말에 계획한 것 있니?

B No, nothing yet. 아니, 아직 없어.

---

24 since
[sins]

prep ~이래로　conj ~한 이래로

A Sarah, I've been trying to give you this file since last week.
사라, 이 파일을 지난주부터 너에게 주려고 했어.

B Is it the file from the main office?
본사에서 온 파일이야?

---

25 until
[əntíl]

prep ~까지　conj ~할 때까지

A How much longer do we have to wait?
우리 얼마나 더 오래 기다려야 해?

B We have to wait until 7 o'clock.
7시까지 기다려야 해.

Word Search

앞에서 배운 어휘를 기억하며 모두 찾아 보세요.

정답

T	Q	R	N	K	Z	Z	N	I	X	L	N	E	G	M
H	C	Z	E	E	L	G	N	Y	T	A	C	C	W	J
T	L	G	P	G	T	J	Y	M	D	A	B	G	K	Y
G	X	C	I	F	O	F	E	K	P	F	Q	U	X	B
N	M	A	Y	N	O	N	O	S	V	U	K	Q	B	U
E	E	Z	O	U	O	R	E	V	G	T	F	R	R	D
L	U	N	T	I	L	T	M	E	F	U	A	Q	A	O
U	N	I	V	E	R	S	E	E	T	R	E	A	N	I
M	O	M	E	N	T	R	H	E	R	E	D	R	C	R
E	C	V	I	S	A	H	T	P	B	U	D	E	I	E
F	E	H	E	F	O	F	U	D	L	E	N	D	E	P
Z	A	L	W	A	Y	S	O	T	L	W	J	L	N	G
R	R	S	O	D	J	P	Y	A	E	G	G	E	T	T
P	Y	H	T	O	N	L	Y	D	O	J	N	L	Y	J

adult	always	ancient	delay
elder	far	former	future
length	moment	often	period
space	universe	until	youth

Word Bubbles

앞에서 배운 어휘를 기억하며 버블을 단어로 채워 보세요.

정답

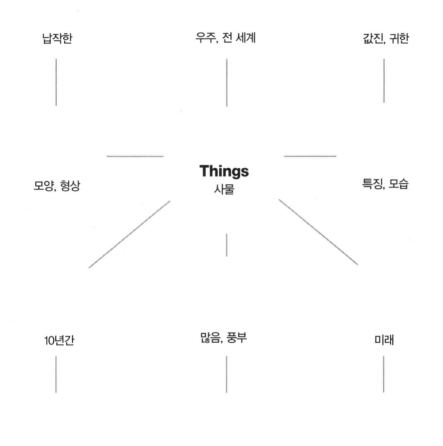

납작한

우주, 전 세계

값진, 귀한

모양, 형상

Things
사물

특징, 모습

10년간

많음, 풍부

미래

1세기, 100년

몇몇의, 몇 개의

기간, 시기

Review Test

A 우리말을 영어로, 영어를 우리말로 쓰시오.

01 길이, 기간 _____ 08 form _____

02 한밤중, 자정 _____ 09 degree _____

03 몇몇의, 몇 개의 _____ 10 belong _____

04 순간 _____ 11 plenty _____

05 뻣뻣한, 경직된 _____ 12 extra _____

06 옛날의, 고대의 _____ 13 period _____

07 10년간 _____ 14 necessary _____

B 빈칸에 알맞은 단어를 쓰시오.

01 소중한 추억 _____ memories

02 인구의 감소 _____ in population

03 일 년 중 내내 the _____ year

04 from dawn till dust _____부터 해질 때까지

05 time and space 시간과 _____

06 tiny fingers _____ 손가락

C 단어의 관계에 맞게 빈칸을 채우시오.

01 항상, 언제나 : 한번도 ~ 않다 = always : _____

02 질 : 양 = quality : _____

03 가득 찬 : 채우다 = full : _____

04 recently : recent = 최근에 : _____

05 valuable : value = 값진, 귀한 : _____

06 quarter : half = 4분의, 4분의 일 : _____

D 배운 단어를 사용하여 문장을 완성하시오. (필요하면 형태를 바꾸시오.)

01 Drinking a lot of water is _____ to our health.
많은 양의 물을 마시는 것은 우리의 건강에 도움을 준다.

02 _____ ten boys were playing basketball one hour ago.
한 시간 전에 약 열 명의 소년이 농구를 하고 있었다.

03 I opened a gift box, but the box was _____.
나는 선물 상자를 열었지만, 그 상자는 비어 있었다.

04 Something strange happened to me last _____.
지난 주말 나에게 이상한 일이 생겼다.

05 He knows _____ about me and my family.
그는 나나 내 가족에 대해서 아는 것이 없다.

E 빈칸에 알맞은 말을 보기에서 찾아 쓰시오.

| another | often | twice | enough | delay |

01 A I don't like this color. Could you show me _____ one?

   B Sure, what about this one?

02 A Do we have _____ money for a taxi fare?

   B I don't think so. We'd better take a bus.

03 A The hurricane is coming. Should I _____ my trip to Florida?

   B If I were you, I would do that.

04 A How _____ do you get your hair cut?

   B I have my hair cut _____ a year.

F 밑줄 친 부분을 우리말로 옮기시오.

01 I think I am going to major in French.

02 In the past, space travel was only a dream.

VOCA Inn!

Express Mathematics 수학 표현

+ 더하기

★ One and one is two.   1+1=2

★ Five and four make (or are) nine.   5+4=9

★ Seven plus two is nine.   7+2=9

— 빼기

★ Thirty minus five equals twenty-five.   30-5=25

★ Thirty minus five is twenty-five.   30-5=25

★ Twenty take away twelve is eight.   20-12=8

× 곱하기

★ Four fives are twenty.   4×5=20

★ Two multiplied by nine makes eighteen.   2×9=18

★ Three times six is eighteen.   3×6=18

÷ 나누기 / 제곱

★ Eighteen divided by nine equals two.   18/9=2

★ Four into sixteen goes four.   16/4=4

★ Two squared is four.   2의 제곱=4

★ Two cubed is eight.   2의 세제곱=8

★ The square of ten is a hundred.   10의 제곱=100

소수점 표현

★ Two point seven.   2.7

★ Eighty-five point five two.   85.52

★ Four ten thousandths.   0.0004

★ Zero point zero zero zero four.   0.0004

★ Seventy-six thousand, sixty-four point eight.   76,064.8

★ Nine thousand seven hundred eighty-two point three five.   9,782.35

Chapter
08

Science & Technology

Convenient Vehicles

city bus tour

Basic Words

- ☐ ride 타다
- ☐ taxi 택시
- ☐ train 기차
- ☐ ferry 연락선
- ☐ wait 기다리다
- ☐ boat 보트
- ☐ car 차
- ☐ ship 배
- ☐ carry 나르다
- ☐ bicycle 자전거
- ☐ bus 버스
- ☐ airplane 비행기

01 arrive
[əráiv]

ⓝ arrival 도착

ⓥ 도착하다　　　**arrive at the airport** 공항에 도착하다

A Has Mr. Roger arrived, yet?
로저 선생님 도착하셨어요?

B No, but he said he would soon.
아뇨, 그런데 곧 도착하신대요.

02 passenger
[pǽsəndʒər]

ⓝ 승객　　　**a passenger train** 여객 열차

A I heard you used to be a pilot.
예전에 비행사였다고 들었어요.

B Yes, this is my first flight as a passenger.
네, 승객으로 비행하기는 이번이 처음이에요.

03 reach
[ri:tʃ]

ⓥ 도착하다, 도달하다
reach the top of the mountain 산 정상에 도착하다

A Did Father call? He is late.
아버지에게서 전화 왔니? 늦으시네.

B Yes, he said he reached the tollgate.
네, 톨게이트에 도착했다고 연락하셨어요.

04 leave
[li:v]

(leave-left-left)

ⓥ 떠나다, 출발하다

A When are you leaving Seoul?
언제 서울을 떠나니?

B I was going to leave tomorrow, but I am not
sure about it. 내일 떠나려고 했는데, 잘 모르겠어.

05 crosswalk
[krɔ́:swɔ̀:k]

ⓝ 횡단보도, 건널목

A Don't you know you should cross the street
at the crosswalk?
횡단보도에서 길을 건너야 한다는 거 모르니?

B I won't do that again. 다시는 안 그럴게요.

06 quickly
[kwíkli]

ⓐ quick 빠른, 급속한

ad 빨리, 서둘러

A We have to get to the party quickly.
우리 파티에 빨리 가야 해.

B I'll go start the car. 가서 차 시동 걸어둘게.

07 subway
[sʌ́bwèi]

n 지하철

A Which subway line should I take to get to Central Station?
센트럴 역에 가려면 지하철 몇 호선을 타야 하나요?

B Take subway line 3. 지하철 3호선을 타세요.

08 seat belt
[síːtbelt]

n 좌석 벨트

A John, put your seat belt on. 존, 좌석 벨트를 매거라.

B Oops. I forgot to. 이런, 매는 걸 잊어버렸어.

09 traffic
[trǽfik]

n 교통, 통행   **traffic jam** 교통 체증

A You must obey the traffic laws to drive safely.
안전하게 운전하려면 교통 법규를 지켜야 해.

B Don't worry, Dad. I will. 걱정 마세요, 아빠. 그렇게 할게요.

10 load
[loud]

ant unload 짐을 내리다

v 짐을 싣다 **n** 짐

A Where do I load my bag, Miss Swan?
스완 선생님, 제 가방은 어디에 싣나요?

B Let's put the bags in the trunk.
가방들은 트렁크에 싣자.

11 signal
[sígnəl]

n v sign 신호, 서명하다

n 신호, 시그널

A Henry, it's a green light. 헨리, 초록불이야.

B Oh, I'm sorry. I wasn't paying attention to the traffic signal. 미안해. 교통 신호에 신경을 안 쓰고 있었어.

12 fasten
[fǽsn]

V 묶다, 잠그다

A Fasten your seat belt, Jim. 짐, 안전벨트 매거라.

B I already did, Mom. 벌써 맸어요. 엄마.

13 gasoline
[gǽsəlíːn]

n 휘발유

A We are running out of gasoline.
우리 휘발유가 바닥나고 있어.

B Turn right here. I know a gas station close by.
여기서 우회전 해. 가까운 데에 있는 주유소를 하나 알아.

14 fare
[fɛər]

n 요금, 운임

A How much is the fare to Four Season Hotel?
포시즌 호텔까지 요금이 얼마입니까?

B That'll be 20 dollars. 20달러입니다.

15 railroad
[réilròud]

n 철도

A I traveled around Russia by railroad last year.
작년에 러시아 여기저기를 철도편으로 여행했어.

B Sounds like fun! 재미있겠구나!

16 station
[stéiʃən]

n 역, 정거장   **at a train station** 기차역에서

A Drop me off at the station. I'll take the
subway from there.
역에서 내려줘. 거기서부터 지하철로 갈게.

B Will you be okay with that? 그렇게 해도 되겠니?

17 repair

[ripέər]

ⓝ repairman 수리공

ⓥ 고치다, 수리하다 **ⓝ** 수리　　　**a repair shop** 수리점

A Why are you so late, honey?

여보, 왜 이렇게 늦었어요?

B My car broke down. I had to take it to the garage to get repaired.

차가 고장 났어. 수리를 하려고 자동차 정비 공장에 맡겨야 했거든.

18 convenient

[kənví:njənt]

ⓝ convenience 편리

ⓐ 편리한　　　　　　　**a convenient store** 편의점

A This device will make our lives more convenient.

이 장치는 우리 삶을 더욱 편리하게 만들 것입니다.

B How does it work? 어떻게 작동하는 건가요?

19 transportation

[trænspərtéiʃən]

ⓝ 운송, 교통기관

A How do you come to work? 어떻게 출근하세요?

B I usually use public transportations.

주로 대중교통을 이용해요.

20 vehicle

[víːikəl]

ⓝ 탈것, 수송 수단　　　　**space vehicles** 우주선

A This vehicle was designed to operate on sand. 이 차량은 모래 위에서 움직이도록 설계되었어.

B It should be useful in desert areas.

사막에서 유용하겠구나.

21 fuel

[fjúːəl]

ⓝ 연료 **ⓥ** 연료를 공급하다

A This engine uses hydrogen as a fuel.

이 엔진은 수소를 연료로 사용해.　　　　　* hydrogen : 수소

B Yes, it's expected to solve the problems of fossil fuel. 응, 화석 연료의 문제점을 해결해줄 것으로 기대되고 있어.

22 ☑ parking
[pάːrkiŋ]

ⓥ park 주차하다

ⓝ 주차, 주차 장소　　　　　**a parking lot** 주차장

A How much is the parking fee?
　주차비가 얼마인가요?

B It's five dollars per hour.
　시간당 5달러입니다.

23 ☑ miss
[mis]

ⓥ 놓치다

A Oh, no! We missed the bus!
　오, 안 돼! 버스를 놓쳤어!

B I hope we're not late. Why don't we just take a taxi? 늦지 않으면 좋겠는데. 그냥 택시를 타는 건 어떨까?

24 ☑ speed
[spiːd]

ⓐ speedy 빠른, 신속한

ⓝ 빠르기, 속력　　　　**at a high speed** 고속으로

A The speed limit is 80km per hour.
　속도제한이 시속 80km이야.

B Be careful not to get a ticket.
　속도위반 딱지 받지 않게 조심해.

25 ☑ transfer
[trænsfə́ːr]

ⓥ 옮기다, 갈아타다

A This is our stop on the subway.
　우리 지하철에서는 이번 역에 내려.

B I guess we transfer to a bus near here.
　이 근처에서 버스로 갈아타는 모양이구나.

Multi-Meaning Word

miss

ⓝ 미혼 여성

Miss Smith is waiting for you in the lobby.
스미스 양이 로비에서 기다리고 계십니다.

ⓥ 놓치다 / 그리워하다

Hurry up not to **miss** the bus. 버스를 놓치지 않도록 서둘러.

I haven't seen her for almost three months, so I **miss** her so much. 그녀를 못 본지 거의 3개월이 되어서 그녀가 몹시 그립다.

Word Search

앞에서 배운 어휘를 기억하며 모두 찾아 보세요.

정답

```
G D L X Z L L C S H T R N T V
M N N A E M K G U C J E X O E
L X I A N S I E B A I F D K H
Z O D K S G Z D W E T S M J I
O C A I R E I G A R V N K O C
T T M V V A A S Y D D A F G L
M Q S I E S P A R Q A R A Z E
P D R F S E R A F Y O T S Q D
Z R M L R E P A I R R T T U E
A R I C I F F A R E L X E I E
N N S T A T I O N O I Q N C P
E F I F U E L B U Z A R H K S
L H B M D T M D P Z R U F L L
O H N L X I M T U L Z V W Y P
```

arrive	fare	fasten	fuel
miss	parking	quickly	railroad
reach	repair	signal	speed
station	subway	transfer	vehicle

Unit 27 Science

01 scientist
[sáiəntist]

ⓝ 과학자

A Many scientists think there is life on other planets. 많은 과학자들은 다른 행성에 생명체가 있다고 생각해.

B That's interesting! 흥미롭구나!

02 device
[diváis]

ⓥ devise 고안하다

ⓝ 장치, 고안

A How do automatic doors work?
자동문의 원리가 뭐야?

B They use devices called "sensors."
'센서'라고 불리는 장치를 사용해.

03 comfortable
[kʌ́mftəbəl]

ⓝ comfort 안락함

ⓐ 편안한

A Does science make our lives healthier and more comfortable?
과학이 우리의 삶을 더 건강하고, 편안하게 해주는 걸까?

B It does in many ways. 여러 가지 면에서 그렇긴 하지.

04 effort
[éfərt]

ⓝ 노력, 수고   **need a lot of effort** 많은 노력이 필요하다

A Why is he making so much effort to make silly things?
왜 그는 바보 같은 것들을 만드는 데 많은 노력을 하는 거지?

B Well, he thinks they could be a big help to people. 글쎄, 사람들에게 큰 도움이 된다고 생각하나 봐.

05 discover
[diskʌ́vər]

ⓝ discovery 발견, 발견물

ⓥ 발견하다

A I cannot imagine life before fire was discovered! 불을 발견하기 이전의 삶은 상상할 수 없어!

B Me, neither. I think it's the most important discovery in history.
나도 그래. 난 불이 역사 상 가장 중요한 발견이라고 생각해.

06 experiment
[ikspérəmənt]

ⓝ 실험, 시험 ⓥ 실험하다

A Why do scientists do experiments so much?
과학자들은 왜 실험을 그렇게 많이 하는 거야?

B They are trying to find something new or better. 그들은 새롭거나 더 나은 무언가를 발견하려고 하는 거야.

07 possible
[pásəbəl]

ⓐ 가능한, 할 수 있는   **as soon as possible** 가능한 빨리

A Now, it is possible to communicate with someone on the other side of the world.
지금은 세계 반대편에 있는 사람과도 의사소통이 가능해졌어.

B Yes, it's thanks to modern technology.
맞아, 현대 과학 기술 덕분이지.

08 create
[kriéit]

ⓝ creation 창조

ⓥ 창조하다, 창시하다

A Many great things were created by science.
과학을 통해 많은 위대한 것이 창조되었어.

B I think I could feel their hard work.
그들의 노력이 느껴지는 것 같아.

09 spaceship
[spéisʃip]

ⓝ 우주선

A Humans have succeeded in sending a spaceship to the moon.
인류는 우주선을 달에 보내는 데 성공했어.

B I wish I could fly to the moon.
나도 달로 날아갈 수 있었으면 좋겠다.

10 chemical
[kémikəl]

ⓐ 화학의, 화학적인 ⓝ 화학물질

A Martin spoiled my chemical experiment.
마틴이 내 화학 실험을 망쳤어.

B What? How did it happen?
뭐라고? 어떻게 그런 일이 발생했니?

11 error
[érər]

n 잘못, 실수　　　　　　　　　　**trial and error** 시행착오

A There is an error in our data.
우리 자료에 오류가 있어요.

B I'll take care of it. 제가 처리하겠습니다.

12 complicated
[kámpləkèitid]

v complicate
복잡하게 하다

a 복잡한, 까다로운

A Women are so complicated. 여자들은 너무 복잡해.

B It's men that are too simple. 남자가 너무 단순한 거야.

13 energy
[énərdʒi]

n 에너지, 에너지원, 활력

A Scientists are trying to use the wind as an energy source.
과학자들은 바람을 에너지원으로 사용하려고 하고 있어.

B They use those machines that look like windmills! 그들은 풍차같이 생긴 기계들을 이용하지!

14 machine
[məʃíːn]

n 기계

A The machine won't work if you design it like this. 기계를 이렇게 설계하면 작동하지 않을 거야.

B Where should I mend it? 어디를 고쳐야 할까?

15 purpose
[pɔ́ːrpəs]

n 목적, 의도　　　　　　　　　　**on purpose** 고의로

A What is the purpose of your project?
네 프로젝트의 목적이 무엇이니?

B It's to make a time machine. 타임머신을 만드는 거야.

16 explore
[iksplɔ́ːr]

n exploration 탐험

v 탐험하다, 탐구하다

A I want to be an astronaut when I grow up.
난 커서 우주비행사가 되고 싶어.

B I guess you want to explore outer space.
우주를 탐험하고 싶은 모양이구나.

17 ☑ **process**
[práses]

❶ 과정, 경과 **go through a process of** ~의 과정을 거치다

A Could you explain the process of making plastic? 플라스틱을 만드는 과정을 설명해 주시겠어요?

B Okay, but it's quite difficult to understand.
좋아. 하지만 이해하기 꽤 어려울 거야.

---

18 ☑ **various**
[véəriəs]

❶ vary 다양하다, 변화하다

ⓐ 가지가지의, 다양한 **various talents** 다양한 재능

A The laboratory has various devices.
실험실에는 다양한 장치가 있어.

B I wonder what they are for.
어디에 쓰이는 것들인지 궁금해.

---

19 ☑ **important**
[impɔ́ːrtənt]

❶ importance 중요성

ⓐ 중요한, 중대한 **important decisions** 중대한 결정

A It is important to measure test results precisely. 실험결과를 정확하게 측정하는 것은 매우 중요해.

B Yes, a small mistake can lead to a big accident. 맞아. 작은 실수가 대형사고로 이어질 수 있지.

---

20 ☑ **electric**
[iléktrik]

❶ electricity 전기

ⓐ 전기의, 전기 장치의

A My dad bought an electric car.
나의 아버지께서 전기 차를 구매하셨어.

B Awesome. How long does it take to charge it? 멋지다. 충전하는 데 얼마나 걸려?

---

21 ☑ **improve**
[imprúːv]

❶ improvement 향상

ⓥ 향상시키다, 개선하다

A Science has improved the quality of human life. 과학은 인간 삶의 질을 향상시켰어.

B I couldn't agree more. 전적으로 동의해.

22 genius
[dʒíːnjəs]

ⓝ 천재, 재능

A It will take a genius to solve this problem!
이 문제는 천재만이 풀 수 있을 거야!

B Is it that difficult? 그렇게 어려워?

23 search
[səːrtʃ]

ⓥ 찾다, 조사하다 **ⓝ** 탐색, 조사

A How can I obtain data here?
내가 여기서 어떻게 자료를 얻을 수 있나요?

B You can use a computer to search for data.
컴퓨터를 사용해서 자료를 찾으면 됩니다.

24 technology
[teknáləbdʒi]

ⓝ 과학 기술, 공학

A We now live in a global village.
우리는 지금 지구촌에 살고 있어.

B Technology makes our world smaller and closer. 과학 기술이 세상을 더욱 작고 가깝게 만들어 줘.

25 when
[wen]

conj ~할 때

A I heard that Edison failed 10,000 times when he tried to invent the light bulb.
에디슨이 전구를 발명할 때 그는 만 번이나 실패했다고 들었어.

B Really? It can't be true. 정말이야? 사실일 리가 없어.

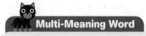
Multi-Meaning Word

energy

ⓝ 에너지
IAEA stands for the International Atomic **Energy** Agency.
IAEA는 국제 원자력 기구를 나타낸다.

ⓝ 활기, 원기
Keep a balance between physical and mental **energy**.
체력과 정신력 사이에 균형을 유지해라.

ⓝ 힘
They put all their **energy** into their work.
그들은 그들의 일에 온 힘을 쏟았다.

Word Search

앞에서 배운 어휘를 기억하며 모두 찾아 보세요.

정답

```
V E T C L P T U N H D P E M E
A V S E T E T O C P O E L A T
R O I P R B C R R Z S N E C A
I R T I Y O A I S R A E C H E
O P N H A E L I M G E R T I R
U M E S S C B P E E I G R N C
S I I E B L T G X F H Y I E R
N G S C E J T T Q E F C C D E
E Y S A P U R P O S E O O F V
H O H P E C I V E D X E R W O
W J D S J G E N I U S V B T C
S S E C O R P R I O J L C J S
T I R Z E G H B E Z M U I O I
U Y S X H B E S W T W H F R D
```

create	device	discover	effort
electric	energy	explore	genius
improve	machine	process	purpose
search	spaceship	various	when

Unit 28 Computer & Tool

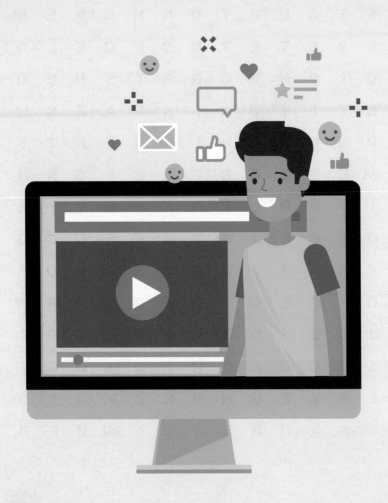

Basic Words

- ☐ computer 컴퓨터
- ☐ monitor 모니터
- ☐ database 데이터베이스
- ☐ nail 못
- ☐ Internet 인터넷
- ☐ fax 팩스
- ☐ software 소프트웨어
- ☐ drill 드릴, 송곳
- ☐ keyboard 키보드
- ☐ homepage 홈페이지
- ☐ hammer 망치
- ☐ toolbox 공구 상자

01 access
[ǽkses]

ⓥ 접근하다 **ⓝ** 접근, 접속

A I can't access your website.
네 홈페이지에 접근할 수 없어.

B Oh, I forgot to tell you the password.
아, 내가 비밀번호 알려주는 것을 잊어버렸구나.

02 invent
[invént]

ⓝ invention 발명품

ⓥ 발명하다   invent the telephone 전화를 발명하다

A Did you know that paper was invented in China? 종이가 중국에서 발명된 거 아니?

B No, I didn't. That's amazing! 아니, 몰랐어. 놀라워!

03 chip
[tʃip]

ⓝ (컴퓨터) 칩, 얇은 조각

A How can computers store so much data?
컴퓨터는 어떻게 그렇게 많은 데이터를 저장할 수 있어?

B It's possible thanks to these small computer chips. 이 작은 컴퓨터 칩 덕분에 가능해.

04 copier
[kápiər]

ⓥ copy 복사하다

ⓝ 복사기

A John, the copier is broken again.
존, 복사기가 또 고장 났어.

B I told you it's not broken. It's just out of paper. 고장 난 것이 아니라고 했잖아. 종이가 다 떨어진 것뿐이야.

05 print
[print]

ⓝ printer 인쇄기

ⓥ 인쇄하다

A I need to print these documents right now.
이 문서들을 지금 당장 인쇄해야 해.

B Sorry, the printer is out of ink.
미안해요, 프린터에 잉크가 떨어졌어요.

06 ☑ design
[dizáin]

ⓝ designer 디자이너

ⓥ 설계하다, 입안하다 **ⓝ** 설계(도), 디자인

A These new computers are designed to be faster. 이 새 컴퓨터들은 속도가 더 빠르도록 설계되었어.

B How fast are they? 얼마나 빠른데?

---

07 ☑ edit
[édit]

ⓥ 편집하다

A Are you done editing the document I gave you? 내가 준 문서 편집 다 했니?

B Give me five more minutes. 5분만 더 줘.

---

08 ☑ file
[fail]

ⓝ (컴퓨터) 파일, 서류철

A Jimmy, I can't find the MP3 file you gave me.
지미, 네가 준 MP3 파일을 못 찾겠어.

B I'll get you a new one. It's only a dollar.
새 것을 받아줄게. 1달러 밖에 안 해.

---

09 ☑ tip
[tip]

ⓝ 비결, 팁

A This computer game is too hard to play.
이 컴퓨터 게임은 너무 어려워서 못하겠다.

B Do you need a few tips? 비결을 알려줄까?

---

10 ☑ laptop
[læptàp]

ⓝ 노트북 컴퓨터

A Did you finish your homework? 숙제 다 했니?

B No, but I brought my laptop. I'm going to do it now. 아니, 하지만 노트북 컴퓨터를 가져왔어. 숙제 지금 하려고.

11 **message**
[mésidʒ]

ⓝ 전갈, 전하는 말

A Send me a text message when you get to the station. 역에 도착하면 나에게 문자 메시지 보내.

B Okay, I will. 알았어, 그렇게.

12 **tool**
[tuːl]

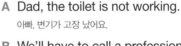

ⓝ 도구, 연장

A Dad, the toilet is not working.
아빠, 변기가 고장 났어요.

B We'll have to call a professional. I don't have my tools. 전문가를 불러야겠다. 연장이 없거든.

13 **document**
[dάkjumənt]
ⓐ documentary 문서의

ⓝ 문서, 서류

A Where did you put that important document?
그 중요한 서류 어디다 뒀어?

B Isn't it on your desk? 책상 위에 없어요?

14 **fix**
[fiks]

ⓥ 수리하다, 고정시키다

A My computer keeps crashing. Can you fix it?
내 컴퓨터가 자꾸 다운돼요. 고칠 수 있나요?

B I think it has a memory problem.
메모리에 문제가 있는 것 같네요.

15 **information**
[ìnfərméiʃən]
ⓐ informative 정보를 주는

ⓝ 정보, 지식　　　**useful information** 유익한 정보

A I'd like some information about the exhibit.
전시에 대한 정보를 얻었으면 좋겠습니다.

B Would you like a pamphlet? 책자를 드릴까요?

16 **delete**
[dilíːt]

ⓥ 삭제하다, 지우다

A Sam, delete your files after you're done with my computer. 샘, 내 컴퓨터 다 쓴 다음에 네 파일들 지워.

B Okay, I will. 응, 그렇게.

17 receive
[risíːv]

ⓥ 받다, 수령하다

A Did you receive my message? 내 메시지 받았니?

B No, I didn't. What was it about?
아니, 못 받았어. 무슨 내용이었니?

18 attach
[ətǽtʃ]

ⓥ 붙이다, 첨부하다 　　　　**attached files** 첨부 파일

A Did you send me the file about the accident?
그 사고에 대한 파일 저한테 보내셨나요?

B Yes, it is attached to the e-mail.
네, 이메일에 첨부되어 있습니다.

19 link
[liŋk]

ⓥ 연결하다 **ⓝ** 고리, 연결로

a link between two parts 두 부품을 잇는 고리

A Rachel, can you link to the Internet?
레이첼, 인터넷에 연결할 수 있니?

B No. There seems to be a problem with the server. 아니, 서버에 문제가 있나 봐.

20 used
[juːzd]
ⓥ use 사용하다
syn second-hand 중고의

ⓐ 중고의 　　　　　　　　　　**a used car** 중고차

A Computers are so expensive!
컴퓨터가 정말 비싸구나!

B Yeah, I think I'll have to buy a used one.
응, 난 중고 컴퓨터를 사야 할 것 같아.

21 on-line
[ánláin]
ant off-line 오프라인의

ad 온라인으로 **ⓐ** 온라인의

A Why can't I go on-line? 왜 접속이 안 되지?

B Your Internet is not connected.
인터넷이 연결돼 있지 않네.

22 technique
[tekníːk]

n 기교, 수법, 기법　　**modern techniques** 현대 기술

A How do you use the shovel? 삽은 어떻게 쓰는 거야?

B There's no technique to it. All you do is dig.
무슨 기교가 있는 건 아냐. 그냥 파면 돼.

23 surf
[səːrf]

n 서핑을[파도타기를] 하다

A Henry, are you busy? 헨리, 바쁘니?

B No, I am just surfing the Internet. Do you need something?
아니, 그냥 인터넷 서핑하고 있어. 필요한 거 있어?

24 switch
[switʃ]

n 스위치, 개폐기　**v** 스위치를 넣다　　**switch off** 끄다

A I can't find the light switch in your bathroom.
화장실에 전등 스위치를 못 찾겠어요.

B It's behind the door. 문 뒤에 있어요.

25 A as well as B

B뿐만 아니라 A도

A He bought a DVD player as well as a new TV.
그는 새 TV뿐만 아니라 DVD 플레이어도 샀어.

B He must have a lot of money.
그는 돈이 많은가 봐.

Multi-Meaning Word

tip

n 끝
I kissed the **tip** of her nose. 나는 그녀 코끝에 키스했다.

n 꼭대기, 정상
We finally reached the mountain **tip**. 우리는 마침내 산꼭대기에 도착했다.

n 팁, 사례금
The old lady gave a five-dollar **tip** to the waiter.
노부인은 웨이터에게 팁으로 5달러를 주었다.

n 비밀정보, 조언
Please give me some **tips** for learning English grammar effectively. 효과적으로 영어 문법을 공부하는 비결을 말해줘.

Word Search

앞에서 배운 어휘를 기억하며 모두 찾아 보세요.

정답

T	I	D	S	U	H	R	B	A	F	I	C	E	J	J
H	D	U	E	C	I	M	V	I	Z	U	O	U	J	Z
M	R	O	A	Z	N	B	L	Q	C	G	P	Q	M	C
F	C	T	K	R	I	E	C	M	I	A	I	I	E	Z
I	T	N	I	E	R	G	G	H	C	S	E	N	W	H
A	I	D	F	C	F	X	N	C	A	B	R	H	P	G
L	G	E	S	E	N	K	E	F	N	P	W	C	F	C
U	B	D	B	I	Q	S	T	I	M	R	P	E	L	T
Z	C	I	A	V	S	N	R	A	N	O	R	T	V	I
E	N	T	T	E	E	P	N	B	T	D	E	S	U	P
R	F	O	B	W	M	V	N	P	D	E	L	E	T	E
B	O	I	N	Q	U	M	A	S	W	I	T	C	H	Y
L	B	I	X	O	E	L	Z	X	O	Z	I	R	Z	Z
F	X	Y	A	D	Z	I	K	U	C	E	J	Q	T	Z

access	attach	copier	delete
edit	file	fix	laptop
link	receive	surf	switch
technique	tip	tool	used

Word Bubbles

앞에서 배운 어휘를 기억하며 버블을 단어로 채워 보세요.

정답

Chapter 8

요금, 운임

역, 정거장

갈아타다

Science & Technology
과학과 기술

교통, 통행

도착하다

장치, 고안

컴퓨터

발명하다

전기의

정보, 지식

창조하다

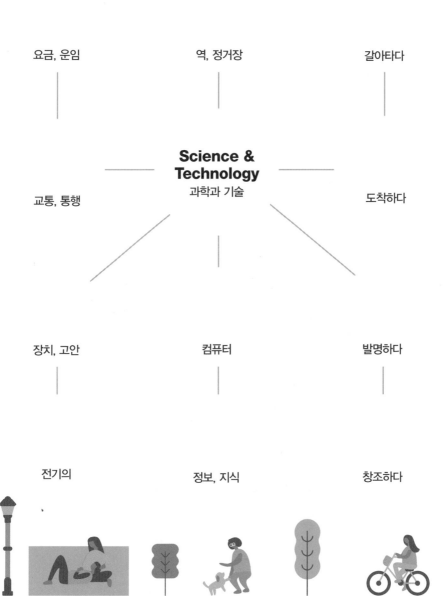

Review Test

A 우리말을 영어로, 영어를 우리말로 쓰시오.

01 설계하다 _____

02 탈것, 수송 수단 _____

03 전기의 _____

04 천재 _____

05 속력, 빠르기 _____

06 찾다, 조사하다 _____

07 도구, 연장 _____

08 fix _____

09 effort _____

10 railroad _____

11 laptop _____

12 quickly _____

13 energy _____

14 access _____

B 빈칸에 알맞은 단어를 쓰시오.

01 시행착오   trial and _____

02 주차장   a(n) _____ lot

03 ~과정을 거치다   go through a _____ of

04 important decisions   _____ 결정

05 traffic jam   _____ 체증

06 print pictures   사진을 _____

C 단어의 관계에 맞게 빈칸을 채우시오.

01 도착하다 : 도착   = arrive : _____

02 다양한 : 다르다   = various : _____

03 복사기 : 복사하다   = copier : _____

04 document : documentary   = 문서, 서류 : _____

05 devise : device   = 고안하다 : _____

06 load : unload   = 짐을 싣다 : _____

D 배운 단어를 사용하여 문장을 완성하시오. (필요하면 형태를 바꾸시오.)

01 The next train for Sydney will _____ in an hour.

다음 시드니행 열차는 한 시간 후에 출발합니다.

02 Traveling by train is more _____ than traveling by bus.

기차 여행이 버스보다 더 편안하다.

03 I couldn't _____ the file because it was too big.

파일이 너무 컸기 때문에 파일을 첨부할 수가 없었다.

04 Douglas Engelbart _____ the first computer mouse in 1964.

더글라스 엔젤바트가 1964년에 최초의 컴퓨터 마우스를 발명했다.

05 The _____ is doing an experiment about heat from the sun.

그 과학자는 태양에서 나오는 열에 대한 실험을 하고 있다.

E 빈칸에 알맞은 말을 보기에서 찾아 쓰시오.

station	discovered	receive	repair	machine

01 **A** When and where shall we meet?

   B Let's meet up at the train _____ at five.

02 **A** Can you _____ this washing _____?

   B Let me see. I don't think I can fix it.

03 **A** Who _____ the earth is round?

   B I know. Galileo Galilei did it.

04 **A** Did you _____ my text message?

   B You mean the message about the meeting?

F 밑줄 친 부분을 우리말로 옮기시오.

01 How much money should I give as a tip to a cab driver?

02 I have been here for only one week, but I miss my parents already.

VOCA Inn!

Signs

★No crossing	횡단 금지
★No parking	주차 금지
★Keep off	접근 금지
★Fire alarm	화재경보기
★No smoking	금연
★Closed today	금일 휴업
★Public telephone	공중전화
★Lavatory	공중 화장실
★Stop, curve ahead	정지, 전방 커브
★Wet paint	페인트 주의
★Unfit for drinking	식수 금지
★No transfer	갈아타지 못함
★No visitors allowed	방문 사절
★Hand off	손대지 마시오
★Watch your step	발밑을 조심하시오
★No spitting	침을 뱉지 마시오
★Information	안내소
★Exit	출구
★Admission free	입장 무료
★Fit for drinking	식수 가능
★Fare forward	요금 선불
★Emergency exit	비상구
★Go slow	서행
★Out of order	고장
★Under repairs	수리 중
★Under construction	공사 중
★Beware of the dog	개 조심

Chapter
09

Nature

Unit 29 Weather & Seasons

- □ spring 봄
- □ hot 더운, 뜨거운
- □ cool 시원한, 서늘한
- □ snow 눈
- □ warm 따뜻한
- □ rain 비
- □ winter 겨울
- □ ice 얼음
- □ summer 여름
- □ fall 가을
- □ rainbow 무지개
- □ wind 바람

01 weather
[wéðər]

n 날씨

A How is the weather in London?
런던의 날씨는 어때?

B It's hard to say. It changes so much in one day! 뭐라고 말하기 어려워. 하루 종일 정말 자주 변하거든!

02 mild
[maild]

a 온화한, 따뜻한

A I like autumn. I like the color of the leaves.
난 가을이 좋아. 나뭇잎 색깔이 좋거든.

B I like spring. I like the mild weather.
난 봄이 좋아. 따뜻한 날씨가 좋아.

03 freeze
[fri:z]
(freeze-froze-frozen)
a freezing 몹시 추운

v 얼다

A Oh, look! The river is frozen over.
와, 봐! 강이 꽁꽁 얼었어.

B Let's go home and get skates.
집에 가서 스케이트 가져오자.

04 temperature
[témpərətʃuər]

n 기온, 체온

A I hope it's not too hot on the weekend.
주말에 너무 덥지 않았으면 좋겠다.

B The weather forecast said the temperature would be around 28 degrees Celsius.
일기 예보에서는 기온이 섭씨 28도 정도일 거라고 했어.

05 storm
[stɔ:rm]
a stormy 폭풍우가 치는

n 폭풍(우)

A Why was the trip to the island cancelled?
섬 여행이 왜 취소되었어요?

B Because there was a storm coming.
폭풍이 오고 있었기 때문이야.

06 rise

[raiz]

(rise-rose-risen)

ⓥ 오르다, 일어나다 **ⓝ** 상승, 향상

A They say polar bears are in danger.
북극곰이 위험에 처해 있다고 해.

B Is it because the temperature rose?
기온이 올랐기 때문이니?

---

07 blow

[blou]

(blow-blew-blown)

ⓥ 불다   **blow one's nose** 코를 풀다

A The wind is blowing hard today.
오늘은 바람이 강하게 부는구나.

B Yes, it's a good thing I brought my gloves.
응. 장갑을 가져오길 잘했어.

---

08 shower

[ʃáuə:r]

ⓝ 소나기, 샤워

A Tom, is it raining a lot?
톰, 비 많이 오고 있니?

B It looks like only a shower.
그냥 소나기인 것 같아.

---

09 thunder

[θʌ́ndə:r]

c.f. lightning 번개

ⓝ 천둥

A What's the difference between lightning and thunder? 천둥과 번개는 어떻게 다른가요?

B Lightning is the light, while thunder is the sound. 번개는 불빛이고 천둥은 소리야.

---

10 season

[síːzən]

ⓝ 계절   **four seasons** 사계절

A What season do you like best?
어떤 계절을 제일 좋아하니?

B I like autumn best because the weather is not too hot or not too cold.
날씨가 너무 덥지도 않고 너무 춥지도 않아서 가을이 제일 좋아.

11 thick
[θik]

ant thin 옅은, 얇은

ⓐ 짙은, 두꺼운

A The fog is too thick to drive today.
오늘 운전하기에는 안개가 너무 짙어.

B Let's take the subway. 지하철을 타자.

12 climate
[kláimit]

ⓝ 기후　　　　　　　　**a wet climate** 습한 기후

A How is the climate in Korea during the summer? 한국의 여름 기후는 어때?

B It is very hot. 매우 더워.

13 flood
[flʌd]

ⓝ 홍수 ⓥ 범람하다

A There was a terrible flood last night.
어젯밤에 끔찍한 홍수가 일어났어.

B I read it in the news, too. 나도 신문에서 읽었어.

14 rainbow
[réinbòu]

ⓝ 무지개

A I saw a rainbow after the rainstorm.
난 폭풍우 후에 무지개를 봤어.

B I couldn't see it because I was inside all day.
난 하루 종일 실내에 있어서 볼 수가 없었어.

15 breeze
[bri:z]

ⓝ 산들바람, 미풍

A There's nothing better than a cool breeze after work.
일 끝난 다음에 시원한 산들바람보다 좋은 것은 없어.

B Yes, it's like I'm in heaven. 응. 마치 천국에 있는 것 같아.

16 cloudy
[kláudi]

ⓝ cloud 구름

ⓐ 흐린, 구름 낀

A It's so cloudy today. 오늘 정말 흐리다.

B I hope it doesn't rain. 비가 안 왔으면 좋겠어.

17 ☑ umbrella
[ʌmbrélə]

ⓝ 우산   **open an umbrella** 우산을 펴다

A It's raining heavily! 비가 정말 많이 왜!

B Oh, no! I forgot to bring my umbrella.
이런! 우산 가져오는 것을 잊어버렸어.

18 ☑ forecast
[fɔ́ːrkæst]

ⓝ 예측, 예보 **ⓥ** 예보하다

     forecast the weather 일기 예보를 하다

A Is it going to rain tomorrow? 내일 비가 올까?

B The weather forecast says it won't.
일기예보에서는 비가 안 온대.

19 ☑ dry
[drai]

ⓐ 마른, 건조한

A The weather has been dry for three weeks.
삼 주 동안 날씨가 건조했어요.

B We should be careful about forest fires.
산불을 조심해야겠어요.

20 ☑ heat
[hiːt]

ⓝ 열, 더위 **ⓥ** 가열하다

A Let's not go outside in the heat.
이 더위에 밖에 나가지 맙시다.

B How about going to the swimming pool?
수영장에 가는 건 어때요?

21 ☑ shine
[ʃain]
ⓐ shiny 빛나는

ⓥ 빛나다, 비치다

A It's such a beautiful day! 오늘 날씨가 너무 좋다!

B Yes, the sun is shining brightly.
응, 해가 밝게 빛나고 있어.

22 wet
[wet]

ⓐ 젖은, 축축한

A I don't like getting my shoes wet on a rainy day. 난 비 오는 날 신발이 젖는 게 싫어.

B Maybe you'd better not go out when it is raining. 아마도 너는 비가 오면 외출을 안 하는 게 낫겠구나.

23 fog
[fɔ(ː)g]
ⓐ foggy 안개가 낀

ⓝ 안개

A I can't see anything because of this fog.
이 안개 때문에 아무것도 안 보여.

B Watch your step! 발 조심해!

24 windy
[windi]

ⓐ 바람이 센, 바람 부는

A Why is your hair in a mess? 왜 머리가 헝클어졌니?

B Because it's very windy outside.
밖에 바람이 아주 세서 그래.

25 in case

~할 경우에   **in case of** ~의 경우에

A Take an umbrella in case it rains.
비가 올 경우를 대비해서 우산을 가져가라.

B I will, thank you. 그렇게 할게. 고마워.

Multi-Meaning Word

thick

ⓐ 두꺼운
I had a **thick** slice of bread with blueberry jam for my lunch.
나는 점심으로 블루베리 잼이 발린 두꺼운 빵 한 조각을 먹었다.

ⓐ 짙은, 진한
The flight for Japan was cancelled because of the **thick** fog.
짙은 안개 때문에 일본행 비행기 운항이 취소되었다.

ⓐ 빽빽한
It can be easy to get lost in the **thick** forest.
울창한 숲에서는 길을 잃기 쉽다.

Word Search

앞에서 배운 어휘를 기억하며 모두 찾아 보세요.

정답

P	X	Y	M	M	O	J	F	W	R	K	C	P	P	W
F	O	R	E	C	A	S	T	A	O	L	C	Y	I	O
R	T	E	R	I	S	E	H	Y	O	M	D	I	N	L
E	A	M	N	P	E	T	L	W	R	N	N	O	H	B
W	E	L	G	I	A	Z	D	E	I	D	S	I	I	T
O	H	G	S	E	H	Y	A	W	J	A	M	C	A	T
H	X	W	W	A	W	S	B	E	E	C	D	J	A	R
S	N	M	R	O	T	S	N	S	R	O	M	I	L	D
E	C	Y	M	Q	W	S	J	S	O	F	V	M	G	S
F	Z	M	Z	K	S	J	I	L	U	N	N	M	Q	D
C	R	E	P	Y	V	E	F	C	R	L	O	W	E	Z
Z	M	Q	E	U	D	K	V	K	Z	B	W	E	T	R
V	B	C	C	R	C	W	F	D	X	S	Z	G	W	N
X	T	N	A	Z	B	Y	C	F	O	G	K	E	W	Z

blow	breeze	dry	flood
fog	forecast	heat	mild
rise	season	shine	shower
storm	thick	wet	windy

Unit 30 Nature

Basic Words

- □ air 대기, 공기
- □ star 별
- □ mountain 산
- □ ground 땅
- □ river 강
- □ sky 하늘
- □ cloud 구름
- □ sand 모래
- □ sun 해
- □ moon 달
- □ sea 바다
- □ dark 어두운

01 natural
[nǽtʃərəl]

ⓝ nature 자연

ⓐ 자연의, 자연스러운

A Where are they taking the bear, Mom?
   엄마, 사람들이 그 곰을 어디로 데려가는 거예요?

B They're taking it back to its natural home.
   자연 서식지로 돌려보내는 거란다.

02 desert
[dézərt]

ⓝ 사막   **the Gobi Desert** 고비사막

A How do animals survive in the desert?
   사막에서 동물들은 어떻게 살아가?

B They mostly live by oases.
   대체로 오아시스를 통해 살아가.

03 soil
[sɔil]

c.f. sand 모래

ⓝ 흙   **rich soil** 기름진 땅

A The flowers in the garden aren't growing well.
   정원에 있는 꽃들이 잘 자라지 않는구나.

B Maybe the soil isn't good. 아마 흙이 좋지 않나 봐요.

04 greenhouse
[gríːnhàus]

ⓝ 온실   **greenhouse effect** 온실 효과

A What causes global warming?
   지구온난화를 일으키는 게 무엇이야?

B The main causes are greenhouse gases.
   주된 원인은 온실 가스야.

05 protect
[prətékt]

ⓝ protection 보호

ⓥ 보호하다

A What can we do to save the earth?
   지구를 살리는 데 우리가 무얼 할 수 있을까?

B I heard many people work together to
   protect the environment.
   내가 듣기로 많은 사람들이 환경을 보호하려고 협력한다고 해.

06 forest
[fɔ́(:)rist]

ⓝ 숲, 산림

A This forest is very nice for a walk.
이 숲은 산책하기에 참 좋아.

B Yes, it's cool even in the summer.
응, 여름에도 시원해.

07 environment
[inváiərənmənt]

ⓐ environmental 환경의

ⓝ 환경, 자연환경

A The natural environment has been changed by human activities.
자연 환경은 인간의 생활에 의해 변화되어 왔어.

B I know. Humans should be aware of that.
나도 알고 있어. 사람들은 그것을 알아야만 해.

08 preserve
[prizə́:rv]

ⓝ preservation 보호, 보존

ⓥ 보호하다, 지키다   **preserve wetlands** 습지대를 보존하다

A We must preserve the environment!
우리는 환경을 보호해야 해!

B Yes, we can't live without the earth!
맞아, 지구 없이는 우리도 살 수 없어!

09 stone
[stoun]

ⓝ 돌, 돌멩이   **trip on a stone** 돌부리에 걸려 넘어지다

A That is a nice castle! 참 멋진 성이구나!

B Yes, the stone walls are so beautiful.
응, 돌 벽이 참 아름다워.

10 pollute
[pəlú:t]

ⓝ pollution 오염

ⓥ 더럽히다, 오염시키다

A Why can't people stop polluting the earth?
사람들은 어째서 지구를 오염시키는 일을 멈추지 못할까요?

B I don't know. 모르겠어.

11 beach
[biːtʃ]

ⓝ 해변, 해안　　　　　　　　　**a sandy beach** 모래사장

A What are you doing this summer?
여름 동안 뭐 할 거니?

B I think I'll go to the beach. 해변에 갈까 해.

12 recycling
[riːsáikliŋ]

ⓥ recycle 재활용하다

ⓝ 재생, 재활용

A Why are there several trash cans?
왜 쓰레기통이 여러 개 있니?

B They are for recycling.
재활용을 위해 있는 거야.

13 destroy
[distrɔ́i]

ⓝ destruction 파괴

ⓥ 파괴하다, 파멸시키다

A Pollution is destroying our earth.
환경오염이 우리의 지구를 파괴하고 있어.

B Yes, it's a serious problem. 맞아, 심각한 문제야.

14 surface
[sə́ːrfis]

ⓝ 표면, 수면

A Isn't the sunset beautiful? 일몰이 참 멋지지 않니?

B Yes, it's like the sun is sitting on the sea
surface. 응, 마치 태양이 해수면 위에 앉아 있는 것 같아.

15 island
[áilənd]

ⓝ 섬　　　　　　　　　**an island country** 섬나라

A Where are you from? 네 고향은 어디니?

B I'm from Jeju Island. 나는 제주도에서 왔어.

16 cliff
[klif]

ⓝ 낭떠러지, 벼랑, 절벽　　　　**a steep cliff** 가파른 절벽

A Wow! This cliff is so beautiful! 와! 이 절벽 참 멋지다!

B Yes, it's one of my favorite places.
응, 내가 가장 좋아하는 곳 중 하나야.

17 trash
[træʃ]

n 쓰레기　　　　　**throw trash away** 쓰레기를 버리다

A What happens to everyday trash?
생활 쓰레기는 어떻게 되니?

B Most of it is buried. 대부분 매장돼.　　* bury : 매장하다

18 effect
[ifékt]

a effective 효과적인

n 효과, 영향　　　　　**have no effect** 아무런 효과가 없다

A Global warming has effects on nature and human life. 지구온난화는 자연과 인간 생활에 영향을 미쳐.

B We should stop global warming.
우리는 지구온난화를 막아야 해.

19 remove
[rimú:v]

n removal 제거

v 옮기다, 제거하다

A If we removed all the cars on the earth, would the air be cleaner?
우리가 지구에 있는 자동차를 모두 없앤다면 공기가 더 깨끗해질까?

B Yes, but that's impossible.
맞아, 하지만 그건 불가능하잖아.

20 coast
[koust]

n 연안, 해안　　　　　**a coast road** 해안 도로

A Let's go to the east coast. I want to see the sunrise. 우리 동해안에 가자. 일출을 보고 싶어.

B That's a good idea. 좋은 생각이야.

21 life
[laif]

pl. lives

n 생명, 생존　　　　　**the origin of life** 생명의 기원

A All the life, from ants to elephants, are so mysterious.
개미부터 코끼리까지 모든 생명체는 너무나 신비로워.

B I totally agree with you. 전적으로 동감이야.

22 ☑ reduce
[ridjúːs]

Ⓥ 줄이다, 축소하다

A What can we do for the environment?
우리는 환경을 위해 무얼 할 수 있나요?

B First, we should reduce the amount of trash.
먼저, 쓰레기의 양을 줄여야 해.

23 ☑ flow
[flou]
(flow-flew-flown)

Ⓥ 흐르다

A Where do all the rivers flow?
강은 모두 어디로 흐르는 건가요?

B They all flow into the sea.
모두 바다로 흘러 들어간단다.

24 ☑ pond
[pɑnd]

Ⓝ 연못

A I heard there used to be a pond here.
내가 듣기로, 예전에는 여기에 연못이 있었대.

B Yes, it was filled up to build a hotel.
응, 호텔을 지으려고 메웠어.

25 ☑ tend
[tend]

Ⓥ 경향이 있다

A People tend to save energy to save money.
사람들은 돈을 아끼려고 에너지를 절약하는 경향이 있어.

B It is one way to protect the environment.
그것은 환경을 보호하는 하나의 방법이야.

Multi-Meaning Word

life

Ⓝ 삶, 생활
What are the big differences between city and country **life**?
도시와 시골 생활에 큰 차이는 무엇일까?

Ⓝ 수명, 목숨
How many **lives** were saved?
몇 사람이 구출되었나?

Ⓝ 활기
She was still full of **life**.
그녀는 여전히 활기에 차 있었다.

Word Search

앞에서 배운 어휘를 기억하며 모두 찾아 보세요.

Unit 30 **Nature**

Y	T	F	E	K	L	P	J	T	X	W	E	W	B	Z
S	E	S	K	N	O	I	S	C	N	B	V	M	H	A
C	O	W	E	L	A	O	X	E	J	M	R	W	D	P
I	Z	I	L	R	C	T	E	T	B	O	E	T	O	Q
C	O	U	L	R	O	I	S	O	E	D	S	R	E	Q
M	T	A	K	P	D	T	O	R	A	W	E	E	D	B
E	A	F	F	I	L	C	M	P	C	W	R	S	N	N
E	C	T	T	E	N	D	A	E	H	A	P	E	A	I
D	F	O	U	E	C	A	F	R	U	S	E	D	L	S
W	N	F	A	R	E	F	I	L	W	C	P	B	S	A
M	I	O	E	S	A	O	A	O	U	R	S	P	I	S
F	J	F	P	C	T	L	L	D	A	K	S	K	U	Y
N	X	V	J	V	T	F	E	S	H	Z	H	G	U	I
Y	F	I	X	X	L	R	H	P	L	O	B	J	J	D

beach	cliff	coast	desert
effect	flow	island	life
pollute	pond	preserve	protect
reduce	soil	surface	tend

Unit 31 Plants & Animals

Basic Words

- animal 동물
- giraffe 기린
- lion 사자
- tiger 호랑이
- zoo 동물원
- tail 꼬리
- monkey 원숭이
- tree 나무
- bird 새
- duck 오리
- fox 여우
- flower 꽃

01 **plant**
[plænt]

ⓝ 식물 ⓥ 심다　　　　　　　**plant trees** 나무를 심다

A What kind of plant is that? 저건 무슨 식물이니?

B It's a tomato plant. 토마토 나무야.

02 **cage**
[keidʒ]

ⓝ 새장, 우리

A Look at that bear. It's so scary.
저 곰 좀 봐. 정말 무섭다.

B I think it looks sad inside that cage.
나는 곰이 우리 속에 있어서 슬퍼 보여.

03 **insect**
[ínsekt]

ⓝ 곤충

A I really hate insects, Jim! 짐. 난 곤충이 정말 싫어!

B But they are so wonderful if you look close
enough, Sally.
하지만, 샐리야, 아주 자세히 보면 아주 멋져.

04 **exist**
[igzíst]
ⓝ existence 존재

ⓥ 존재하다

A I can't believe that big animals like dinosaurs
existed on the earth.
나는 공룡과 같은 큰 동물이 지구 상에 존재했다는 것이 안 믿어져.

B Why did they disappear? 왜 사라진 걸까?

05 **raise**
[reiz]

ⓥ 기르다, 올리다

A My father used to raise cows on his farm.
저희 아버지는 예전에 농장에서 소를 길렀어요.

B What does he do now? 지금은 뭐 하시는데요?

06 **pet**
[pet]

ⓝ 애완동물

A Do you have a pet at home?
집에 애완동물 있니?

B I want a pet snake, but my parents won't let me. 나는 애완용 뱀을 키우고 싶은데 부모님이 허락하지 않으셔.

07 **seed**
[siːd]

ⓝ 씨, 종자, 열매　　　　　　　　**sow seeds** 씨를 뿌리다

A Do you want to try some sunflower seeds?
해바라기 씨 한번 먹어 볼래?

B Are they good? I've never had any.
맛있어? 나 한 번도 안 먹어 봤어.

08 **survive**
[sərvaiv]
ⓝ survival 생존, 살아남음

ⓥ 살아남다

A How do polar bears survive in the cold temperature? 어떻게 북극곰은 추운 온도에서 살아남는 거지?

B A thick layer of fat under their skin keeps them warm. 그들의 두꺼운 피하 지방 층이 그들을 따뜻하게 해 줘.

* layer : 층

09 **beast**
[biːst]

ⓝ 짐승, 동물　　　　　　　　**a wild beast** 야수

A Why is the lion called the king of the beasts?
왜 사자는 동물의 왕이라 불릴까?

B Well, I have no idea. 글쎄, 나도 잘 모르겠는데.

10 **bud**
[bʌd]

ⓝ 꽃봉오리, 싹　　　　　　　　**come into bud** 싹이 트다

A The rose buds survived the cold winter.
장미 꽃봉오리들이 추운 겨울 살아남았구나.

B Yes, they did. New life is born after every winter. 맞아. 매 겨울이 지나면 새로운 생명이 탄생하지.

11 root
[rut]

n 뿌리

A What is the role of plant roots?
식물의 뿌리 역할은 무엇이에요?

B They take in water and food from the soil.
뿌리는 흙에서 물과 양분을 흡수한단다.

12 wild
[waild]

a 야생의, 야만의   **wild animals** 야생 동물

A I heard there was an accident at the zoo.
동물원에서 사고가 났다고 들었어요.

B Yes, one of the wild zebras got loose.
네, 야생 얼룩말 한 마리가 탈출했어요.

13 male
[meil]

ant female 암컷의

a 수컷의, 남성의 **n** 수컷, 남자

A How can you tell a male horse from a female? 수컷 말과 암컷을 어떻게 구분하죠?

B The male and female are different in size.
수컷과 암컷은 크기가 달라.

14 branch
[bræntʃ]

n 나뭇가지   **spread branches** 가지를 뻗다

A Look at the cute koala on the tree branch!
나뭇가지에 있는 귀여운 코알라 좀 봐!

B She is sleeping again. I have never seen a koala awake! 또 자고 있네. 깨어있는 코알라를 본 적이 없어!

15 wing
[wiŋ]

n 날개

A How are birds and airplanes similar?
새와 비행기는 어떻게 닮았을까?

B First of all, they both have wings.
첫째로 둘 다 날개를 가지고 있어.

16 ☑ worm
[wəːrm]

ⓝ 벌레, 기생충

A I found a worm in my sandwich!
내 샌드위치 안에 벌레가 들어 있었어!

B It's better than finding half a worm.
벌레 반쪽만 있는 것보단 낫잖아.

17 ☑ jungle
[dʒʌŋgl]

ⓝ 정글, 밀림

A He traveled through the Amazon jungle when he was young. 그는 젊었을 때 아마존 밀림을 여행했어.

B He must love nature very much.
자연을 굉장히 사랑하나 봐.

18 ☑ leaf
[liːf]
pl. leaves

ⓝ 잎

A Why do the leaves turn red or yellow in fall?
왜 가을에 잎이 빨강이나 노랑으로 변할까?

B It is one of their ways of preparing for winter.
그것이 그들이 겨울을 준비하는 하나의 방법이야.

19 ☑ feed
[fiːd]

ⓥ 먹을 것을 주다, 먹이다

A Don't forget to feed the dog, Frank.
프랭크, 강아지 먹이 주는 거 잊지 마라.

B Yes, Mom. 네, 엄마.

20 ☑ nest
[nest]

ⓝ 둥지, 보금자리

A I found a sparrow nest in the attic.
다락방에 참새 둥지를 발견했어.

B I hope you left it alone. 가만히 놔뒀기를 바라.

21 hatch
[hætʃ]

ⓥ (알을) 까다, 부화하다

A Most birds sit on their eggs until they hatch.
대부분의 새들은 알이 부화할 때까지 품고 있어.

B I guess it's never easy to be a parent.
부모가 되는 일은 절대로 쉽지 않구나.

22 bush
[buʃ]

ⓝ 관목, 수풀, 덤불　　　　**hide in the bush** 덤불에 숨다

A Your front yard looks better with the bushes.
관목이 있으니까 앞마당이 더 보기 좋네요.

B Really? Thank you. 정말이에요? 감사합니다.

23 bloom
[bluːm]

ⓥ (꽃이) 피다 **ⓝ** 꽃　　　　**in full bloom** 활짝 피어

A Do you see the flowers? It's finally spring!
꽃들이 보이니? 드디어 봄이야!

B Yes, they bloomed early this year.
응, 올해는 꽃이 일찍 폈어.

24 mate
[meit]

ⓥ 짝지어주다 **ⓝ** 상대, 배우자

A Is it possible to mate a lion and a tiger?
사자와 호랑이가 짝짓기 하는 게 가능할까?

B Haven't you heard of a liger?
라이거라고 못 들어보았니?

25 species
[spíːʃi(ː)z]
pl. species

ⓝ 종류, 종

A How many species of animals are there on the earth? 지구 상엔 몇 종의 동물이 존재할까?

B Well, more than ten million. 글쎄. 천만 종 이상.

Word Search

정답

앞에서 배운 어휘를 기억하며 모두 찾아 보세요.

W	W	T	I	C	O	M	R	L	T	M	H	X	C	W
L	O	X	T	P	C	X	E	H	S	T	S	F	E	I
H	D	R	X	H	Q	A	P	N	I	L	F	S	A	L
Y	A	J	S	E	F	D	N	C	X	G	I	T	P	D
Y	U	T	G	H	S	U	B	W	E	A	S	F	A	Y
H	L	A	C	Z	K	D	A	R	E	U	S	V	M	
M	C	T	K	H	V	H	D	E	N	H	I	T	B	B
D	E	A	F	R	T	P	J	L	P	G	H	E	P	M
S	Z	D	O	X	U	H	G	G	E	U	A	P	S	A
A	U	O	B	M	E	G	N	N	T	S	L	R	E	K
D	T	Q	L	I	L	T	I	A	T	A	U	M	E	Y
I	E	T	A	M	A	E	W	J	N	J	M	F	D	F
I	V	U	S	K	M	A	E	T	C	X	L	B	Y	V
R	A	S	I	F	L	Q	A	S	L	I	Y	I	Q	X

beast	bush	cage	exist
hatch	leaf	male	mate
nest	pet	plant	raise
root	seed	wild	wing

Word Bubbles

앞에서 배운 어휘를 기억하며 버블을 단어로 채워 보세요.

정답

얼다

빛나다

홍수

Nature
자연

(바람이)불다

예측하다

오염시키다

보호하다

온실

파괴하다

동물

식물, 심다

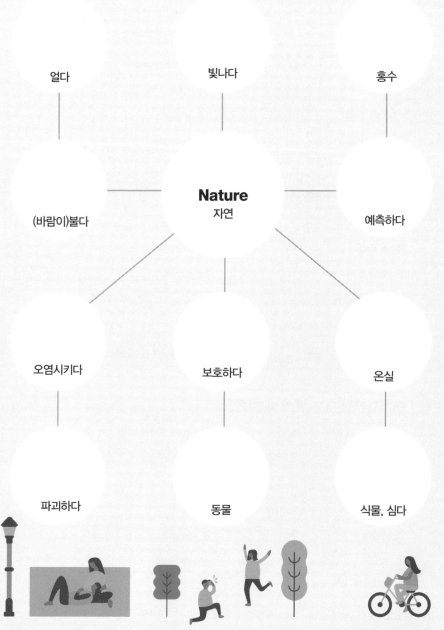

A 우리말을 영어로, 영어를 우리말로 쓰시오.

01 숲, 산림 _____
02 건조한 _____
03 절벽 _____
04 관목, 수풀 _____
05 홍수 _____
06 짐승, 동물 _____
07 파괴하다 _____

08 shower _____
09 pollute _____
10 shine _____
11 tend _____
12 wild _____
13 plant _____
14 climate _____

B 빈칸에 알맞은 단어를 쓰시오.

01 우산을 펴다   open a(n) _____
02 돌부리에 걸려 넘어지다   trap on a(n) _____
03 싹이 트다   come into _____
04 sow seeds   _____을/를 뿌리다
05 a rise in temperature   _____의 상승
06 preserve wetland   습지대를 _____

C 단어의 관계에 맞게 빈칸을 채우시오.

01 두꺼운 : 얇은 = thick : _____
02 존재 : 존재하다 = existence : _____
03 효과, 영향 : 효과적인 = effect : _____
04 fog : foggy = 안개 : _____
05 male : female = 수컷의 : _____
06 soil : sand = 흙 : _____

D 배운 단어를 사용하여 문장을 완성하시오.

01 How did people _____ the Ice Age?

어떻게 사람들은 빙하기를 살아남았을까?

02 The Nile _____ into the Mediterranean Sea.

나일강은 지중해로 흘러 들어간다.

03 How much _____ is produced each day in New York?

뉴욕에서는 하루에 얼마나 많은 쓰레기가 만들어집니까?

04 His shoes and socks became _____ from the rain.

비 때문에 그의 신발과 양말은 축축해졌다.

05 If I cut a(n) _____ off a tree and water it, will it grow into a new tree?

제가 나뭇가지를 꺾어 물을 주면, 새 나무로 자랄까요?

E 빈칸에 알맞은 말을 보기에서 찾아 쓰시오.

| beach | raised | windy | weather | desert |

01 **A** What is the _____ like in winter in Seoul?

B It is cold and _____ .

02 **A** Did you have a good weekend?

B Nothing special, I just went to the _____ for a swim.

03 **A** Why is the _____ so cold at night?

B I'm not sure. It is probably because of the dry air.

04 **A** How long have you _____ the chickens?

B For about ten years.

F 밑줄 친 부분을 우리말로 옮기시오.

01 Wearing a seat belt could save your life in a car accident.

02 Three men went into the thick jungle and never showed up.

VOCA Inn!

외국인은 소리도 다르게 듣는가?

어느 나라 말이나 사물의 소리나 형태를 표현하는 말들이 있다. 이를 의성어, 의태어라고 부른다. 특히, 영어에서 발음하는 소리들은 우리가 알고 있는 그것과 다른 경우가 많다. 자주 사용되는 동물이나 사물의 소리를 알아보자.

★bow wow (yap yap) 개   멍멍 (깽깽)

★mew mew (purr) 고양이   야옹야옹 (그르렁)

★caw caw 까마귀   까악까악

★quack quack 오리   꽥꽥

★moo moo 소   음매

★tweet tweet 새   짹짹

★peep peep 병아리   삐약삐약

★cluck cackle 암탉   꼬꼬

★cock-a-doodle-doo 수탉   꼬끼오

★hoo hoo 부엉이   부엉부엉

★oink oink 돼지   꿀꿀

★chirp chirp 꾀꼬리   꾀꼴꾀꼴

★croak croak 개구리   개굴개굴

★tick tack 시계   째깍째깍

★ting a ring a ring 방울   딸랑딸랑

★pitter patter 소나기   타닥타닥

★crack rumble kabon 번개   번쩍 우르릉 꽝

★ding dong 종   땡땡

★squeak 쥐   찍찍

★z z z z 잠자기   쿨쿨

★pit-a-pat 심장   두근두근

★tap tap 노크   똑똑

★bang bang 총   탕탕

Chapter
10

Places & Motions

Basic Words

□ street 거리	□ road 길	□ country 국가
□ city 도시	□ move 이사하다	□ City Hall 시청
□ busy 바쁜	□ rush hour 혼잡한 시간	□ warehouse 창고
□ tower 탑	□ crowd 사람들, 무리	□ corner 모퉁이, 구석

01 avenue
[ǽvənjùː]

c.f street 거리

ⓝ 대로, 큰 길

A Where's your house? 너희 집 어디에 있어?

B It's the second house on Fifth Avenue.
5번가에 있는 두 번째 집이야.

02 capital
[kǽpitl]

ⓝ 수도, 중심지

A Is your home, Seoul, a big city?
네 고향 서울은 큰 도시니?

B Yes, it's the capital of Korea. 응. 한국의 수도야.

03 suburb
[sʌ́bəːrb]

ⓝ 교외, 근교　　　　　**in a suburb of Paris** 파리 근교에

A What kind of city is Queens?
퀸즈는 어떤 도시인가요?

B It is a suburb of New York. 뉴욕의 근교에요.

04 downtown
[dáuntáun]

ad 시내에, 도심지에

A Weren't you at home last night?
어젯밤에 집에 없었니?

B No, I went downtown to do some shopping.
응. 나 쇼핑 좀 하려고 시내에 갔었어.

05 region
[ríːdʒən]

ⓐ regional 지역의, 지방의

ⓝ 지역, 지대, 지방

A What part of London do you live in, Miss
Margaret? 마가렛 선생님은 런던 어느 지역에 사시나요?

B I live in the northeast region.
저는 북동쪽 지역에 살아요.

06 citizen
[sítəzən]

ⓝ 시민　　　　　**citizens of Seoul** 서울 시민

A What country are you from, sir?
손님, 어느 나라에서 오셨습니까?

B I am a citizen of the Republic of Korea.
저는 대한민국 시민입니다.

07 countryside
[kʌ́ntrisàid]
syn the country 시골

ⓝ 시골, 지방   **live in the countryside** 시골에 살다

A How is the life in the countryside?
시골에서의 생활은 어때?

B It's like having an endless backyard.
끝없는 뒤뜰이 있는 것과도 같지.

08 building
[bildiŋ]
ⓥ build 짓다, 건축하다

ⓝ 건물

A I didn't see that building the last time I was here. 지난번에 여기 왔을 때는 저 건물 못 봤는데.

B They built it last year. 작년에 지었어.

09 settle
[sétl]
ⓝ settlement 정착

ⓥ 자리잡다, 정착하다

A It must be hard to live in a foreign country.
외국에서 사는 건 힘들겠다.

B Only, at first. It's all right after you settle down. 처음에만 그래. 정착한 다음에는 괜찮아.

10 bridge
[brídʒ]

ⓝ 다리, 교량, 육교   **build a bridge** 다리를 건설하다

A Where does this bridge go to?
이 다리가 어디로 이어지나요?

B It goes to San Francisco.
샌프란시스코로 이어집니다.

11 farm
[fɑːrm]
ⓝ farming 농업

ⓝ 농장, 농지   **a farm worker** 농장 노동자

A I heard you were born in the countryside, Sally. 샐리, 너 시골에서 태어났다고 들었어.

B Yes, my dad used to own a huge corn farm.
응, 우리 아빠가 예전에 엄청 큰 옥수수 밭을 가지고 있었어.

12 everywhere
[évriwὲər]

ad 어디에나, 도처에

A There are Starbucks everywhere in this city.
이 도시 어디에나 스타벅스가 있어.

B I know. It's really a global company.
나도 알아. 정말 세계적인 기업이야.

---

13 center
[séntər]

a central 중심의

n 중심, 핵심, 중앙　　　**in the center of** ~의 한 가운데에

A This plaza is the center of city life.
이 쇼핑센터는 도시 생활의 중심이야.

B Are there lots of shops and beautiful cafes
around it? 주위에 많은 상점과 아름다운 카페가 있니?

---

14 square
[skwɛəːr]

n (거리의) 광장, 사각형　　　**a square table** 사각형 테이블

A What is the fastest way to the square?
광장으로 가는 가장 빠른 길이 뭐죠?

B Take a right at the next corner.
다음 모퉁이에서 우회전 하세요.

---

15 rural
[rúərəl]

ant urban 도시의

a 시골의, 지방의　　　**rural life** 전원생활

A What will you do after you quit your job?
일을 그만두고 나서 무엇을 할 거니?

B I want to move to a rural area. I am sick of
city life. 시골 지역으로 이사를 가고 싶어. 도시 생활에 지쳤어.

---

16 highway
[háiwèi]

n 고속도로, 큰길

A How do I get to the airport?
공항에 어떻게 가죠?

B You have to take the highway.
고속도로를 타야 합니다.

17 ☑ **mall**
[mɔːl]

ⓝ 쇼핑센터

A What did you do at the mall today?
오늘 쇼핑센터에서 뭘 했니?

B I bought some clothes and had dinner.
옷을 좀 사고 저녁을 먹었어요.

18 ☑ **map**
[mæp]

ⓝ 지도   **a map of the world** 세계 지도

A I can't find your village on the map.
지도에서 너의 마을을 찾을 수 없어.

B All right, give me the map. 좋아. 지도를 나에게 줘 봐.

19 ☑ **underground**
[ʌndərgràund]

ⓝ 지하 **ⓐ** 지하의, 지하에 있는

A What is that noise coming from
underground? 지하에서 나는 저 소리는 뭐지?

B The city is building a new subway station.
시에서 새로운 지하철역을 짓고 있어.

20 ☑ **roadway**
[róudwèi]

ⓝ 도로, 차로

A It's hard to drive on such a narrow roadway.
이렇게 좁은 도로에서 운전하려니까 힘들어.

B At least it's not a dirt road.
적어도 비포장도로는 아니잖아.

21 ☑ **sidewalk**
[sáidwɔ̀ːk]

ⓝ (포장된) 보도, 인도

A Why is this sign blocking the sidewalk?
왜 이 표지판이 인도를 막고 있나요?

B There has been an accident.
사고가 있었습니다.

22 local
[lóukəl]

ⓐ 지방의, 한 지방 특유의   **local food** 지역 음식

A I read your interview. 당신의 인터뷰를 읽었습니다.

B It was only in a local newspaper.
지방 신문에 실렸을 뿐이었는데요.

---

23 field
[fiːld]

ⓝ 들판, 벌판

A I love to walk through the green grass fields.
난 초록 잔디 늘판을 걷는 것이 정말 좋아.

B I also like the smell of green fields.
나는 초록 들판 냄새도 좋더라.

---

24 crowded
[kráudid]

ⓝ crowd 군중, 다수

ⓐ 붐빈, 혼잡한

A Why do you always drive your car to work?
너는 왜 항상 출근할 때 차를 몰고 오니?

B Because the bus is always crowded.
왜냐하면 버스는 항상 혼잡하기 때문이야.

---

25 into
[íntu/íntə]

prep 안으로   **go into the house** 집안으로 들어가다

A Where can I find an ATM?
어디서 현금자동입출금기를 찾을 수 있죠?   * ATM : 현금자동입출금기

B Walk into this building and you will see it.
이 건물 안으로 들어가면 볼 수 있습니다.

 **Multi-Meaning Word**

capital

ⓝ 수도
What's the **capital** of Canada?
캐나다의 수도가 어디지?

ⓝ 대문자
Please fill in your name and address in **capitals**.
이름과 주소를 대문자로 채우세요.

ⓝ 자본, 원금
He lost both **capital** and interest.
그는 원금과 이자를 모두 잃었다.

Word Search

앞에서 배운 어휘를 기억하며 모두 찾아 보세요.

정답

Unit 32 Country & City

```
C G C Z L S E T T L E D E R A
W I G H B R I D G E L T E T V
L A T K O Z V B K E I T Y B G
N O K I F W U Z I X N L E M T
U P C F Z A D F R E T A W A U
P Q L A L E D E C U S T D L O
Y B A D L O N O D T Q I A L Z
T H I S I D E W A L K P O W A
N N A P E L K X B K L A R V Q
G O E G J R R R X R Q C E R L
R F I C H K A E S W U N L A M
D V U G C W D U C G U B R A R
V X H X E R A G Q E W U U N A
M A P V Z R O Y C S R J C S F
```

avenue	bridge	capital	center
citizen	farm	field	local
mall	map	region	rural
settle	sidewalk	square	suburb

Basic Words

□ peace 평화　　　　□ Pacific 태평양　　　　□ Europe 유럽

□ America 아메리카　□ Asia 아시아　　　　　□ Africa 아프리카

□ Oceania 오세아니아　□ Atlantic 대서양　　　□ Indian Ocean 인도양

□ Earth 지구　　　　□ war 전쟁　　　　　　□ tribe 부족

01 abroad
[əbrɔ́ːd]

ad 외국에, 해외에   **go abroad** 외국에 가다

A My dream is to travel through Europe.
내 꿈은 유럽을 여행하는 거야.

B Me, too. I have never been abroad.
나도 그래. 나 해외에 나가본 적이 없어.

02 border
[bɔ́ːrdər]

n 테두리, 경계, 국경

A The border between Korea and China has changed throughout history.
역사 속에서 한국과 중국의 국경이 변화해왔어.

B Yes, it was further north during the Koguryo Dynasty. 응. 고구려 왕조 때는 더 북쪽이었지.

03 global
[glóubəl]

n globe 지구, 세계

a 전 세계의, 지구의

A Environmental pollution is becoming a global problem. 환경 오염은 전 세계적인 문제가 되고 있어.

B We should do what we can.
우리는 우리가 할 수 있는 것을 해야 해.

04 international
[ìntərnǽʃənəl]

ad internationally
국제적으로

a 국제적인, 국가 간의

A It's important to keep a friendly relationship with other countries.
다른 나라와 우호적인 관계를 유지하는 것은 중요해.

B Yes, international relationships are getting more complex. 응. 국제 관계는 점점 복잡해지고 있어.

05 extend
[iksténd]

v 연장하다, 확장하다

A How long will you stay in Korea?
한국에 얼마나 오래 머물거니?

B I have another month. I decided to extend my stay. 한 달 더 남았어. 머무르는 시간을 연장하기로 결정했거든.

06 foreign
[fɔ́(:)rin]
ⓝ foreigner 외국인

ⓐ 외국의, 외국산의　　　　**a foreign country** 외국

A Do you speak any foreign languages?
외국어를 할 줄 아십니까?

B I speak Chinese and Italian.
저는 중국어와 이탈리아어를 합니다.

---

07 unite
[juːnáit]
ⓝ unity 단결, 일치

ⓥ 결합하다, 합치다　　　　**unite into one** 합쳐서 하나가 되다

A Several people united to preserve the environment. 여러 사람이 환경을 보호하기 위해 힘을 합쳤어.

B I want to take part, too. 나도 동참하고 싶어.

---

08 race
[reis]

ⓝ 인종, 민족

A It's hard to tell the difference between the races of westerners.
서양인들의 인종을 구별하는 것은 참 어려워.

B We feel the same about Asians.
우리도 동양인에 대해서 그렇게 느껴.

---

09 invade
[invéid]
ⓝ invasion 침입, 침략

ⓥ 침입하다, 침략하다

A When did the Second World War break out?
언제 세계 2차 대전이 발발했니?

B It was 1939 when Germany invaded Poland.
독일이 폴란드를 침략한 1939년이야.

---

10 polar
[póulər]

ⓐ 극의, 극지의

A Why is global warming such a problem?
지구온난화가 왜 그렇게 문제가 되니?

B Because if ice in polar regions melts, it can change our climate.
극지방의 얼음이 녹으면 기후 변화를 일으킬 수 있기 때문이야.

11 earth
[ə:rθ]

n 지구

A How many planets are in the solar system?
태양계에는 몇 개의 행성이 있니?

B There are eight planets and the earth is the third one. 여덟 개의 행성이 있고 지구가 태양에서 세 번째야.

12 official
[əfíʃəl]

a 공식적인 **n** 공무원

A Where did you hear that news?
그 소식 어디서 들었어?

B I visited their official website.
그 쪽의 공식 웹사이트에 들어갔었어.

13 ocean
[óuʃən]

n 대양, 해양   **the Pacific Ocean** 태평양

A What did you do this summer? 올 여름에 뭘 했니?

B I went to see the ocean. 바다를 보러 갔어요.

14 nation
[néiʃən]

a national 국가의, 민족의

n 국가, 민족   **Western nations** 서방 국가들

A How many nations are in the UN?
국제 연합에는 몇 개 국가가 소속돼 있습니까?

B There are 193. 193개국이 있습니다.

15 native
[néitiv]

a 토착의, 본국의; 본래의

A You speak English well like a native speaker.
영어를 원어민처럼 잘하네요.

B That's because I was born in England.
그건 제가 영국에서 태어났기 때문이에요.

16 aid
[eid]

n 원조 **v** 원조하다, 돕다

A Many counties give food aid to Africa.
많은 국가들이 아프리카에 식량 원조를 하고 있어.

B Is there any way for us to help hungry Africans?
우리가 굶주린 아프리카인을 도와줄 수 있는 방법이 없을까?

17 continent
[kántənənt]

ⓝ 대륙, 육지   **the Old Continent** 구대륙(유럽)

A Which of the seven continents have you
been to? 일곱 개의 대륙 중 어느 곳을 가봤니?

B I have been to Asia, North America, and
Africa. 아시아, 북미 그리고 아프리카에 가봤어.

---

18 spread
[spred]
(spread-spread-spread)

ⓥ 퍼지다, 퍼뜨리다

A Where did that virus spread from?
그 바이러스는 어디서 퍼진 건가요?

B Experts are researching at this moment.
전문가들이 현재 연구 중입니다.

---

19 common
[kámən]

ⓐ 공통의, 공동의   **a common language** 공통 언어

A What is the most common concern of the
world's people?
세상 사람들의 가장 큰 공통 관심사는 무엇일까?

B Probably, protecting the environment.
아마도, 환경 보호하는 거.

---

20 rotate
[róuteit]

ⓥ 회전하다, 교대하다

A The earth rotates once every 24 hours.
지구는 스물 네 시간마다 한 번씩 회전해.

B That's why we have a day and a night.
그것 때문에 낮과 밤이 있는 거구나.

---

21 history
[hístəri]

ⓐ historic 역사의

ⓝ 역사, 역사학   **Korean history** 한국 역사

A I am very interested in world history, so I
often watch the History Channel.
난 세계 역사에 관해서 관심이 많아서 종종 히스토리 채널을 봐.

B You do? I like it, too. 그래? 나도 좋아하는데.

22 ☑ tropical
[trɑ́pikəl]

ⓐ 열대지방의, 열대산의 tropical plants 열대 식물

A Where do you want to travel?
어디로 여행을 가고 싶나요?

B I want to visit a tropical island.
열대 섬을 방문해보고 싶어요.

23 ☑ peaceful
[píːsfəl]

ⓝ peace 평화

ⓐ 평화로운, 태평한

A When can we live in a peaceful world?
언제면 우리가 평화로운 세상에서 살 수 있을까?

B After all the wars are over. 모든 전쟁이 끝나고 난 후.

24 ☑ worldwide
[wə́ːrldwáid]

ad 전 세계로 ⓐ 세계적인, 세계 속의
worldwide success 전세계적인 성공

A My dream is to introduce Korea worldwide.
내 꿈은 전 세계로 한국을 소개하는 거야.

B Good luck! 행운을 빌어!

25 ☑ combination
[kɑ̀mbənéiʃən]

ⓥ combine 결합하다

ⓝ 결합

A Why is America also called the United States? 미국을 왜 미합중국이라고 부르기도 하나요?

B That is because America is a combination of 50 different states.
그것은 미국이 50개 다른 주의 결합이기 때문이란다.

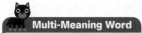
Multi-Meaning Word

race

ⓝ 경주
He will be the youngest runner in the **race**.
그는 경주에 참가한 가장 어린 선수일 것이다.

ⓥ 경주하다
Let's **race** to the end of the road.
도로 끝까지 경주를 하자.

ⓝ 인종, 종족
This event will unite people of all **races,** ages, and genders.
이 행사는 모든 인종과 연령, 그리고 성별의 사람들을 화합시킬 것이다.

Word Search

앞에서 배운 어휘를 기억하며 모두 찾아 보세요.

정답

```
W  T  N  Z  N  T  E  S  W  K  E  P  B  M  I
F  A  K  J  V  A  G  T  N  N  O  M  M  O  C
E  A  R  T  H  T  T  M  I  G  R  R  D  K  G
D  M  Z  A  M  P  L  I  M  N  I  A  A  I  E
Y  R  O  T  S  I  H  A  V  D  U  E  L  C  A
E  L  R  W  R  H  E  B  B  E  A  I  R  O  E
M  Q  F  K  A  W  A  L  O  O  N  E  N  O  T
T  R  O  P  I  C  A  L  U  R  L  A  R  D  F
K  B  U  O  V  Z  K  D  N  F  D  G  E  T  S
O  I  H  Z  L  X  Y  U  N  E  E  E  X  E  S
E  O  F  F  I  C  I  A  L  E  T  C  R  R  O
J  C  A  X  M  P  N  W  N  Y  T  I  A  L  M
A  B  R  O  A  D  V  U  I  K  L  X  O  E  G
E  T  A  T  O  R  R  O  O  E  I  T  E  N  P
```

abroad	aid	border	common
earth	extend	foreign	global
history	native	official	peaceful
race	rotate	tropical	unite

Unit 34 Movements

01 **shake**
[ʃeik]

ⓥ 흔들다　　　　　　　　**shake hands** 악수하다

A The apples are too high on the tree.
사과가 나무의 너무 높은 곳에 있어.

B Try shaking the branches. 나뭇가지를 흔들어 봐.

02 **nod**
[nɑd]

ⓥ (고개를) 끄덕이다

A Just nod when you're ready.
준비되면 머리만 끄덕이면 돼.

B Okay, I will. 알았어. 그렇게 할게.

03 **spill**
[spíl]

ⓥ 쏟다, 엎지르다

A Do you have a towel? I spilled juice on my shirt. 수건 있어요? 셔츠에 주스를 쏟았어요.

B Yes, wait for a minute. 네, 잠깐만 기다리세요.

04 **bend**
[bend]

ⓥ 굽히다, 구부러지다　　　　**bend over** 허리를 구부리다

A You have to bend your knees when you shoot. 슛할 때 무릎을 구부려야 해.

B Oh, basketball is so hard. 아, 농구는 정말 어렵다.

05 **movement**
[múːvmənt]
ⓥ move 움직이다

ⓝ 운동, 활동, 움직임

A Body movements are important when we communicate. 의사소통할 때 신체의 움직임은 중요해.

B They help people express their thoughts.
그것들은 사람들이 생각을 표현하는 데 도움을 줘.

06 **point**
[pɔint]

ⓥ 가리키다, 지목하다

A What do you call the finger you point with?
물건을 가리킬 때 쓰는 손가락을 뭐라고 하니?

B It's called the forefinger. 집게손가락이라고 불러.

07 ☑ throw
[θróu]
(throw-threw-thrown)

ant catch 받다

V 던지다, 버리다

A Never throw things at people!
절대로 물건을 사람에게 던지면 안 돼!

B I'm sorry. I didn't mean to.
죄송해요. 일부러 그런 것은 아니에요.

08 ☑ lean
[liːn]

V 기대다, 의지하다　　**lean against the wall** 벽에 기대다

A You shouldn't lean against the door on the
subway. 지하철에서 출입문에 기대면 안 돼.

B You're right. I could get hurt.
네 말이 맞아. 다칠 수도 있어.

09 ☑ hurry
[hə́ːri]

N 서두름 **V** 서두르다

A I think people these days are in too much of
a hurry. 나는 요즘 사람들이 너무 서두른다고 생각해.

B Me, too. They need more rest.
나도 그렇게 생각해. 그들에겐 더 많은 휴식이 필요해.

10 ☑ clap
[klæp]

V 손뼉을 치다

A How will I know when you're ready?
네가 준비됐는지 어떻게 알지?

B I'll clap my hands twice. 내가 손뼉을 두 번 칠게.

11 ☑ appear
[əpíər]

ant disappear 사라지다

V 나타나다, 출현하다

A Where did the magician appear from?
마술사가 어디서 나타났니?

B Where is he? I can't see him.
그가 어디 있니? 난 안 보이는데.

12 rush
[rʌʃ]

n 돌진, 급습 **v** 돌진하다, 급하게 행동하다

A Why are you in such a rush? 왜 그렇게 급해?

B I'm late for school. 학교에 늦었어요.

13 escape
[iskéip]

v 벗어나다, 달아나다   **escape from prison** 탈옥하다

A It's so nice to be on the beach!
해변에 오니 너무 좋구나!

B Yes, we really need to escape from the city.
응. 우린 정말 도시에서 벗어나야 해.

14 cover
[kʌ́vər]

v 덮다, 감추다, 싸다   **cover one's face** 얼굴을 가리다

A Why is the floor covered with newspapers?
왜 바닥이 신문으로 덮여 있습니까?

B I was planning to paint the wall today.
오늘 벽을 페인트칠할 계획이었습니다.

15 still
[stil]

a 정지한, 움직이지 않는   **still life** 정물화

A A bee is on my left shoulder! Do something!
벌이 내 왼쪽 어깨에 있어! 어떻게 좀 해 봐!

B Sit still until it flies away.
날아갈 때까지 움직이지 말고 앉아있어.

16 march
[maːrtʃ]

v 행진하다, 행군하다

    march along the street 거리를 행진하다

A Why is this street closed off?
이 도로가 왜 통제됐습니까?

B The soldiers will march down here soon.
곧 군인들이 여기로 행진할 겁니다.

17 ☑ wave
[weiv]

Ⓥ 흔들다, 물결치게 하다 **wave one's arms** 팔을 흔들다

A I can't find him among all these people.
이 사람들 사이에서 그를 찾을 수 없어.

B Look! He is waving to us.
봐! 그가 우리에게 손을 흔들고 있어.

18 ☑ grab
[græb]

Ⓥ 부여잡다, 움켜잡다

A How did you get that doll? They were all sold out. 그 인형 어떻게 구했니? 품절이었는데.

B I grabbed the last one. 마지막 남은 한 개를 움켜잡았지.

19 ☑ hug
[hʌg]

Ⓝ 포옹 Ⓥ 꼭 껴안다 **hug each other** 서로 껴안다

A Come here and give me a hug.
이리 와서 나를 안아줘.

B No, not in front of other people.
안 돼, 다른 사람들 앞에서는 안 돼.

20 ☑ release
[rilíːs]

Ⓥ 풀어 놓다, 석방하다

A The mall is full of people. Don't release my hand, Dan. 쇼핑몰이 사람들로 꽉 찼구나. 댄, 내 손을 놓지 마라.

B I won't, Mom. 알았어요, 엄마.

21 ☑ crawl
[krɔːl]

Ⓥ 기어가다, 포복하다

A Watch your step! A worm is crawling on the ground. 발 조심해! 땅에 벌레가 기어가고 있어.

B I almost stepped on it and I would have killed it. 밟아서 죽일 뻔했어.

22 knock
[nɑk]

V 치다, 두드리다　　**knock on the door** 문을 두드리다

A You should knock before you enter.
들어오기 전에 노크를 해야지.

B Excuse me. 미안해.

23 twist
[twist]

V 뒤틀다, 비틀다

A What happened to your leg? 다리가 왜 그래?

B I twisted my ankle while hiking.
등산 중에 발목이 뒤틀렸어.

24 press
[pres]

V 누르다, 밀다

A How do I turn the TV off?
TV를 끄려면 어떻게 해야 하나요?

B Simply press this button.
이 버튼을 누르기만 하면 됩니다.

25 tie
[tai]

V 매다, 묶다　　**tie a ribbon** 리본을 묶다

A Teddy, tie your shoelaces before you go.
테디, 나가기 전에 신발끈을 묶어라.

B Okay, Mom. I will. 네, 엄마. 그럴게요.

Multi-Meaning Word

still

a 정지한
Diana stood **still** without saying a word.
다이애나는 한 마디도 안 한 채 가만히 서 있었다.

a 말 없는, 조용한
Still waters run deep. 고요한 물이 깊이 흐른다.

ad 여전히
Even though his brain is badly injured, he is **still** alive.
그의 뇌에 심한 부상을 입었지만, 그는 아직도 살아있다.

ad 훨씬
Two heads are **still** better than one.
혼자보다 두 사람의 머리가 낫다. (백지장도 맞들면 낫다.)

Word Search

앞에서 배운 어휘를 기억하며 모두 찾아 보세요.

Y	F	T	W	I	S	T	C	N	H	U	R	R	Y	K
E	T	A	H	S	D	K	L	L	O	O	L	U	I	N
L	L	G	B	N	R	P	I	A	A	D	E	X	Y	O
U	U	R	E	C	S	U	J	B	I	P	A	X	D	C
H	P	B	R	T	Z	T	S	P	M	P	N	N	S	K
R	T	A	M	R	M	P	E	H	L	O	S	R	P	Y
W	S	W	S	Z	Q	O	J	R	B	S	T	I	L	L
L	Z	A	O	R	E	V	O	C	P	A	J	L	S	G
V	W	P	X	R	G	F	Z	I	W	E	R	A	W	B
C	G	O	J	G	H	U	S	W	E	A	U	G	O	U
G	C	I	C	Y	S	T	N	Z	H	B	V	Q	J	B
E	F	N	B	Q	X	R	Q	E	P	X	H	E	L	O
D	I	T	S	H	A	E	Q	N	G	T	G	W	C	Y
R	V	T	T	U	E	R	J	N	M	Z	X	R	Y	Y

bend	clap	cover	grab
hug	hurry	knock	lean
nod	point	rush	still
throw	tie	twist	wave

Unit 35 Directions & Locations

Basic Words

- □ up 위쪽으로
- □ high 높은
- □ down 아래로
- □ low 낮은
- □ south 남쪽
- □ east 동쪽
- □ west 서쪽
- □ north 북쪽
- □ in front of ~의 앞쪽에
- □ by ~옆에
- □ alongside 나란히
- □ on ~위에

01 surround

[səráund]

ⓥ 둘러싸다, 에워싸다

A I had a hard time finding his house.
그의 집을 찾느라 애를 먹었어.

B I know why. His house is surrounded by tall trees. 이유를 알겠다. 그의 집은 큰 나무로 둘러싸여 있지.

02 above

[əbʌ́v]

prep ~의 위에, 보다 높이

A Which light was out? 어떤 전구가 나갔지?

B The one above the kitchen table.
식탁 위쪽에 있는 거.

03 inside

[ínsáid]

ant outside 밖에, 외부에

ad 내부에, 안쪽에

A Oh, no! The door is locked! 오, 안 돼! 문이 잠겼잖아!

B Did you leave your keys inside?
너 열쇠를 안에 두고 왔니?

04 beyond

[bijánd]

prep ~을 넘어서

A What is there beyond the universe?
우주 너머엔 뭐가 있을까?

B Maybe, there is another universe.
아마도 또 다른 하나의 우주가 있지 않을까.

05 direction

[dirékʃən]

ⓥ direct 가리키다

ⓝ 방향, 방위

A Fly the kite east before the wind changes direction! 바람이 방향을 바꾸기 전에 연을 동쪽으로 날려!

B Which way is east? 어느 쪽이 동쪽이야?

06 behind

[biháind]

prep ~뒤에

A How did you do that card trick?
그 카드 마술 어떻게 한 거야?

B I was hiding a card behind my hand.
내 손 뒤에 카드를 숨기고 있었어.

07 beside
[biséid]

prep ~ 옆에

A Who is that girl sitting beside Joshua?
조슈아 옆에 앉아 있는 여자애 누구야?

B I don't know. She must be a new student.
모르겠어. 전학생인가 봐.

08 below
[bilóu]

prep ~보다 아래에

A Did you see your test scores? 네 시험 점수 확인했니?

B Yes, they were below the class average.
응. 반 평균보다 낮아.

09 bottom
[bátəm]

n 밑, 바닥   **the bottom line** 핵심, 요점

A What happened to the *Titanic*?
타이타닉 호는 어떻게 되었어요?

B It sank to the bottom of the sea.
바다의 밑바닥에 가라 앉았단다.

10 hang
[hæŋ]
(hang-hung-hung)

v 걸다, 매달다

A Mr. Patrick, where can I hang my coat?
패트릭 선생님, 코트 어디에 걸면 되나요?

B There's a coat hanger on the door.
문에 옷걸이가 있어.

11 draw
[drɔː]
(draw-drew-drawn)

v 당기다

A How did you know I was cooking?
내가 요리하고 있는 것을 어떻게 알았어?

B I was drawn by the smell. 냄새가 나를 끌어 당겼어.

12 ☑ **follow**
[fálou]

Ⓥ 따라가다, 따르다

A How can I get to the radio station?
라디오 방송국에 가려면 어떻게 해야 하죠?

B Follow me. 저를 따라오세요.

---

13 ☑ **turn**
[təːrn]

Ⓥ 회전하다, 돌리다 **Ⓝ** 회전, 순번　　**by turns** 교대로

A Honey, can you turn the car around?
여보, 차를 돌릴 수 있어?

B Why? Did you leave something at home?
왜? 집에 두고 온 것 있어?

---

14 ☑ **position**
[pəzíʃən]

Ⓝ 위치, 입장　　**the position of the town** 마을의 위치

A Why doesn't a submarine sink?
잠수함은 왜 가라앉지 않아?

B It keeps air inside to hold a certain position.
일정한 위치를 유지하기 위해 함 내에 공기를 가지고 있어.

---

15 ☑ **under**
[ʌndər]

prep 아래에, 밑에　　**under the sea** 바다 속에

A Where did you find this book?
이 책을 어디서 찾았어?

B It was under the bed. 침대 밑에 있었어.

---

16 ☑ **place**
[pleis]

Ⓝ 장소, 곳 **Ⓥ** 두다
place a book on the table 책을 탁자 위에 두다

A Do you remember this bridge? 이 다리 기억해?

B Sure. This is the place we met first.
그럼. 우리가 처음 만난 곳이잖아.

17 **left**
[left]
ant right 오른쪽의

ⓐ 왼쪽의, 왼편의　　　　　　　**the left hand** 왼손

A Where is the grocery store?
식료품점이 어디 있나요?

B It is on the left of the movie theater.
영화관의 왼쪽에 있습니다.

---

18 **middle**
[mídl]

ⓐ 한가운데의, 중간의　　**in the middle of ~** ~의 한가운데

A Where is Las Vegas? 라스베이거스는 어디에 있나요?

B It is located in the middle of a desert.
사막 한 가운데에 위치해 있어요.

---

19 **along**
[əlɔ́ːŋ]

prep ~을 따라　　　　　**along the river** 강을 따라

A Come along with me. You don't want to get
lost. 자 나를 따라 와. 길을 잃고 싶진 않지.

B Where are we going, grandpa?
할아버지, 우리 어디로 가는 건가요?

---

20 **drop**
[drɑp]

ⓥ 떨어뜨리다, 내리다　　**drop one's head** 고개를 떨구다

A Why is the floor covered in water?
왜 바닥에 물이 흥건하지?

B I dropped the bucket.
내가 양동이를 떨어뜨렸어.

---

21 **toward(s)**
[təwɔ́ːrd]

prep ~ 쪽으로, ~로 향하여

A Where is the post office? 우체국이 어디 있나요?

B Walk towards City Hall, and you will find the
post office. 시청 쪽으로 걸어가면 우체국이 있을 것입니다.

22 opposite
[ápəzit]

ad ~의 맞은편에 **a** 맞은편의, 정반대의

A Where is the bank?
은행이 어디에 있죠?

B It is opposite the police station.
경찰서 맞은편에 있습니다.

23 lift
[líft]

v 들어 올리다 **n** 승강기

A I can't lift this machine. It's too heavy.
이 기계를 들어 올릴 수 없어. 너무 무거워.

B That's why it has wheels. 그래서 바퀴가 달려 있는 거야.

24 locate
[lóukeit]

n location 장소, 위치

v 위치하다, 위치를 정하다

A Where is the hospital? 병원이 어디 있죠?

B The hospital is located next to the park.
병원은 공원 옆에 위치해 있어요.

25 through
[θrú:]

prep ~을 통하여, ~을 뚫고

A Will you take a walk through the forest with me? 나와 함께 숲을 통과해 산책을 할래?

B Only if we get back before dark.
어두워지기 전에 돌아올 수 있다면.

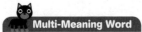
Multi-Meaning Word

turn

v 회전시키다, 돌리다

Turn your head around and look back.
고개를 돌려 뒤를 돌아보라.

v 뒤엎다

Turn your hand so the palm faces downward.
손을 뒤집어서 손바닥이 아래를 향하도록 해 봐.

n 순번, 차례

Wait for your **turn**.
너의 차례를 기다려.

Word Search

앞에서 배운 어휘를 기억하며 모두 찾아 보세요.

정답

I	K	F	W	P	D	V	D	R	S	Q	Z	B	F	K
N	Y	C	Z	O	D	N	X	M	G	V	E	X	Y	U
S	R	G	N	R	I	T	E	Z	U	H	W	J	E	V
I	F	V	Q	D	R	B	N	Y	I	O	T	H	L	L
D	T	B	V	O	E	E	O	N	E	B	R	F	X	N
E	R	F	A	R	C	R	D	T	L	B	K	R	E	Z
W	E	E	I	J	T	C	V	F	T	O	D	P	U	L
O	D	I	N	L	I	Z	B	M	P	L	C	R	V	S
L	N	E	H	Y	O	N	I	E	B	L	M	A	A	D
L	U	A	D	G	N	D	R	P	L	S	A	I	T	W
O	L	L	A	I	D	G	S	U	A	O	L	C	V	E
F	Y	O	K	L	T	M	N	T	T	O	W	S	E	D
E	J	N	E	N	L	E	L	A	G	V	X	I	E	P
B	M	G	D	R	D	L	B	P	H	O	D	U	X	W

along	behind	below	direction
draw	drop	follow	hang
inside	left	lift	locate
middle	place	turn	under

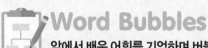

수도

대로, 큰 길

지방의

Places & Motions
장소와 이동

도시

시골

세계

굽히다,
구부러지다

~보다 아래에

인종, 민족

기대다, 의지하다

~보다 위에

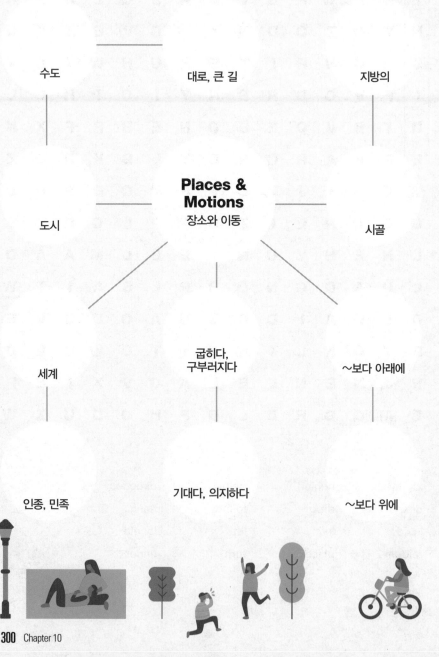

A 우리말을 영어로, 영어를 우리말로 쓰시오.

01 기대다   _____   08 shake   _____

02 국경, 테두리   _____   09 downtown   _____

03 위치하다   _____   10 highway   _____

04 극의, 극지의   _____   11 settle   _____

05 서두르다   _____   12 tropical   _____

06 어디에나, 도처에   _____   13 spread   _____

07 교외, 근교   _____   14 countryside   _____

B 빈칸에 알맞은 단어를 쓰시오.

01 집안으로 들어가다   go _____ the house

02 탈옥하다   _____ from prison

03 외국   a(n) _____ country

04 march along the street   거리를 _____

05 citizens of Seoul   서울 _____

06 a common language   _____ 언어

C 단어의 관계에 맞게 빈칸을 채우시오.

01 지대, 지방 : 지역의, 지방의 = region : _____

02 평화스런 : 평화 = peaceful : _____

03 움직임 : 움직이다 = movement : _____

04 building : build = 건물 : _____

05 throw : catch = 던지다 : _____

06 combination : combine = 결합 : _____

D 배운 단어를 사용하여 문장을 완성하시오. (필요하면 형태를 바꾸시오.)

01 The _____ is the home of about 1.8 million species of creatures. 지구는 약 백팔십만 종의 생물체의 안식처이다.

02 _____ connects the past to the present.
역사는 과거를 현재와 연결시켜준다.

03 People _____ their hands when the singer appeared on the stage. 가수가 무대에 오르자, 사람들은 박수를 쳤다.

04 The city was so _____ because of the New Year Festival.
신년 축제 때문에 도시는 정말 붐볐다.

05 I _____ coffee on my computer yesterday.
나는 어제 내 컴퓨터에 커피를 쏟았다.

E 빈칸에 알맞은 말을 보기에서 찾아 쓰시오.

follow	abroad	knocking	map	opposite

01 A Can you tell me where the bank is?
   B Oh, I'm on my way there, too. Just _____ me.

02 A Someone is _____ on the door.
   B It must be James.

03 A Have you ever been _____?
   B Yes, I have. I went to some places in Europe.

04 A I think we are lost.
   B The _____ says the train station is in the _____ direction.

F 밑줄 친 부분을 우리말로 옮기시오.

01 We use <u>capitals</u> at the beginning of a sentence.

02 It was <u>my turn to wash the dishes</u>, but suddenly we decided to go out.

Chapter
11

Society

Unit 36 Society

Basic Words

- □ join 가입하다
- □ person 개인
- □ world 세계
- □ network 네트워크(통신망)
- □ club 동호회
- □ help 돕다
- □ group 단체, 그룹
- □ connect 연결하다
- □ meet 만나다
- □ town (소)도시
- □ manner 태도
- □ persuade 설득하다

01 folk
[fouk]

ⓐ 민속의, 민간의   **folk music** 민속 음악

A What do Koreans do when they catch a cold? 한국 사람들은 감기에 걸리면 어떻게 하니?

B A popular folk remedy is to drink green tea.
유명한 민간요법으로 녹차를 마셔.

02 master
[mǽstər]

ant servant 하인

ⓝ 주인, 대가, 거장 **ⓥ** 숙달하다

A Master, I will grant you three wishes. What would you like?
주인님, 제가 세 가지 소원을 들어드리겠습니다. 무엇을 원하십니까?

B I wish I were a princess.
내가 공주였으면 좋겠어.

03 general
[dʒénərəl]

ad generally 일반적으로

ⓐ 일반의, 대체적인

A Why do you want to be a reporter, Mr. Mark?
마크 씨, 왜 기자가 되고 싶나요?

B I want to inform the general public about the truth. 일반 대중에게 진실을 알리고 싶습니다.

04 slave
[sleiv]

ⓝ slavery 노예 제도

ⓝ 노예

A This is so unfair. We shouldn't be treated as slaves. 이건 너무 불공평해. 우리는 노예 취급을 받아서는 안 돼.

B I agree. Let's go talk to the boss.
나도 그렇게 생각해. 사장님하고 이야기하러 가자.

05 president
[prézidənt]

ⓝ 대통령, 장관, 의장

A I thought the king of England was like a president. 나는 영국의 왕이 대통령 같은 것인 줄 알았어.

B No, but the royal family is an important symbol of England.
아냐. 하지만, 왕족은 영국의 중요한 상징이지.

06 develop
[divéləp]

n development
발달, 발전

V 발달시키다, 발전시키다

A Why do you want to study in Europe?
왜 유럽에서 공부하고 싶니?

B That is because many countries in Europe are more developed.
그것은 유럽에 있는 많은 나라들이 더 발전했기 때문이야.

07 duty
[djú:ti]

n 의무　　　　　　　　**do one's duty** 의무를 다하다

A Thank you, officer! 감사합니다, 경찰관님!

B I'm just doing my duty, ma'am.
부인, 제 의무일 따름입니다.

08 social
[sóuʃəl]

n society 사회

a 사회의, 사회적인

A Recently, health has become a major social issue in Korea.
최근에 한국에서 건강은 중요한 사회적인 이슈가 되었어.

B I guess it's because health is so important.
건강이 매우 중요하기 때문일 거야.

09 culture
[kʌ́ltʃər]

a cultural 문화의, 문화적인

n 문화, 교양

A What is the hardest thing about living in Korea, Sam?
샘, 한국에서 사는 데 가장 어려운 점이 무엇이니?

B I'd say the difference in culture is the biggest thing. 내 생각에는 문화 차이가 가장 큰 것 같아.

10 system
[sístəm]

n 체계, 조직, 제도

A Every country has its system of law.
모든 나라는 고유의 법체계를 가지고 있어.

B So you mean each system is different from another? 그러니까 네 말은 그 체계는 서로 다르다는 말이니?

11 tradition
[trədíʃən]
ⓐ traditional 전통적인

ⓝ 전통

A What do Americans do on Christmas, Sally?
샐리, 미국인들은 크리스마스 때 뭐하니?

B We meet with our family for Christmas dinner by tradition.
전통적으로 집안 식구들이 모여 크리스마스 저녁 식사를 해.

12 power
[páuər]
ⓐ powerful 강력한

ⓝ 권력, 힘, 능력

A Which do you prefer, power or fame?
너는 권력과 명예 중 어느 걸 더 선호하니?

B I only want to be rich. 난 부자만 되면 돼.

13 action
[ǽkʃən]
ⓥ act 행동하다

ⓝ 행동, 동작

A She's all talk but no action.
그녀는 말만 하지 실천은 하지 않아.

B Actions speak louder than words.
말보다 행동으로 보여주는 것이 더 효과적인데.

14 right
[rait]

ⓐ 옳은, 올바른 **ⓝ** 권리

demand equal rights 동등한 권리를 요구하다

A You should always do the right thing.
항상 올바른 일을 해야 해.

B How do you know what is right?
넌 무엇이 올바른지 어떻게 아니?

15 liberty
[líbərti]

ⓝ 자유   the Statue of Liberty 자유의 여신상

A There is a saying in English, "Freedom is not free." 영어에는 '자유는 공짜가 아니다'라는 말이 있어.

B I see that you value liberty.
너희는 자유를 소중히 여기는구나.

16 ☑ affair
[əfɛ́ər]

ⓝ 사건, 업무　　the beginning of an affair 사건의 발단

A What is the purpose of your travel, sir?
여행 목적이 어떻게 됩니까?

B It's a business affair. 사업상의 업무입니다.

17 ☑ custom
[kʌ́stəm]

ⓝ 관습, 습관

A Our custom is to bow our heads to elders.
우리 관습은 웃어른께 고개를 숙이는 거야.

B I got it. I'll try to do that, too.
알았어. 나도 그렇게 해볼게.

18 ☑ provide
[prəváid]

ⓥ 제공하다

A The government should provide its people with the freedom of choice.
정부는 자국민들에게 선택의 자유를 부여해야 해.

B I agree with you. 네 말에 동의해.

19 ☑ lead
[liːd]

ⓥ 이끌다, 인도하다

A Don't you think he is too young?
그가 너무 어리다고 생각하지 않습니까?

B He is experienced enough to lead the team.
그는 팀을 이끌 만큼 충분한 경험이 있습니다.

20 ☑ gap
[gæp]

ⓝ (의견 따위의) 차이, 간격

A There is a growing gap between rich and poor people. 빈부의 격차가 심해지고 있어.

B It is one of the biggest social problems.
그게 가장 큰 사회 문제 중의 하나지.

21 organization
[ɔ̀:rɡənizéiʃən]

ⓝ 조직, 구성

A Our organization works to help homeless people.
우리 조직은 집이 없는 사람들을 도와주기 위해 노력합니다.

B How do you help them? 그들을 어떻게 도와주시나요?

22 government
[ɡʌ́vərnmənt]

ⓝ 정부, 내각, 정치

A The government is trying to make more jobs.
정부는 일자리를 늘리려고 노력하고 있어.

B I hope it does. 그랬으면 좋겠다.

23 people
[píːpl]

c.f person (개개의) 사람

ⓝ (복수 취급) 국민, 사람들

A The president vowed to serve the people.
대통령은 국민을 섬기기로 맹세했어.

B I hope he keeps his word. 자기가 한 말을 지키길 바라.

24 force
[fɔːrs]

ⓐ forceful 강제적인

ⓝ 힘, 세력 **ⓥ** 강요하다

A Taking land by force is against the law.
땅을 무력으로 차지하는 것은 법에 위반 돼.

B I know, but sometimes that happens in real life. 알아, 하지만 가끔 그런 일이 실생활에서 발생하기도 하잖아.

25 rule
[ruːl]

ⓝ 규칙, 관례 **ⓥ** 통치하다　　　**rule by law** 법으로 통치하다

A Why do we need all the rules?
왜 모든 규칙이 필요할까?

B Well, that's probably because we are only humans not gods.
글쎄, 아마도 우리가 신이 아니라 단지 인간이기 때문에 그런 것 같아.

Word Search

앞에서 배운 어휘를 기억하며 모두 찾아 보세요.

E	E	E	N	F	E	E	L	U	R	E	C	R	G	R
W	O	Z	S	O	Y	Z	X	J	K	R	E	I	A	R
T	Y	N	E	A	I	A	A	V	R	U	D	A	P	L
A	C	T	I	O	N	T	M	L	L	T	I	F	R	V
D	E	V	E	L	O	P	I	I	S	L	V	F	F	S
L	O	T	O	A	Y	X	B	D	P	U	O	A	K	B
J	A	Y	H	O	C	E	Q	O	A	C	R	I	L	K
M	K	I	T	G	R	R	O	R	L	R	P	E	O	I
Q	O	S	C	T	I	P	O	E	W	J	T	I	F	G
Q	U	V	Y	O	L	R	A	F	D	U	T	Y	A	H
C	Q	R	C	E	S	D	S	Y	S	T	E	M	I	S
R	E	T	S	A	M	Z	G	C	R	I	L	K	L	G
K	X	A	O	O	C	N	F	L	J	H	O	V	C	R
T	L	Y	K	Z	T	H	Y	E	C	Y	F	V	X	I

action	affair	culture	develop
duty	folk	gap	lead
liberty	master	provide	right
rule	social	system	tradition

Basic Words

- □ actor 배우
- □ beauty artist 미용사
- □ pilot 조종사
- □ pianist 피아니스트
- □ programmer 프로그래머
- □ barber 이발사
- □ firefighter 소방관
- □ soldier 군인
- □ postman 우체부
- □ farmer 농부
- □ musician 음악가
- □ vet 수의사

01 able

[éibəl]

ant unable ~할 수 없는

ⓐ 능력 있는, ~할 수 있는

be able to ~ ~할 수 있다

A I don't think she is able to do this job.
난 그녀가 이 일을 할 능력이 안 된다고 생각해.

B I don't agree with you. 난 네 말에 동의하지 않아.

02 earn

[ə:rn]

ⓥ 벌다, 일해서 얻다

A I should spend money more wisely.
나는 돈을 더 현명하게 써야 할 텐데.

B Yes, remember how hard you earned it.
응. 얼마나 힘들게 벌었는지를 기억해.

03 income

[ínkʌm]

ⓝ 소득

A What do you think is important for your future? 네 미래에 있어서 중요한 게 무엇이니?

B I just want a high income.
단지 높은 소득을 원할 뿐이야.

04 interview

[íntərvjù:]

ⓝ interviewer 면접관

ⓝ 면접, 회견 **ⓥ** 면접하다

A Did you find a job, Susan? 수잔, 일자리는 구했니?

B No, not yet. But I have an interview this Thursday. 아니, 아직. 하지만 목요일에 면접이 있어.

05 salary

[sǽləri]

ⓝ 봉급, 급료

get a raise in salary 급료가 오르다

A It's hard to live on such a small salary.
이렇게 적은 봉급으로 살아가는 건 쉽지 않아.

B Cheer up, John. It'll get better if you work harder. 기운 내, 존. 더 열심히 일하면 나아질 거야.

06 manage
[mǽnidʒ]

ⓝ manager 관리인, 매니저

ⓥ 관리하다, 해내다

A How is your business going? 사업은 어때?

B Not bad. I had a hard time managing workers at first.
괜찮아. 처음에는 직원들을 관리하는 데 힘들었어.

07 talent
[tǽlənt]

ⓐ talented 재능 있는

ⓝ 재능, 재주   **a native talent** 천부적인 재능

A I believe hard work is more important than talent. 저는 재능보다 열심히 노력하는 것이 중요하다고 생각합니다.

B I like how you think. 자네 생각하는 것이 마음에 드네.

08 wage
[wéidʒ]

ⓝ 임금, 노임

A The government sets the minimum wage to protect the poor.   * minimum : 최저의
정부는 가난한 사람들을 보호하기 위해 최저임금을 지정해.

B Doesn't the minimum affect the economy?
그 최저치가 경제에 영향을 끼치지 않니?

09 hardworking
[háːrdwə̀ːrkiŋ]

ⓐ 열심히 일하는

A The newcomer is very hardworking.
신입사원이 아주 열심히 일하네.

B Yes, it seems that he really likes his work.
응, 자기 일을 정말 좋아하는 모양이야.

10 failure
[féiljər]

ⓥ fail 실패하다

ⓝ 실패   **end in failure** 실패로 끝나다

A I ruined the whole project.
내가 모든 프로젝트를 망쳤어.

B Chin-up! One failure isn't the end of the world. 기운 내! 실패 한 번 했다고 세상이 끝나진 않아.

11 ☑ quit
[kwit]

ⓥ 그만두다, 중지하다

A I have not seen Jane since May.
5월부터 제인을 보지 못했어.

B She quit her job and went traveling to India.
그녀는 일을 그만두고 인도로 여행하러 떠났어.

---

12 ☑ labor
[léibər]

ⓐ laborious 힘든, 고된

ⓝ 노동, 근로　　　　　　　　**physical labor** 육체노동

A How were labor conditions in the past?
과거의 노동 조건은 어땠습니까?

B They were very poor. 아주 열악했습니다.

---

13 ☑ skilled
[skild]

ⓝ skill 숙련, 기술

ⓐ 숙련된

A Tony, why would a skilled bartender like you quit your job?
토니, 너 같이 숙련된 바텐더가 왜 일을 그만두니?

B I'm sorry, but I'm planning to go to college.
죄송하지만, 저 대학에 갈 계획이에요.

---

14 ☑ require
[rikwáiər]

ⓝ requirement 필요, 요건

ⓥ 필요로 하다

　　　　require special care 각별한 주의를 필요로 하다

A What is required for this job?
이 일에 무엇이 필요하죠?

B You need to speak both Korean and English.
한국어와 영어를 모두 하셔야 합니다.

---

15 ☑ employ
[emplɔ́i]

ⓝ employer 고용주
　　employee 종업원

ⓥ 고용하다

A How did Peter get a job so quickly?
피터는 어떻게 그렇게 빨리 취직했니?

B The company employed him because of his programming skills.
그 회사는 그의 프로그래밍 능력 때문에 그를 고용했어.

16 chief
[tʃiːf]

ⓝ 우두머리, 장, 상사 **ⓐ** 주요한, 최고의

A Is your chief nice to you?
너희 부장님은 너에게 잘해주니?

B Yes, she is a good person. 응, 좋은 분이셔.

17 business
[bíznis]

ⓝ 사업, 상업, 장사   **business hours** 영업 시간

A Is your business doing well? 사업이 잘 되십니까?

B No, the economy isn't helping.
아니오, 경제가 도움이 안 되고 있어요.

18 service
[sə́ːrvis]

ⓥ serve 봉사하다, 섬기다

ⓝ 봉사, 편의

A Your son did a great service for his country.
댁의 아드님은 국가에 크나큰 봉사를 했습니다.

B I am proud of him. 저는 그 녀석이 자랑스러워요.

19 apply
[əplái]

ⓝ applicant 지원자

ⓥ 지원하다, 적용하다

A What kind of companies did you apply to?
너는 어떤 회사에 지원했니?

B I applied to electronics companies mostly.
나는 주로 전자제품 회사에 지원했어.

20 succeed
[səksíːd]

ⓝ success 성공

ⓥ 성공하다

A I will succeed in this project. I promise!
이 프로젝트에 성공하겠습니다. 약속합니다!

B I wish you good luck! 행운을 비네!

21 hire
[haiər]

ⓥ 고용하다

A Chief, we need to hire a reporter.
편집장님, 기자를 고용해야 합니다.

B Do you have anyone in mind?
자네가 생각해 둔 사람 있나?

22 chairman
[tʃɛ́ərmən]

ⓝ 의장, 사회자, 회장

A Who is the new chairman of the corporation?
누가 그 기업의 새로운 회장입니까?

B His son took over after he died.
그가 죽은 후 그의 아들이 맡았습니다.

23 office
[ɔ́(:)fis]

ⓝ 사무실, 관청, 공직

A The office is closed on weekends.
사무실은 주말에 문을 닫아.

B But I don't have time to go on weekdays.
하지만, 평일에는 내가 갈 시간이 없어.

24 fire
[fáiər]

ⓥ 내쫓다, 해고하다

A Bob was fired for being late for work too often. 밥은 직장에 너무 자주 지각해서 해고됐어.

B You should be more careful, too.
너도 더 조심해야겠네.

25 than
[ðǽn]

conj ~보다

A Who do you think I should give the project to? 자네 생각에는 프로젝트를 누구에게 주는 게 좋을 것 같나?

B I think Mr. Gibbons will be better than anybody else.
제 생각에는 기번스 씨가 다른 누구보다 나을 것 같습니다.

Multi-Meaning Word

fire

ⓝ 화재, 불
Most animals are afraid of **fire**. 대부분 동물들은 불을 두려워한다.

ⓥ 사격하다
Soldiers **fired** on the crowd. 병사들이 군중들에게 사격을 가했다.

ⓥ 해고하다
He claimed he was **fired** because of his age.
그는 자신의 나이 때문에 해고되었다고 주장했다.

Word Search

앞에서 배운 어휘를 기억하며 모두 찾아 보세요.

정답

E	E	E	T	F	F	V	K	Y	A	V	S	P	W	D
M	R	M	R	G	C	A	D	Q	C	V	N	Z	T	C
K	Y	I	P	I	Q	K	V	X	D	Y	G	O	V	G
J	N	J	U	L	H	V	N	M	E	N	K	L	X	T
P	E	S	H	Q	O	Z	B	D	C	V	B	U	K	M
Z	V	C	C	A	B	Y	G	E	R	U	L	I	A	F
T	A	L	E	N	T	R	O	E	E	O	W	M	D	Q
S	K	I	L	L	E	D	T	H	M	F	H	W	E	D
F	S	O	L	F	A	I	B	E	O	F	P	A	E	U
T	W	A	E	A	V	P	G	C	C	I	U	F	C	Q
V	A	I	L	R	B	A	P	A	N	C	N	I	C	Q
Y	H	U	E	A	N	O	B	L	I	E	R	R	U	A
C	G	S	Q	A	R	C	R	A	Y	J	A	E	S	M
H	D	R	M	Z	E	Y	W	A	G	E	E	R	I	A

apply	chief	earn	employ
failure	fire	hire	income
labor	manage	office	salary
skilled	succeed	talent	wage

Basic Words

□ gold 금	□ rich 부자	□ money 돈
□ dollar 달러	□ bank 은행	□ poor 빈곤한
□ lend 빌려주다	□ rise 오르다	□ choice 선택
□ tax 세금	□ elect 선출하다	□ politics 정치

01 company
[kʌ́mpəni]

ⓝ 회사　　**start a new company** 새로운 회사를 시작하다

A The world-famous company went bankrupt.
그 세계적으로 유명한 회사가 파산했어.　　* bankrupt : 파산한

B I remember seeing it on the news.
뉴스에서 본 기억이 나.

02 factory
[fǽktəri]

ⓝ 공장　　**a toy factory** 장난감 공장

A Are there any changes in your hometown, Jim? 짐. 고향에는 변한 것 없어?

B People say that a big factory will be opening.
큰 공장 하나가 가동한다더라.

03 loss
[lɔ́(:)s]
ⓥ lose 잃다

ⓝ 손실, 손해

A If you want to be rich, always think about your gains and losses.
부자가 되고 싶다면, 언제나 이익과 손해에 대해서 생각하도록 해.

B I'll keep that in mind, Father.
기억하고 있을게요, 아버지.

04 produce
[prədjúːs]
ⓝ production 생산
product 제품

ⓥ 만들다, 생산하다

A The factory started to produce the new product last week, sir.
사장님. 공장에서 지난주에 신제품을 생산하기 시작했습니다.

B Nice work. I hope it succeeds.
수고했네. 신제품이 성공해야 할 텐데.

05 goods
[gudz]

ⓝ 상품, 물품　　**lack of goods** 물자 부족

A The prices of goods have risen recently.
최근에 물품 가격이 올랐어.

B Yes, people are worried about that.
응. 사람들이 그것에 대해 걱정을 하고 있어.

06 profit
[práfit]

n 이익   **a profit organization** 영리 단체

A We are losing profit. What should I tell the boss? 우리 이익이 줄고 있네. 사장님께 뭐라고 해야 하지?

B I'll find the reason. 제가 원인을 찾아내겠습니다.

07 industry
[índəstri]

n 산업

A The game industry in Korea is growing very fast. 한국의 게임 산업은 굉장히 빠르게 성장하고 있어.

B Many countries try to learn from Korea now. 여러 나라들이 한국에게 배우려고 해.

08 save
[seiv]

n saving 절약, 저축

v 저축하다, 절약하다

       save up for a rainy day 만일의 경우를 대비해 저축하다

A What is the secret to saving so much money? 그렇게 많은 돈을 모은 비결이 뭐니?

B I have saved a few dollars each week. 나는 매주 몇 달러씩 저축하고 있어.

09 election
[ilékʃən]

v elect 선출하다

n 선거   **mayor election** 시장 선거

A The election is coming up soon. 곧 선거기간이야.

B Did you decide who to vote for? 누구에게 투표할지 결정했어?

10 economy
[ikánəmi]

a economic 경제의

n 경제   **global economy** 세계 경제

A More and more tourists are visiting Korea these days. 요즘 점점 더 많은 관광객이 한국을 방문하고 있어.

B I hope that will help Korean economy. 그게 한국 경제에 도움이 되었으면 좋겠다.

11 market
[máːrkit]

ⓝ 시장, 구매층

A I'm afraid there is not a large market for this product. 이 제품을 위한 큰 시장이 없어서 유감입니다.

B What about exporting it to other countries?
다른 나라로 수출하는 건 어떨까요?   * export : 수출하다

12 demand
[dimǽnd]

ⓝ 수요, 요구 ⓥ 요구하다 **demand a refund** 환불을 요구하다

A Why do prices rise, Mr. Thomson?
톰슨 선생님, 가격은 왜 오르는 건가요?

B Basically, prices rise when the demand rises.
기본적으로 수요가 오를 때 가격도 오른단다.

13 benefit
[bénəfit]
ⓐ beneficial 유익한, 유리한

ⓝ 이로움, 이익

A I can't decide whether I should buy the house or not. 그 집을 사야 할지 말아야 할지 결정을 못 하겠어.

B What are the benefits if you do?
그 집을 사면 이익이 무엇인데?

14 material
[mətíəriəl]

ⓝ 재료, 물질   **building materials** 건축 자재

A How can we reduce the costs of material?
어떻게 하면 재료비를 줄일 수 있을까요?

B We can use recycled paper.
재생지를 사용할 수 있습니다.

15 wealth
[welθ]
ⓐ wealthy 부유한

ⓝ 부, 재산

A He is a man of wealth, but died young.
그는 부자였지만, 젊었을 때 죽었어.

B We have to remember "Health is above wealth."
우리는 '건강이 재산보다 더 중요하다'라는 말을 기억해야 해.

16 supply
[səplái]

ⓝ 공급 **ⓥ** 공급하다   **supply power** 전력을 공급하다

A What determines prices? 무엇이 가격을 결정하지?

B It is influenced by supply and demand.
공급과 수요의 영향을 받아.

17 affect
[əfékt]

c.f. effect ~을 초래하다

ⓥ ~에 영향을 미치다

A The new economic policy will affect us all.
새 경제 정책은 우리 모두에게 영향을 미칠 거야.

B When was it changed? 정책이 언제 바뀌었어?

18 vote
[vout]

ⓝ 투표, 표결 **ⓥ** 투표하다

A I will not vote for that politician.
나는 저 정치인에게 투표하지 않을 거야.

B He never thinks about the environment.
그는 환경을 전혀 생각하지 않아.

19 gain
[gein]

ⓥ 얻다, 획득하다   **gain knowledge** 지식을 얻다

A What have you gained from this project?
이 프로젝트를 통해 무엇을 얻었니?

B It is the value of working together. 협력의 가치야.

20 issue
[íʃuː]

ⓝ 논쟁, 쟁점, 문제

A What is our issue? 우리의 문제는 무엇입니까?

B The biggest issue is that we don't have
enough time. 가장 큰 문제는 충분한 시간이 없다는 것입니다.

21 select
[silékt]

ⓝ selection 선출

ⓥ 선출하다

A Be careful who you select for the class
president. 누구를 반장으로 선출할지 신중히 생각해.

B I have someone in mind. 생각해 둔 사람이 있어.

22 progress
[prágrəs]

ⓝ 전진, 진행   **make progress** 전진하다, 진보하다

A What is the progress on our marketing plan?
우리 마케팅 기획은 어떻게 진행되고 있나요?

B People are responding very well.
사람들이 아주 잘 호응하고 있습니다.

23 trade
[treid]

ⓝ 무역, 장사, 거래   **foreign trade** 외국 무역

A Where does she work? 그녀는 어디서 일하지?

B She works for a large trade company.
그녀는 큰 무역회사에서 일해.

24 advertise
[ǽdvərtàiz]

ⓝ advertisement 광고

ⓥ 광고하다, 선전하다

A Is there a movie you want to watch?
보고 싶은 영화 있니?

B No, I don't like the ones that are being advertised these days.
아니, 요즘 광고하는 것들은 마음에 안 들어.

25 among
[əmʌ́ŋ]

prep ~의 사이에

A Johnnie won the election among four people.
네 사람 중에서 조니가 선거에서 당선됐어.

B He must be very happy. 그는 정말 행복하겠구나.

Multi-Meaning Word

issue

ⓥ 발행하다
The U.S. **issues** millions of passports each year.
미국은 매년 수백만 개의 여권을 발행한다.

ⓝ 문제, 쟁점
We should raise the **issue** of pollution.
우리는 오염 문제를 제기해야 한다.

ⓝ 발행, 판
I'm looking for the May **issue** of Vogue.
보그지 5월 호를 찾고 있습니다.

Word Search

앞에서 배운 어휘를 기억하며 모두 찾아 보세요.

정답

H	S	R	M	A	W	E	T	K	C	G	D	Q	S	F
T	S	X	I	N	C	I	S	D	O	E	N	H	E	N
L	O	M	L	O	F	G	Y	A	M	O	G	E	L	Y
A	L	H	N	O	S	X	E	G	P	D	A	D	E	G
E	R	O	R	A	A	V	J	R	A	S	I	A	C	H
W	M	P	V	R	E	E	J	J	N	P	N	R	T	N
Y	K	E	T	R	X	X	W	O	Y	P	Z	T	O	M
M	Q	N	T	B	E	N	E	F	I	T	D	I	T	V
Y	B	I	I	S	S	U	E	D	K	Q	P	R	C	S
M	S	E	T	O	V	Q	V	V	N	C	Z	F	E	U
E	I	N	D	U	S	T	R	Y	E	A	Y	I	F	P
H	F	N	C	V	G	O	P	L	P	N	M	K	F	P
L	X	A	Q	N	P	K	E	J	A	K	N	E	A	L
T	E	S	R	A	M	U	X	P	P	X	U	V	D	Y

affect	benefit	company	demand
economy	gain	industry	issue
loss	profit	save	select
supply	trade	vote	wealth

Unit 39 Rules & Belief

- □ god 신
- □ police 경찰
- □ break 어기다
- □ heaven 천국

- □ angel 천사
- □ church 교회
- □ thief 도둑, 절도범
- □ bless 축복하다

- □ devil 악마
- □ believe 믿다
- □ reward 보상
- □ ban 금지하다

01 cheat

[tʃiːt]

ⓝ cheater 사기꾼

ⓥ 속이다, 부정행위를 하다

A I will not allow anybody to cheat on the test.
누구든 간에 시험에 부정행위 하는 것을 허용하지 않을 것이다.

B Yes, Mr. Thomson. 네, 톰슨 선생님.

02 steal

[stiːl]

(steal-stole-stolen)

c.f. thief 도둑

ⓥ 훔치다

A Where were you? I was looking for you.
너 어디 있었어? 찾았잖아.

B I was at the police station. Someone stole
my wallet. 경찰서에 있었어. 누군가 내 지갑을 훔쳐갔어.

03 obey

[oubéi]

ⓥ 복종하다, 따르다

A What is it like to be in the army?
군대에 들어간다는 것은 어떤 것일까?

B You can learn to obey orders.
명령을 따르는 것을 배우게 돼.

04 pray

[prei]

ⓥ 기도하다

A What are you praying for, Ally?
앨리, 무슨 기도를 하니?

B I am praying for my sick grandfather.
편찮으신 할아버지를 위해 기도하고 있어.

05 holy

[hóuli]

ⓐ 성스러운

A The people of Chosun thought that this area
was holy.
조선시대 사람들은 이 지역이 신성하다고 생각했어.

B I didn't know it had such history.
그렇게 역사가 깃든 곳 인줄 몰랐어.

06 crime
[kraim]

n criminal 범인

n 죄, 범죄

A It's a crime to steal from others.
다른 사람의 물건을 훔치는 것은 범죄야.

B Greed is always the problem.
욕심이 언제나 문제야.

07 punish
[pʌ́niʃ]

n punishment 벌

v 벌하다, 응징하다

punish for telling a lie 거짓말을 한 것에 대해 벌하다

A Why are you cleaning the restroom, Sam?
샘, 왜 화장실 청소를 하는 거니?

B I'm being punished by Mr. Brian.
브라이언 선생님께서 벌을 주시는 거야.

08 magic
[mǽdʒik]

n magician 마술사

n 마술 **a** 신기한, 마술의

A I used to believe in magic until I was ten.
나는 열 살 때까지 마술이 진짜라고 믿었어.

B How did you find out it was fake?
가짜라는 것을 어떻게 알게 되었니?

09 evil
[íːvəl]

a 나쁜 **n** 악   **an evil spirit** 악령

A You should forgive James. He's not an evil
person. 제임스를 용서해줘. 악한 사람은 아냐.

B I know, but he makes me so mad.
나도 아는데, 제임스가 나를 너무 화나게 해.

10 ghost
[goust]

n 유령, 영혼   **a scary ghost story** 무서운 유령 이야기

A Sally! I saw a ghost yesterday!
샐리야! 나 어제 유령을 봤어!

B Are you sure? You might be mistaken.
확실해? 착각하고 있을지도 몰라.

11 **court**
[kɔːrt]

ⓝ 법정, 공판, 안뜰

A I don't know why I should appear in court.
내가 왜 법원에 출두해야 하는지 모르겠어.

B They probably think you saw the bank robber. 아마도 당신이 은행 강도를 보았다고 생각하나 봐요.

---

12 **promise**
[prάmis]

ⓝ 약속 **ⓥ** 약속하다　　　**break a promise** 약속을 어기다

A I'm sorry. I won't be late again.
미안해. 다시는 늦지 않을게.

B Can you make that a promise?
그거 약속할 수 있어?

---

13 **limit**
[límit]
ⓝ limitation 제한

ⓝ 제한 **ⓥ** 제한하다

A Slow down! You're close to the speed limit.
속도를 줄여! 제한속도에 너무 가까워.

B Okay, I will. 알았어, 그렇게 할게.

---

14 **false**
[fɔːls]
ant true 참된, 사실의

ⓐ 틀린, 오류의, 거짓의　　　**false information** 거짓 정보

A It turned out that it was a false advertisement.
그거 알고 보니 거짓광고였어.

B How could they do something like that?
어떻게 그런 짓을 할 수 있을까?

---

15 **mystery**
[místəri]
ⓐ mysterious 신비한

ⓝ 신비, 비밀, 수수께끼

　　　the mystery of Pyramids 피라미드의 신비

A Whether the monster exists or not is still a mystery. 그 괴물이 실재하는지는 여전히 수수께끼야.

B That's fascinating! 신기하다!

16 belief
[bilíːf]
ⓥ believe 믿다

ⓝ 확신, 신념　　　　　**beyond belief** 믿을 수 없는, 놀라운

A I don't think I'll succeed as an actor.
나는 배우로 성공할 수 없을 것 같아.

B Have belief in your dream. 너의 꿈에 대한 확신을 가져.

---

17 law
[lɔː]
ⓝ lawyer 변호사

ⓝ 법률, 법　　　　　**obey the law** 법을 지키다

A The law limits free speech in court.
법은 법정에서 자유로운 발언을 제한합니다.

B We'll be quiet, officer. 조용히 할게요, 경찰관님.

---

18 kill
[kil]
ⓝ killer 살인자

ⓥ 죽이다, 살해하다

A Have you heard the news? Sam was killed on the street the other day.
그 소식 들었니? 샘이 길거리에서 며칠 전에 살해되었대.

B Has the killer been caught, yet? 범인은 잡혔니?

---

19 rob
[rɑb]
ⓝ robber 강도

ⓥ 훔치다, 빼앗다

A I heard someone robbed James yesterday.
어제 누가 제임스에게서 물건을 빼앗았대.

B Is he okay? That's terrible.
그는 무사하니? 끔찍해.

---

20 prison
[prízn]
ⓝ prisoner 죄수

ⓝ 교도소, 감옥

A Jimmy became a new man after he got out of prison. 지미는 교도소에서 나온 뒤로 새사람이 되었어.

B We'll see about that. 한번 두고 보자.

21 **faith**
[feiθ]

ⓐ **faithful** 충실한

ⓝ 신념, 충실   **have a faith in ~** ~에 신념을 가지다

A Do you think I can do well without you?
내가 너 없이도 잘 할 수 있을 거라고 생각해?

B Have faith in yourself. 네 자신을 믿어.

22 **temple**
[témpl]

ⓝ 절, 사원, 전당

A The temple burned down because of the forest fire. 산불 때문에 절이 불타 없어졌어.

B We have lost a national treasure.
우리는 국보 하나를 잃어버렸어.

23 **religion**
[rilídʒən]

ⓝ 종교, 신앙   **the freedom of religion** 종교의 자유

A What is your religion? 너는 종교가 뭐니?

B I am a Catholic. 나는 천주교 신자야.

24 **responsible**
[rispánsəbl]

ⓝ **responsibility** 책임

ⓐ 책임 있는, 신뢰할 수 있는

     a responsible person 믿을 수 있는 사람

A Who broke this window? 누가 이 창문을 깼어?

B I am responsible for it. 제 책임입니다.

25 **therefore**
[ðέəːrfɔːr]

ad 그러므로, 따라서

A Sam is such a terrible liar. Therefore I don't trust him.
샘은 정말 지독한 거짓말쟁이야. 따라서 나는 그를 신뢰하지 않아.

B Really? I didn't know that. 정말이야? 난 몰랐는데.

🐱 **Multi-Meaning Word**

court   ⓝ 정원/법정/(테니스 등의) 코트

We walked into the beautiful **court**yard with tall trees.
우리는 큰 나무가 있는 아름다운 정원으로 걸어 들어갔다.

I'd rather solve our differences without going to **court**.
나는 법정에 가지 않고 우리의 견해 차이를 풀고 싶다.

The players will appear in the **court** in an hour.
선수들은 한 시간 후에 코트에 나타날 것이다.

Word Search

앞에서 배운 어휘를 기억하며 모두 찾아 보세요.

정답

A	W	R	I	E	N	Y	G	F	M	K	H	O	U	T
E	A	A	M	E	J	B	I	C	A	W	H	C	Z	L
B	K	I	L	K	L	I	J	V	O	I	I	D	Y	I
L	R	H	I	B	E	L	I	E	F	G	T	Q	A	K
C	T	Z	M	O	P	W	U	V	A	P	W	H	R	T
T	R	U	O	C	B	B	L	M	R	M	C	W	P	I
A	T	K	X	H	T	E	J	P	T	L	L	A	V	M
H	B	C	B	J	I	X	Y	F	N	N	T	K	T	I
Z	H	G	V	Z	O	Y	R	E	T	S	Y	S	E	L
P	U	N	I	S	H	N	O	S	I	R	P	T	M	H
T	P	C	F	Y	T	A	U	R	O	O	S	F	P	O
H	L	A	E	T	S	G	B	G	W	O	S	R	L	L
W	V	L	I	V	A	N	I	X	H	Z	L	Q	E	Y
C	O	T	A	E	H	C	W	G	F	C	P	S	D	G

belief	cheat	court	crime
faith	ghost	holy	law
limit	magic	obey	pray
prison	punish	steal	temple

의무

자유

따르다,
복종하다

Society
사회

전통

법

경제

고용하다

정치

이익

노동, 근로

투표

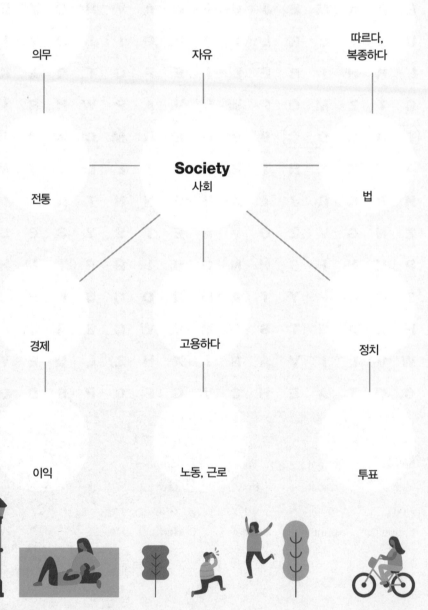

Review Test

A 우리말을 영어로, 영어를 우리말로 쓰시오.

01 노예 _____ 08 earn _____

02 숙련된 _____ 09 advertise _____

03 공장 _____ 10 duty _____

04 벌하다 _____ 11 lead _____

05 선거 _____ 12 belief _____

06 문화, 교양 _____ 13 business _____

07 시장 _____ 14 promise _____

B 빈칸에 알맞은 단어를 쓰시오.

01 법으로 통치하다 _____ by law

02 세계 경제 global _____

03 육체노동 physical _____

04 false information _____ 정보

05 make progress _____ 하다

06 get a raise in salary _____ 이/가 오르다

C 단어의 관계에 맞게 빈칸을 채우시오.

01 이익 : 유익한 = profit : _____

02 손실, 손해 : 잃다 = loss : _____

03 성공하다 : 성공 = succeed : _____

04 action : act = 행동, 동작 : _____

05 power : powerful = 힘 : _____

06 demand : supply = 수요, 요구 : _____

D 배운 단어를 사용하여 문장을 완성하시오. (필요하면 형태를 바꾸시오.)

01 Dan is working for a computer _____ as a programmer.
댄은 컴퓨터 회사에서 프로그래머로 일한다.

02 Susan _____ half of her salary every month.
수잔은 매달 자신의 급료의 절반을 저축하다.

03 People _____ for the world peace.
사람들은 세계의 평화를 위해 기도 드린다.

04 I think I saw a(n) _____ last night.
나 어젯밤에 유령을 본 것 같아.

05 Hannah is a(n) _____ person, and she always helps other people.
한나는 열심히 일하는 사람이고 그녀는 항상 다른 사람들을 도와준다.

E 빈칸에 알맞은 말을 보기에서 찾아 쓰시오.

interview	stole	among	customs	able

01 **A** What color will you choose _____ blue, yellow, and red?

  B I will take red.

02 **A** I have a job _____ tomorrow. I am so nervous.

  B Don't worry! You will be _____ to get the job.

03 **A** Someone _____ my car in front of my house!

  B Let's call the police first, okay?

04 **A** What are Christmas _____ and traditions?

  B Setting up a Christmas tree is one of them.

F 밑줄 친 부분을 우리말로 옮기시오.

01 A ball hit <u>my right eye</u>, and it really hurts.

02 There was <u>a big fire</u> in the forest near the national park.

Appendices

Answers

Index

Answers

Chapter 1   p. 43

A

01 secret	08 결혼하다
02 cousin	09 손님
03 memory	10 존경, 존경하다
04 refuse	11 식사를 하다
05 neighbor	12 대화
06 scream	13 교우, 우정
07 depend	14 환영, 환영하다

B

01 twins	04 취소하다
02 together	05 불평하다
03 festival	06 일생

C

01 wife	04 축하
02 invite	05 기혼의, 결혼한
03 warmth	06 졸업하다

D

01 held	04 member
02 blames	05 fence
03 children	

E

01 accept
02 between
03 holidays, grandparents
04 birthday

F

01 빠른우편	02 친한 친구들

Chapter 2   p. 68

A

01 strict	08 블라우스
02 perfect	09 기분 좋은, 명랑한
03 clothes	10 호기심 있는
04 bald	11 다른, 상이한
05 blond	12 면직물, 솜
06 careful	13 적합하다, 꼭 맞는
07 height	14 추한, 추악한

B

01 sweater	04 의심
02 cruel	05 얼룩
03 curly	06 매력적인

C

01 light	04 불친절한
02 loose	05 우아한
03 polite	06 무게를 달다

D

01 brave	04 changed
02 beard	05 pocket
03 similar	

E

01 proud
02 attractive
03 wonder
04 trousers, size

F

01 폭설	02 7대 불가사의

336

A

01 skin
02 noise
03 disappointed
04 cough
05 understand
06 bone
07 sense
08 감정

09 부끄러운, 수줍어
　　하는
10 추측하다, 추측
11 땀을 흘리다, 땀
12 관찰하다
13 지배하다, 억제하다
14 독, 독약

B

01 chest
02 sound
03 heal

04 기분
05 결정하다
06 약

C

01 breath
02 blind
03 bleed

04 침묵하는, 고요한
05 기쁜
06 마음

D

01 cheeks
02 aware
03 healthy

04 regret
05 intend

E

01 nervous, worry
02 imagine
03 voice
04 rest

F

01 감자 칩을 건네다　02 힘든 일

A

01 restaurant
02 roof
03 greet
04 fresh
05 arrange
06 dessert
07 usually

08 과일
09 씹다
10 엉망인, 어질러진
11 버릇
12 휘젓다
13 집세
14 식사, 한 끼니

B

01 food
02 recipe
03 activities

04 쓰레기
05 커튼
06 식욕

C

01 borrow
02 salty
03 decorate

04 맛있는
05 야채
06 목욕

D

01 thirsty
02 rotten
03 dream

04 address
05 acts

E

01 habit
02 weekdays
03 boil
04 wiping, toilet

F

01 내 취향　　　02 4층

Chapter 5 p. 159

A

01 report	08 교과서
02 uniform	09 결과, 결말
03 attempt	10 나누다
04 mean	11 평균, 보통
05 lesson	12 계산하다
06 homework	13 복습하다
07 solve	14 계속하다

B

01 count	04 교육
02 elementary	05 마치다
03 break	06 시험

C

01 explanation	04 정확하게
02 difficulty	05 입학하다
03 answer	06 ~을 뺀, 마이너스의

D

01 classmate	04 praise
02 subject	05 Even though /
03 excellent	Although

E

01 college, advise
02 playground
03 mistakes
04 absent

F

01 10개의 문제	02 높은 점수

Chapter 6 p. 191

A

01 match	08 판매원, 점원
02 deliver	09 위험
03 popular	10 비용, 값
04 travel	11 현대의, 근대의
05 cheer	12 득점, 점수
06 proper	13 놀랄 만한, 굉장한
07 sale	14 공항

B

01 wrap	04 연습하다
02 museum	05 여행
03 cheap	06 사진

C

01 collect	04 예술가
02 safety	05 자유로운
03 choice	06 패배

D

01 spend	04 exchange
02 Both	05 newspaper
03 hobbies	

E

01 passport
02 ballet
03 favorite, well-known
04 cash

F

01 내 휴대전화를 충전하다
02 금메달을 놓고 경쟁하다

Chapter 7 p. 216

A

01 length
02 midnight
03 several
04 moment
05 stiff
06 ancient
07 decade

08 형태, 형식
09 정도, 도
10 ~에 속하다, 소유이다
11 많음, 풍부
12 여분의, 규정 외의
13 기간
14 필요한, 필수의

B

01 precious
02 decrease
03 whole

04 새벽
05 공간
06 조그마한

C

01 never
02 quantity
03 fill

04 최근의
05 가치
06 반, 절반

D

01 helpful
02 About
03 empty

04 weekend
05 nothing

E

01 another
02 enough
03 delay
04 often, twice

F

01 프랑스어를 전공하다
02 우주여행

Chapter 8 p. 242

A

01 design
02 vehicle
03 electric
04 genius
05 speed
06 search
07 tool

08 고치다
09 노력
10 철도
11 노트북 컴퓨터
12 빨리, 서둘러
13 에너지, 활력
14 접근하다, 접근

B

01 error
02 parking
03 process

04 중대한
05 교통
06 인쇄하다

C

01 arrival
02 vary
03 copy

04 문서의
05 장치
06 짐을 내리다

D

01 leave
02 comfortable
03 attach

04 invented
05 scientist

E

01 station
02 repair, machine
03 discovered
04 receive

F

01 팁, 봉사료   02 부모님이 그립다

A

01 forest	08 소나기
02 dry	09 오염시키다
03 cliff	10 빛나다, 비치다
04 bush	11 경향이 있다
05 flood	12 야생의
06 beast	13 식물, 심다
07 destroy	14 기후

B

01 umbrella	04 씨
02 stone	05 온도
03 bud	06 보호하다

C

01 thin	04 안개 낀
02 exist	05 암컷의
03 effective	06 모래

D

01 survive	04 wet
02 flows	05 branch
03 trash	

E

01 weather, windy
02 beach
03 desert
04 raised

F

01 너의 생명	02 울창한 정글

A

01 lean	08 흔들다
02 border	09 도심지의, 시내의
03 locate	10 간선도로
04 polar	11 자리잡다, 정착하다
05 hurry	12 열대지방의,
06 everywhere	열대산의
07 suburb	13 퍼뜨리다
	14 시골, 지방

B

01 into	04 행진하다
02 escape	05 시민
03 foreign	06 공통

C

01 regional	04 짓다
02 peace	05 받다
03 move	06 결합하다

D

01 earth	04 crowded
02 History	05 spilled[spilt]
03 clapped	

E

01 follow
02 knocking
03 abroad
04 map, opposite

F

01 대문자
02 내가 설거지 할 차례

A

01 slave	08 벌다
02 skilled	09 광고하다
03 factory	10 의무
04 punish	11 이끌다
05 election	12 확신, 신념
06 culture	13 사업
07 market	14 약속, 약속하다

B

01 rule	04 거짓
02 economy	05 전진/진보
03 labor	06 급료

C

01 profitable	04 행동하다
02 lose	05 강력한
03 success	06 공급

D

01 company	04 ghost
02 saves	05 hardworking
03 pray	

E

01 among
02 interview, able
03 stole
04 customs

F

01 내 오른쪽 눈	02 큰 불

Index

Memo

이것이 THIS IS 시리즈다!

THIS IS GRAMMAR 시리즈
▷ 중·고등 내신에 꼭 등장하는 어법 포인트 분석 및 총정리

강남인강
강의교재

THIS IS READING 시리즈
▷ 다양한 소재의 지문으로 내신 및 수능 완벽 대비

강남인강
강의교재

THIS IS VOCABULARY 시리즈
▷ 주제별로 분류한 교육부 권장 어휘

THIS IS 시리즈

무료 MP3 및 부가자료 다운로드
www.nexusbook.com
www.nexusEDU.kr

THIS IS GRAMMAR 시리즈
Starter 1~3 영어교육연구소 지음 | 205×265 | 144쪽 | 각 권 12,000원
초·중·고급 1·2 넥서스영어교육연구소 지음 | 205×265 | 250쪽 내외 | 각 권 12,000원

THIS IS READING 시리즈
Starter 1~3 김태연 지음 | 205×265 | 156쪽 | 각 권 12,000원
1·2·3·4 넥서스영어교육연구소 지음 | 205×265 | 192쪽 내외 | 각 권 13,000원

THIS IS VOCABULARY 시리즈
입문 넥서스영어교육연구소 지음 | 152×225 | 224쪽 | 10,000원
초·중·고급·어원편 권기하 지음 | 152×225 | 180×257 | 344쪽~444쪽 | 10,000원~12,000원
수능 완성 넥서스영어교육연구소 지음 | 152×225 | 280쪽 | 12,000원
뉴텝스 넥서스 TEPS연구소 지음 | 152×225 | 452쪽 | 13,800원

LEVEL CHART

	초1	초2	초3	초4	초5	초6	중1	중2	중3	고1	고2	고3
VOCA	초등필수 영단어 1-2 · 3-4 · 5-6학년용									WORD PASS		
			The VOCA + (플러스) 1~7									
		THIS IS VOCABULARY 입문 · 초급 · 중급					고급 · 어원 · 수능 완성 · 뉴텝스					
				WORD FOCUS 중등 종합 5000 · 고등 필수 5000 · 고등 종합 9500								
Grammar	초등필수 영문법 + 쓰기 1~2											
	OK Grammar 1~4											
	This Is Grammar Starter 1~3											
			This Is Grammar 초급~고급 (각 2권: 총 6권)									
			Grammar 공감 1~3									
			Grammar 101 1~3									
			Grammar Bridge 1~3 (NEW EDITION)									
			The Grammar Starter, 1~3									
				한 권으로 끝내는 필수 구문 1000제								
				구사일생 (구문독해 Basic) 1~2								
					구문독해 204 1~2 (개정판)							
						고난도 구문독해 500						
				그래머 캡처 1~2								
				[특급 단기 특강] 어법어휘 모의고사								

	초1	초2	초3	초4	초5	초6	중1	중2	중3	고1	고2	고3

Writing

공감 영문법+쓰기
1~2

도전만점
중등내신 서술형 1~4

영어일기 영작패턴
1-A, B · 2-A, B

Smart Writing 1~2

Reading

Reading 101 1~3

Reading 공감 1~3

This Is Reading Starter 1~3

This Is Reading
전면 개정판 1~4

원서 술술 읽는
Smart Reading Basic 1~2

원서 술술 읽는
Smart Reading 1~2

[특급 단기 특강]
구문독해 · 독해유형

[앱솔루트 수능대비
영어독해 기출분석]
2019~2021학년도

Listening

Listening 공감 1~3

The Listening 1~4

넥서스 중학 영어듣기
모의고사 25회 1~3

도전! 만점
중학 영어듣기 모의고사
1~3

만점 적중
수능 듣기 모의고사
20회 · 35회

TEPS

NEW TEPS 입문편 실전 250⁺
청해 · 문법 · 독해

NEW TEPS 기본편 실전 300⁺
청해 · 문법 · 독해

NEW TEPS 실력편 실전 400⁺
청해 · 문법 · 독해

NEW TEPS 마스터편 실전 500⁺
청해 · 문법 · 독해

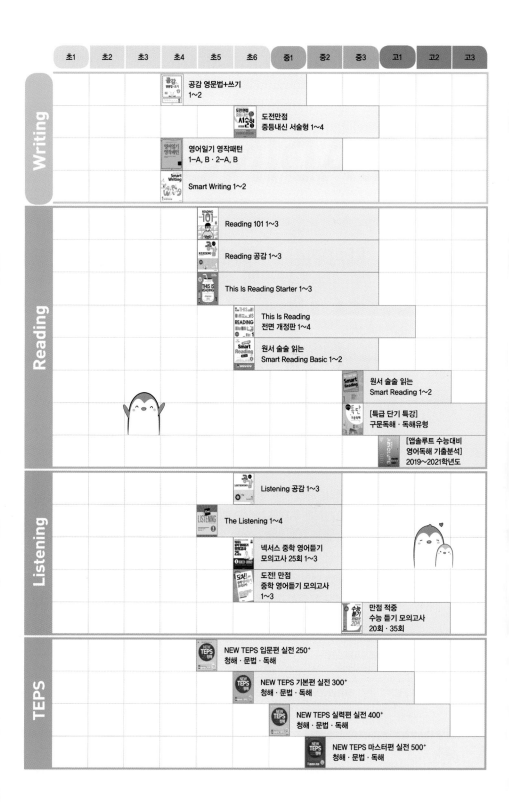